JAPAN
Nation
Building
Nature

JAPAN Nation Building Nature

自然をつくる国日本

Joachim Nijs

nai010 publishers

Contents

Prologue:
A Work in Progress

The past few years I have been living on and off in Japan. I discovered the country as a travelling volunteer, then came back for a year-long traineeship in a large Japanese architecture office. During my spare time, I laid the groundwork for this book, which I originally drafted as a Master's dissertation at the University of Ghent upon my return to Belgium. After obtaining my degree in architecture and urban design, I was able, thanks to this dissertation, to come back to Japan once more, and start working for Florian Busch Architects in Tokyo, where I am doing my best to refine and put into practice some of the ideas put forward in this book. The work is never finished.

Although every step in my gradual acquaintance with Japan still comes with new lessons and experience, I have only made minor amendments to the original manuscript. Looking back from a point where I now have a stable routine in this country, I can see that I started writing at the best possible time—right in the middle of my transition between Europe and Japan. I was no longer in the comfortable position of a visitor, looking in from the outside. It was a time when keeping interest in Japan was not merely a matter of fascination for me: it had turned into an active effort to make myself at home in an absolutely foreign country.

In my view, this meant that I had to relearn the very basics of human interaction, at least to a certain extent. For instance, I grew up fluent in five European languages but learning Japanese demanded more of me than simply adding a sixth to the mix: it was an immersion in a whole new system of thought... Just like I had to relearn how to read people, their manners, their expressions, their values, I also had to relearn how to read the cityscape. How do the Japanese house and street express themselves? What stories do they tell?

I discovered that, even as a beginner, the ability to switch between two sets of cultural norms offers more than a choice between one or the other, or even the ability to pick and choose. The real opportunity here is to take a step back and critically address the invisible ideas and habits at the core of your being. This experience, while humbling, was a source of freedom for me. It sparked curiosity and creativity. A young expat, I spent my time getting to know this country in a playful state of mind, where Japan could be what it was, there to discover... but also what I consciously decided to make of it. This playful attitude shaped *Japan: Nation Building Nature*. At a base level, the book explores a new way of writing history, taking joy in bending the rules of convention.

Like many books, the original manuscript has been overtaken by time. When I was writing, I was looking at the 'present' time frame between 2016 and 2018, wondering how that situation would extend into the future, up until 2020 and beyond. Soon, 2020 will have passed and ended in a way no-one could have expected. The relative isolation we experienced this summer has been a shocking turn of events, around the globe yes, but in Tokyo in particular since we were expecting a mass influx of tourists when hosting the 2020 Olympics. The cancellation of the Games has somewhat shaken up the premise of this book, the publication of which was originally geared towards this potentially era-defining mega-event. Nevertheless, I am confident that the crisis has added an additional layer of meaning to the book.

Although it is too early to make definite statements about the long-term impact of the coronavirus outbreak on architecture in Japan and abroad, we are already getting a glimpse of how, rather than triggering a complete change in course, this pandemic is only accelerating existing social and economic trends. This historical pattern corresponds the societal impact big earthquakes have had in Japan, as we discuss in chapter one. Many parallels to what is happening in the world at this very moment can be found throughout the book. History and travel always help bring the 'here' and 'now' into perspective. That is why I hope the story told will stay alive, taking on new meanings in the years to come. I think that, by its nature, this book is open to change, eager to absorb additions and interpretations. It is by no means comprehensive and should lead to a broader discussion and debate, opening doors to follow-up projects.

In the meantime, I want to thank all those who helped me keep this project alive through years past, as it took on many different forms. First of all, I would like to thank my thesis promoters, professor Johan Lagae, professor Andreas Niehaus, and professor Tijl Vanmeirhaeghe from the University of Ghent, who guided me in my research and later encouraged me to pursue a publication. I especially thank professor Johan Lagae for keeping in touch with me while I was abroad, even though my studies were officially on hold. I would also like to thank Hera Van Sande who joined my professors in the jury, for her feedback on the manuscript, and her kind support as I made my way back to Japan.

I want to thank Yasuhiko Kumagai and all the staff at Yasui Architects and Engineers for inviting me to Japan and mentoring me as a young apprentice, before I had even graduated. Many thanks to my Japanese teachers at the Naganuma Language School in Shibuya, who always looked after my classmates and me, and taught us much more than how to speak Japanese—as if that was not hard enough in itself. Professor William Steele and doctor Kishi Yu from the Christian University in Tokyo have also been very generous with their council and helped me put my research on the right track in the very early stages. I am especially grateful to one of my favourite architects and my current employer, Florian Busch, who offered me a chance to come back to Tokyo after my graduation, and has always trusted and encouraged me to explore a wide range of interests at the office.

I want to thank everyone who later on helped publish the book, including of course the team at nai010 who have been extremely professional and kept the project on course despite ongoing disturbances due to the coronavirus outbreak. I want to thank Marcel Witvoet, for believing in my manuscript and guiding me through the publication process, and Laurence Ostyn for carrying the book over the finish line on a tight schedule. Many thanks to Sander Boon for his careful work on the graphic layout and to Leo Reijnen for the final edit of the text. I am indebted to Sami Biwer, CEO and founder of TourInJapan and TourInTravel, as he generously helped me advertise my crowdfunding campaign at the exact right time. I thank all of the backers who helped me fund this publication via Kickstarter. This book would not be here without you.

I am extremely grateful to my mother, my father, my brother, and my grandparents who have been there all the way, and helped me move forward at every step. Finally, I want to thank all my other friends and acquaintances who have been involved in any way, big or small.

Introduction

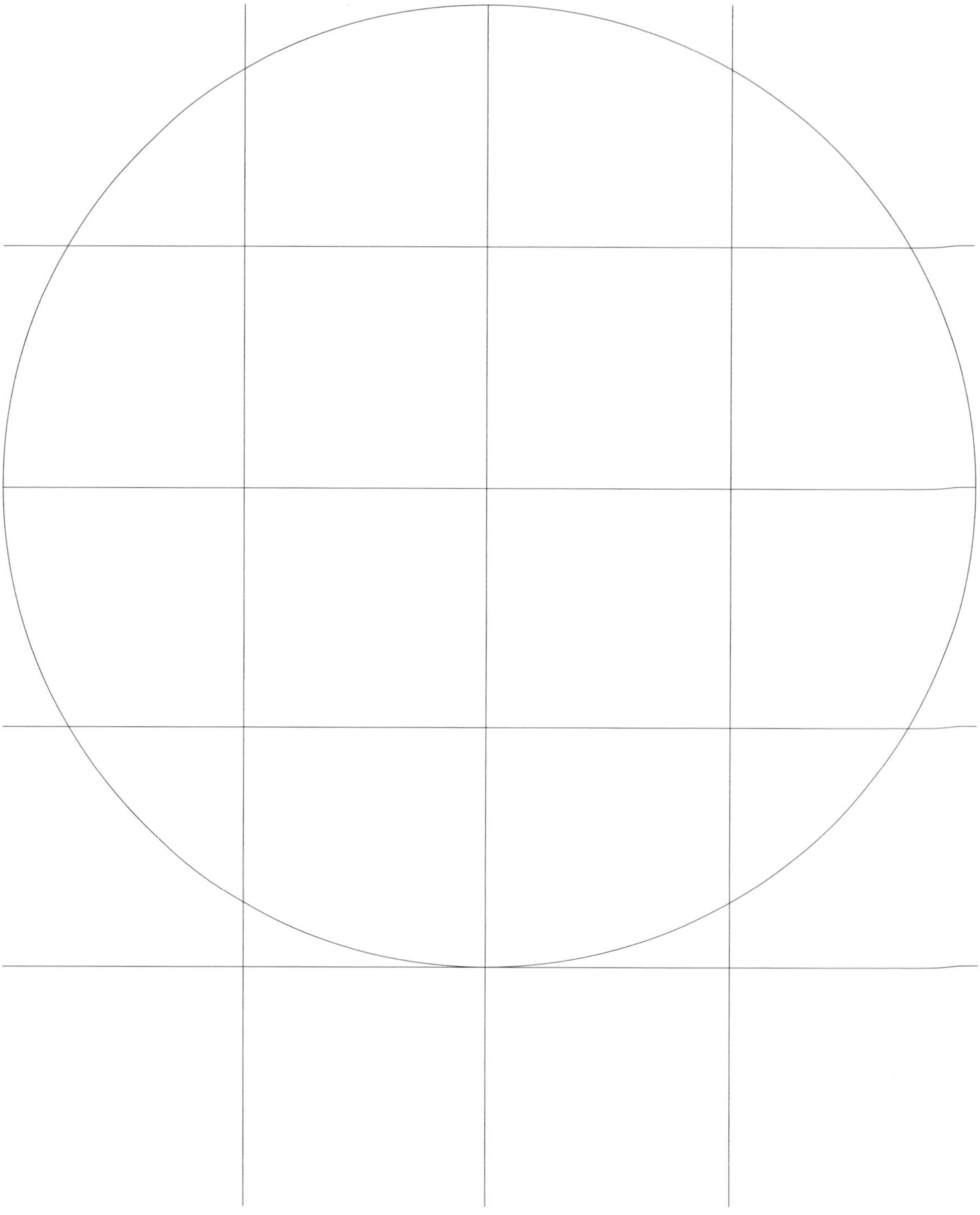

Matrix

Nation Building Nature is the first book dedicated to mapping out the views of nature that have shaped the widely acclaimed—but often misunderstood—modern architecture of Japan. How can collective efforts to build a metropolis of gleaming skyscrapers on shaking ground be justified? Is the city part of nature, and should it be treated as such? Do machines have souls? This book investigates the various ways in which Japanese culture can shed new light on our understanding of ecology in construction, and vice-versa. Largely based on a Master's dissertation I presented at the University of Ghent in 2018, it is the product of a long-standing interest in Japanese architecture. I have been fascinated by this country and its beautiful, bizarre, at times simply baffling buildings since I started studying architecture at university. After my fourth year of studies, I was awarded a European scholarship to go live and work in Tokyo for a year. That is when I started taking notes for this book. I decided early on to write about Japanese architecture, but found every aspect of it so interesting that it seemed a pity to narrow it down to one specific subject. Instead, I decided to do the opposite: I would use Japanese architecture as evidence to address a broader, and perhaps more important topic. How do we humans relate to nature? It is a question echoed across the globe and the answer is reflected in the houses, the streets, and the cities we build. It is a timeless question and yet it seems more appropriate than ever, with our environment on the brink of collapse. Instead of using this ecological lens to project a straight path into the future, as is common, I used it to travel back in time. It led me to uncover an alternative Japanese architectural history, from which we can come back to the now, with fresh questions and ideas for the future.

To tackle the global environmental crisis, expansion of the sustainability paradigm is currently leading to a revival of local responses to climate. Since each regional ecosystem comes with its specific constraints, it seems natural for Japan and other countries to look into their respective building traditions, rather than follow a universal model. Yet Japan presents a special case, as some deep ecologists[1] go so far as to promote Japan's alleged 'oneness with nature' as a cultural model for the whole world to emulate. This points to a particular interest in Japanese culture within Western ecological circles. We see this reflected in the popularity of Buddhist philosophy as a response to our unbalanced lifestyle, or even in the typical section dedicated to Japanese products in many organic shops. With this in mind, expectations to find in Japan a goldmine of ecological inspiration could not be higher. Furthermore, the Japanese have a long history of dealing with earthquakes, tsunamis and typhoons. After an earthquake, entire cities built of wooden houses would burn down on an almost regular basis. In times of environmental crisis, it makes sense to turn to Japan for inspiration. That is why I was shocked to discover how at first sight, ecology often did not appear to be a major concern in this country.

This impression was mitigated as I got acquainted to Japanese life, and found that clues to the Japanese business and design ethics presented themselves to me at the office, as well as during casual walks in quiet neighbourhoods, in conversations that struck me, and in practicing the language. Japanese ecological ethics are popular, meaning not only that they have an aesthetic appeal both in and outside Japan, thriving on a new era of Japonism. They are popular in the literal sense that they belong to a folklore that is entrenched in the daily customs of the population. This has both positive and negative implications. On the one hand, the popular character of ecological ethics in Japan can be a delightful antidote to the reductionism that, among other things, equates ecology to quantifying carbon dioxide emissions. On the other hand, the emphasis on the natural environment as a matter of representing the nation exposes citizens to populist political discourse that idealises aesthetic aspects of a so-called harmonious relation to nature while concealing the actual material harm done to nature by a heavily industrialized, consumerist society.[2]

In Japan, the construct of an overlap between nation and nature has been instrumental in modern nation-building efforts ever since the mid-nineteenth century and architecture was quickly recognized as a medium through which this overlap could be affirmed. In fact, as of 1869, architectural and agricultural space played a joint role in 'naturalizing' the Northern Island of Hokkaidō, modern Japan's first colonial conquest, as part of the Japanese archipelago.[3] Until recently, the former Prime Minister Shinzō Abe still often referred to the beauty of the Japanese landscape in his speeches and, upon taking office, pledged to create 'a beautiful country, Japan'.[4] This rhetoric aims at tapping into a nationalist sentiment to introduce reactionary policies while simultaneously seeking international economic expansion by showing a progressive and ecologically engaged nation to the world.[5] Beyond the political arena, the nature-nation debate has opened up a contested field of scholarly research of its own. In recent years, Japan's alleged unique relationship with nature is once again drawing the attention of scholars who claim to find valuable elements in Japanese culture for the world to learn from.[6] This idealistic stance in prospect of a necessary paradigm shift as we face environmental disaster finds itself at odds with studies that take the materialistic point of view.[7] The latter emphasize the constructed nature of these cultural ideals and the material harm done in spite of them. The implicit left-right political divide in the views above should not distract us from the fact that in architecture, critical and poetic approaches can be mutually supportive rather than exclusive, allowing us to engage in multiple points of view.

History shows that idealized Japanese images of nature are, to a certain extent, modern productions, invented through Japanese encounters and exchanges with the West[8], and many of these ideas can be categorized as nationalist propaganda or even marketing techniques. But Japanese views of nature also take shape in a concrete reality, reflecting—and responding to—concerns of daily life. In placing 'building' at the crossroads of nation and nature, *Nation Building Nature* aims to take due account of this reality. As previous histories of the Japanese nature-nation hinge have primarily focused on an exchange of ideas among politics, arts, and sciences, this study presents a complementary point of view by examining the interaction of these higher spheres with the construction of a physical environment. Correspondingly, most of the questions, interests, and insights guiding the narrative of this story arose during a year-long experience of interning and travelling in Japan. While spending a week there would be enough to realize that in accounts of Japan and its architecture received abroad much is left unsaid, living through day-to-day struggles (and delights)—learning the language, fitting in the corporate culture, enduring hour-long commutes in packed trains, conversing with neighbours, and so on—have inspired an assessment of the built environment as a support structure for the characteristic way of life on the spot. The work below reflects my attempt to make sense of these first-hand impressions of Japanese architecture and urbanity, and investigates into how these personal interests might fit into a larger narrative by systematically confronting my subjective experience with the macro perspective found in history books.

To achieve a balance between personal impressions and more objective points of view, the structure of the text is conceived as a two-dimensional matrix anchoring a heterogeneous collection of texts that confront and complement each other. Each of the topics, while carefully selected, is nevertheless replaceable and can always be complemented by additional investigations and new perspectives. In presenting this potentially infinite matrix, we avoid trying to offer a comprehensive history. Because it is impossible to reconcile all aspects of Japanese architecture's relation to nature within a single story, or a single volume, we only aim at juxtaposing fragments in a coherent and sensible way. This structure conjures up new associations, and allows readers to draw their own conclusions, reading between the stories. Japanese culture, and by extent its architecture, have been fiercely criticized and also strongly idealized. But seeing cultural differences in black and white only perpetuates views of Japan as strange, remote, and alien. The matrix that organizes the knowledge below is in itself an encouragement to look at Japan, at cultural differences, and at ourselves in a particular way. It is a tool designed to give an outlet to different points of view, thus letting Japanese architecture emerge in a frame aimed at understanding, rather than at imposing a value judgment.

Time X Space

Our matrix is defined by two axes, spanning across space and time. Four chapters stretch out horizontally in 'space' as so-called ecologies: Earthquake, Monsoon, Post-Nuclear and Island. These ecologies are traversed vertically by three complementary narratives unfolding on the 'time' axis. This space-time structure is inspired by two historical analyses that seek to highlight the role of the natural environment as a determinant factor in the historical production of culture and architecture. The first is Reyner Banham's *Los Angeles: Architecture of Four Ecologies* (1971), and the second Tetsurō Watsuji's *Fūdo*[9] (1935). At first glance these two books do not seem to hold much in common. The object of study and historical context of the books differ as does their message to the world. Nevertheless, the authors seem to share a fundamental assumption that structures their work and leads them to comparable research methods. Essentially, both Banham and Watsuji point to the tendency of previous accounts to read history as a chain of events in time while overlooking the effects of spatial factors in what Banham calls 'ecologies' and Watsuji calls fūdo or a 'climate', a concept that overlaps with Banham's loose definition of ecology.

Like this book, Banham and Watsuji's works were inspired by a journey. In his journey, the British Reyner Banham falls in love with L.A. and learns how to drive a car in order to navigate the city like a local. It makes him look at the city through movement, as a system of flows. A living system if you will, which is the larger definition of ecology. The construct of 'four ecologies' frames the way he sees Angelenos relate to the beach, the freeways, the flatlands, and the foothills. The architectural historian looks beyond the interminable footprint of L.A.'s rectangular urban grid to recover its underlying territories.[10] His discovery of these territories goes hand in hand with an 'embrace of everyday pop and a celebration of indigenous and overlooked phenomena'. Watsuji, too, sees in everyday objects and rituals the expression of a living system bound to a certain territory. In *Fūdo*, a product of his journey through Asia and Europe, the Japanese scholar writes: 'A style distinctive to a certain locality, perhaps because of the latter's cultural supremacy, may be transplanted to another locality with a different climate. (This can occur more readily with dress than with architectural styles.) But to whatever locality it may be transplanted, the fact that the style is conditioned by the climate which produced it can never be effaced. European-style clothes remain European, even after more than half a century of wear in Japan.'[11]

In his preface to *Fūdo*, Watsuji recalls coming across the problem of climate while reading Martin Heidegger's 'Sein und Zeit', in the summer of 1927 in Berlin. Intrigued by the German philosopher's attempt to treat the structure of man's existence in terms of time, Watsuji wonders why space is not also postulated as part of this basic structure of existence: 'Indeed it would be a mistake to allege that space is never taken into account in Heidegger's thinking, for 'Lebendige Natur' was given fresh life by the German Romantics, yet even so it tended to be almost obscured in the face of the strong glare to which time was exposed. I perceived that herein lay the limitations of Heidegger's work, for time not linked with space is not time in the true sense.'[12] In 'In the Rear-view Mirror', Banham's foreword to his reading of Angeleno architecture, the architectural historian uses a similar assumption as a point of departure. The author blames the fact that L.A. has been systematically cast out of the league of great architecture cities on the insistence of the architectural establishment to place L.A.'s architecture on a timeline of the general evolution they see in architecture. Instead of seeing Los Angeles as a mistake, a shameful episode that does not want to fit within the logical series of events that constitutes the history of modern architecture and planning, Banham explains that Angeleno architecture should be understood and appreciated as a response to spatial and climatic factors as well. In his foreword he declares: 'What I have aimed to do is to present the architecture (in a fairly conventional sense of the word) within the topographical and historical context of the total artefact that constitutes Greater Los Angeles, because it is this double context that binds the polymorphous architecture into a comprehensible unity that cannot often be discerned by comparing monument with monument out of context.'[13]

In the process of integrating 'space' in the structure of history in the form of 'ecologies' and 'climates', Banham and Watsuji blur the boundaries of the scientific definitions of these concepts. Watsuji explicitly claims that 'it is proper that natural science should treat climate as a natural phenomenon, but it is another question whether the phenomena of climate are in essence objects of natural science.'[14] This is echoed for Banham in the foreword to his 2009 edition of *Los Angeles: Architecture of Four Ecologies*, written by architectural theorist Joe Day. The latter notes that 'there is something bordering on blithe dismissal in Banham's use of the term: Ecologies, he seems to imply, are simply what we make of them.'[15] When Banham's book first came out in 1971, ecology was already a societal concern and this concern has increased ever since. It is therefore not surprising that Banham received a lot of criticism, including from ecologists, regarding his relaxed appropriation of the term. In his inflammatory review 'Ecology of Evil' of 1972, Peter Plagens condemns Banham for his apparent hypocrisy: 'In a more humane society where Banham's doctrines would be measured against the subdividers' rape of the land and the lead particles in little kids' lungs, the author might be stood up against a wall and shot; as it is we must try to laugh through our tears at ... Four Ecologies' nearly comic ineptness.'[16] Likewise, *Fūdo* and the works inspired by Watsuji's philosophical study are dismissed by serious scholars as dangerous pseudo-science. Indeed, although Watsuji's environmental determinism seems naïve or even comical today, it endorsed the totalitarian imperial rule of colonial and wartime Japan, a subject that will be analysed in chapter two. It may be surprising therefore that despite their unscientific character Banham's and Watsuji's approach have received renewed interest and approval in light of the contemporary environmental crisis.

Addressing the sceptics who do not see how Banham's usage of ecologies could be read in terms of sustainable design, Joe Day reminds us in his foreword to a 2009 edition of *Los Angeles: Architecture of Four Ecologies* that Banham's attitudes actually closely compare to the assumptions underlying the environmental movement today: 'that consumers must "buy into" sustainability, not be hounded out of their tastes; that new technologies can replace and remedy many of the ills of older, more wasteful or polluting modes of transit, agriculture, and so on; and that raising standards of living are the best defences against ecological blight'.[17] Similarly, architectural theorist Jin Baek, author of *Architecture as the Ethics of Climate* explains that Watsuji sees his concept of fūdo not merely as a collection of natural features—climatic, scenic, and topographical—of a given land, but also as 'the metaphor of subjectivity', or 'who I am'.[18] Since in fūdo this 'self-discovery' is inter-personal rather than individual, Baek argues that Watsuji's concept of fūdo could be revisited as 'a lesson that without considering the collective humane characteristic of a natural climatic phenomenon, any sustainable act is flawed and inefficient'. Viewing it as a work that challenges Eurocentrism and Cartesian dualism, Baek goes so far as to call fūdo an 'East-Asian notion of sustainability'.[19]

This points to the potential value of continuing to think ecology as a broader reality today, to reach beyond technical interpretations and think ecology in a cultural sense, one that may not always be quantifiable. The question is not whether the positive sciences are correct or not, nor can we deny that we will heavily depend on science and technology to protect ourselves from environmental disaster in the future. Revisiting a broader view of ecology is about realizing the full potential of adapting our relationship to nature. The urgency of climate change and pollution have turned ecology into a widespread dogma, that is being integrated into all kinds of fields including architecture. From the Kyoto protocol to the Paris climate agreement, ecology is being (re)assigned to society and architecture as a new, mainstream, progressive, and often purely technical issue. But as the sustainability and smart city assignments increasingly tend to hand over the responsibility of building the living environment to technicians, rediscovering how ecology can intersect with identity and politics has the potential to restore ecology as an essentially architectural challenge. Watsuji would explain that climatic phenomena are expressed in all kinds of human activities ranging from the arts to daily manners and customs and that 'it is evident therefore that climatic phenomena understood in this light differ from phenomena studied by natural science. To consider a sea-food diet as a climatic phenomenon is not to regard climate merely as natural environment. To interpret artistic style in relation to climate is to indicate the inseparability of climate from history.'[20] Grounded in the belief that 'history and climate in isolation from each other are mere abstractions'[21] Watsuji's philosophical study aims to return to a holistic view of history by repairing this broken link. In this study however, bringing time and space together is intended as a reversal of Watsuji's thinking. The purpose of confronting the abstractions of time and space is to underline the fact that these are in fact abstractions. The time-space matrix is here to remind us that reality can and must be apprehended in multiple ways. The 'spaces' or ecologies described below are not objectively definable places. These 'constructed' ecologies are in fact imagined and idealized abstractions that have been built up in the course of history as a result of top-down and bottom-up cultural adaptations to outside forces, resulting in a distinctive, yet ever-changing relationship to nature.

Space X 4

Our research is confined to four of the most stereotypical natural phenomena said to have influenced the Japanese building culture: earthquakes, the monsoon climate, nuclear erasure of life (and its reappearance), and insularity. A separate chapter is dedicated to each of these phenomena, analysing how architecture has been complicit in the construction of their respective 'ecology', or their sphere of interaction within the physical, political, scientific, and social realms. To reveal the dynamic between the nation and its alleged natural space, each of these four chapters opens with a simple map zooming out on Japan in its surroundings. Looking at a globe, we tend to think of Japan as a clearly defined entity, isolated by the ocean. The maps presented below intend to show how the boundaries of what is perceived as part of Japan have actually been very flexible over the course of the past century. Characterizing Japan as an 'earthquake ecology' or a 'monsoon ecology', has helped redefine the Japanese sphere of influence, and even its territorial boundaries. Even the border of contemporary Japan as an 'island ecology' has a completely unexpected and artificial shape when we look at Japan's Exclusive Economic Zone granted by the UN Convention of the Sea in 1982. Although the specific confines of each ecology as a contested subject of debate cannot be objectively delineated, the maps are a convenient way to provide the reader with a reference of how the phenomena and events described in the text lock into each other spatially by giving an overview of the scale and distances involved.

While all ecologies coexist as a latent presence, at least in contemporary discussions, each of them also emerges as a prominent theme in the architectures of a specific era. Therefore, each chapter closes with a timeline summing up the significant events that have brought the ecology in question to the fore, as well as the (geo)political events influencing the architecture of that period. As the sequence of heterogenous texts—alternating points of view while making leaps from the past to the present—can be disorienting, the map at the beginning and the timeline at the end support the reading of each chapter by 'sandwiching' it in a space-time frame of reference. Within this boundary, analysis proceeds in three steps:

1. **An introduction essaying peculiar spaces of contemporary Tokyo serves as an initial concept-finding exercise, hinting at how research into this ecology could lead to a greater understanding of the Japanese city, or even enrich design practice.**

2. **What follows is a historical analysis, exposing how the ecology in question has impacted the development of Japanese architecture during a certain period, with a series of case studies.**

3. **Using this historical background, a fictional dialogue is set up between architects and scientists of the past and the protagonists of contemporary movements, showing if and how the ecology continues to influence projected futures in the age of environmentalism.**

Time X 3

Essaying Presence

Zen gardens, cherry blossom viewing, and naked bathing in natural hot springs: Japanese intimacy with nature is not hard to picture with eyes closed. Eyes wide open, the cliché quickly dissolves. It is replaced with overhead power lines obstructing the sky, and concrete embankments cutting off streams and rivers from human contact. Available land is covered in cheap construction, leftovers are stuffed with vending machines. Here and there, an unexpected pocket of green survives on the sacred land of a temple or shrine. At first sight, Japan seems more addicted to concrete than to its natural riches. In some places, Japan's sprawling concrete infrastructure is a vital protection against natural disasters such as earthquakes, floods, and tsunamis. In others, it is a superfluous product of Keynesian economic policy that uses the construction industry as a lever to boost the country's productivity and crush unemployment. The difference is hard to tell and, in any case, neither are truly ecological. As architect Toyo Itō points out in the wake of the Great East-Japan Earthquake in 2011: 'We cannot win a fight against nature'[22], implying that human settlement patterns must be integrated in the natural system instead of trying to resist it. In order to understand the motivations behind this kind of statement, everyday experience is essential.

The beauty and intelligence of Japanese architecture is too often looked at in an abstract way that is disconnected from the context of everyday life. A Japanese house for example, may delight us on a picture with its open and light aesthetic. However, once we experience this building in person, the cold of winter or the summer heat will draw our attention to the fact that the walls are poorly insulated and the slick windows don't have double glazing. From the point of view of a European architect, who will maximize the lifespan of the building with sustainable materials and minimize loss of energy with thermal insulation, the flimsy houses of Japan appear to be the antithesis of ecological construction. In contrast to European buildings that have historically used thick walls to protect the interior climate from exterior influences, Japanese houses wrapped in paper were always designed in a way that welcomes the weather inside the house. Although this is our expectation, the structure in itself is not the finished product that should be evaluated here. It is the users' performance of the house which is ecological. Take the *tatami*[23] floors that provide a neutral ground in the house on which all domestic activities can take place. Their flexible use allows indoor activities to follow the sunlight entering the space from dawn until dusk. Ideally, the void of the home becomes a stage for the family to come together in a shared embrace of climate.

Of course, contemporary reality diverges significantly from this ideal. Inside spaces are now equipped with electrical air-conditioning, which is completely unsustainable, especially in the absence of thermal insulation. But that is beside the point. Accepting and using the weather as part of

E
Essay

Concept
+
Experience

無常
Mujō

風土
Fūdo

共生
Kyōsei

勿体無い
Mottainai

the indoor experience and protecting the inside from the weather are very different approaches. Perhaps they were influenced by differences in the natural environment. In the humid air of Japan it is harder to keep out the cold and heat.[24] It is also a reflection of cultural differences of which there are still traces. For instance, a common conversation starter in Japan is a comment about the weather. This does not necessarily have the same awkward connotation of lack of inspiration as it does in the West. It is considered the best way to start an interaction because the shared experience of the weather makes the conversation inclusive and accessible to everyone. The ecological reflex to accept climate as a shared experience in daily life remains a part of popular culture and, since in architecture critical and poetic approaches don't have to be exclusive, this kind of sensibility deserves attention.

Travelling to Japan with a preconceived notion of what this culture 'in harmony with nature' should live up to is most likely going to be a disappointing experience. Instead of simply turning to critique, this investigation finds solace in the kind of 'aha' moments described above, which can only arise by letting go of expectations and maintaining a non-judgmental awareness of details in the turmoil of everyday life. As these seemingly trivial observations add up, they culminate in a fresh perspective on what Japan potentially has to offer. So before scrutinizing the past or making speculations about the future, each chapter is introduced by giving the present, which is all we have, a second chance. The essay—open-ended and intuitive—is adopted here as a strategic tool able to bridge the gap between loose fragments of direct experience and their conceptual consolidation. To this effect, each essay borrows a popular Japanese notion related to the 'ecology' in question—Earthquake, Monsoon, Post-Nuclear, and Island—and gives it concrete meaning by letting this borrowed concept frame the narration of tangible urban qualities. By suggesting how they find a pragmatic expression in some of the most mundane, yet distinctive spaces of Tokyo, the compiled concepts of Mujō, *Fūdo*, Kyōsei, and Mottainai add up to a mini guide to the Japanese city as an ecological resource. The text is documented with photographs taken during a year of working and living in Tokyo. As the literary and the photographic essays unfold in parallel, the link between both is left implicit. While the photos convey the immediate sense of curiosity and excitement at discovering something new, something different, the text concludes a period of reflection on the meaning of these spaces in the wider context of contemporary Japanese society.

Historians' Past

After re-evaluating the present built environment through the conceptual lens of ecology, we dive into the history books to retrace the infiltration of earthquakes, climate, nuclear power, and insularity into the discourse and design of Japanese architecture. Although this section follows the historical timeline chronologically, the story told is not one of linear progress nor of a one-sided technology transfer. Involved in nostalgic reactions and shifting stances towards Western influences in society at large, Japanese architecture has historically adopted a highly ambivalent stance. From the time Western architecture is introduced to Japan, architecture's relation to nature is identified as a cross-cultural project in which Japan can showcase its indigenous knowledge acquired over the centuries. Relying on the four 'ecologies' has enabled Japan to question and criticize foreign knowledge and create certain niches for the development of Japanese expertise. This evolution is recorded here in a string of architectural case studies, grouped chronologically, with an introduction outlining the major trends for each period. In order to provide an overview of one-and-a-half centuries of Japanese modern architecture, without losing track of the complexities of the socio-economical contexts, deemed essential in this research, this study is heavily indebted to a number of in-depth historical analyses focusing on Japanese architectural movements within the confines of a specific era of Japanese history.

William Coaldrake's *Architecture and Authority in Japan* (1996) is an exception to this rule as it covers Japanese architecture from the Middle Ages to the modern post-war era. As a reference however, Coaldrake's study of the Japanese state's major public buildings was particularly helpful to cover the early stages of adoption of Western construction techniques and architectural styles during the Meiji period. While each case study in *Architecture and Authority in Japan* is provided with ample background, the context provided remains limited because Coaldrake needs to stick to the 'classics' in light of the scope of his work, and due to the fact that the narrative is written from the perspectives of these singular buildings.

To balance out these deficiencies, Gregory Clancey's *Earthquake Nation: The Cultural Politics of Japanese Seismicity* (2006) was a truly eye-opening work. Zooming in on the Meiji era, Clancey centres his story around the Great Nobi Earthquake, dubbed the 'Big Bang', which he views as the catalyst for the first generation of Japanese architects to question the influx of Western technology and reconsider the qualities of traditional techniques. The study of 'Earthquake Nation'-Japan does not take the point of view of architects however, but frames developments in architectural discourse as collateral to the development of the science of seismology on Japanese soil. Clancey's examination of the co-evolution of architectural and scientific discourse provided a valuable lesson for the subsequent chapters, as did the way he maps these discourses onto nation-building and colonial aspirations of the time. While the new connections Clancey draws between architecture, seismology, and politics give us a completely new view on the architecture of the period, there is much left unsaid about the big earthquakes before and after Nobi.

To dive deeper into the aftermath of the Great Kantō Earthquake of 1923, Gennifer Weisenfeld's *Imaging Disaster: Tokyo and the Visual Culture of Japan's Great Earthquake of 1923* (2012) was an excellent source. Although architecture is not central to her argument, as she focuses on the representations of the 1923 disaster in visual media, her study clearly exposes how earthquakes in Japan serve as a catalyst for change, and how their meaning can be manipulated to point future development in certain directions. Besides providing the necessary knowledge on how the visual imagery of earthquakes has been used as propaganda for and against the reconstruction of Tokyo as a modern metropolis, the book also gave valuable insights into the interpretation of earthquakes in the premodern era.

Jordan Sand's *House and Home in Modern Japan* (2004) made up for the lack of architectural information in Weisenfeld's book. In a rare study of domestic space in early twentieth-century Japan, Sand gives a detailed account of the gradual Westernization and commodification of the Japanese housing stock, showing among other things how this transition was accelerated by the disaster of 1923. The central interests of the book are the actors and policies guiding the general reform of domestic life starting in the 1880s up to the 1930s when, as Sand exposes, growing anxiety about radically transformed lifestyles and social structures start to trigger a backlash against Westernization and cosmopolitanism.

While Watsuji Tetsurō's *A Climate: A Philosophical Study* (1935) falls out of Sand's scope, the latter's conclusion on alienation and anxiety in reaction to the reform of 'everyday life', especially among older male intellectuals, provided an interesting point of view to reconsider Watsuji's seminal work. Usually criticized as an offshoot of a radicalizing political regime, Watsuji's discourse on fūdo, which discusses the Japanese house and the infrastructural Westernization of Tokyo at length, could now be viewed as part of a bottom-up reaction as well, expressing generalized fears spreading among the Japanese population. Jin Baek's *Architecture as the Ethics of Climate* (2016) further supported the reading of Watsuji, providing interpretations already discussed above. Baek's positive reception of *Fūdo/A Climate* was especially helpful in maintaining a balanced view of Watsuji's ideas, which are heavily criticized and cast of as ultranationalist propaganda in most of the scientific articles on the subject. A major inspiration, not only for the content of this book but also for its format and the interests taken was *Project Japan: Metabolism Talks* (2011) by Rem Koolhaas and Hans Ulrich Obrist, who travelled to Japan to meet and interview the members of the Metabolist movement who have by now reached the age of retirement. The book alternates conversations with the former members of the movement with historical sections providing context or illustrating typological innovations. Although his work is not put in the spotlight, *Project Japan* revolves around the puppet master of the group, 'national architect' Kenzō Tange, acknowledging his role as a pioneering architect, a teacher, a mentor, and an 'ambassador' for the export of Japanese architecture. The main interest of the book is the interplay between a (non-Western) architectural avant-garde and what is considered a 'hyper creative' Japanese bureaucracy.

H
History

Context
+
Cases

Auto-colonisation
(1868-1889)

Discovery of
Wooden Japan
(1891-1923)

Domesti-city
(1918-1930)

Climate and Colonial
Architecture
(1930-1945)

Resurrection of the
Construction State
(1945-1960)

Cold War Architecture
(1952-1973)

Architecture of Dispersal
(2011-2020)

After Growth
(1992-2050)

Despite featuring all kinds of facts and figures, *Project Japan* does not offer much insight into the relationship between Metabolism as a Utopian movement and the actual construction culture of the time. In that respect Zhongjie Lin's preceding, shorter account *Kenzō Tange and the Metabolist Movement: Urban Utopias of Modern Japan* (2010), did provide helpful information as Lin shows that while visionary, Metabolist proposals were not that unrealistic. He places Metabolism in the context of mass urban reconstruction, economic miracle, a socio-political reorientation, and a fast-growing construction industry. Put together, Lin's work and *Project Japan* give a good overview of the interaction between state planning, industry, and architectural invention and expose the roots of this interaction in pre-war colonial planning.

The doctoral dissertation of Hyunjung Cho elucidates a key aspect influencing the architecture of that period that is often left out of the picture in the previous two books. In *Competing Futures: War Narratives in Post-war Japanese Architecture* (2011) Cho provides a completely new perspective, showcasing Japanese post-war architecture as a symptom of wartime trauma and nuclear anxiety. The doctoral thesis was an invaluable asset in the attempt to expose a relation between the build-up of nuclear power, a construction culture, and subconscious reactions to nuclear anxiety in avant-garde architectural design. Other authors have written about post-war Japanese architecture from this psychological perspective but what sets Cho's work apart is the fact that she does not view wartime trauma as a static entity but as a notion evolving according to a dynamic geopolitical context. For the last chapter, *Cities, Autonomy and Decentralization in Japan* (2006) edited by Carola Hein was inspirational by bringing attention to the paradox of Japan as an archetypically centralized nation with a modern history full of plans for decentralization. The book gives a detailed overview of decentralization in modern planning history, including scales varying from the neighbourhood to the island. While Hein's book does not include an analysis of this kind of 'starchitecture', the debates surrounding decentralization and grassroots movements such as *machizukuri* described in the book were unexpectedly helpful in putting the contemporary architectures of Toyo Itō and Kengo Kuma in a much wider perspective, and helped to frame the stylistic debates surrounding the architecture of the upcoming 2020 Olympics, now postponed to 2021.

Furthermore, as we frame the current situation in Japan as an 'Island Ecology', Eiji Oguma's sociological study on Japanese ethnicity, entitled *A Genealogy of 'Japanese' Self-images* (2002), was enlightening in the way it retraces the Japanese self-description as an 'island people' throughout modern history. The book presents a refreshing counter-argument to widely held views in Japan as well as abroad, that the Japanese have believed that they are a homogeneous nation since the onset of modernity. Oguma's book also provides a background story to the character of Tetsurō Watsuji and his theories preceding *Fūdo.*

Finally, *Inventing Japan* (2003), a small but densely packed book by Ian Buruma, has been of use throughout the four chapters. As the title suggests, the book swiftly outlines how Japan has reinvented itself as a modern nation, from the time it was forced out of isolationism up to the 1964 Olympics, when Japan 'rejoined the world' and beyond. Focusing on politics and the general trends in popular culture, Buruma eloquently describes how Japan participates in the global process of modernization and the internal conflicts that arise as a result. Buruma does spend a lot of time describing the surface of Japan's historical evolution, giving more importance to political personas or cinema and literature than to the economical foundations of infrastructure, trade, and production processes. But as a vivid summary of Japanese modern history it was of great value as a guiding compass through its various episodes to keep track of the coherence of it all.

The aim here is not to give the books cited above a critical review. Instead, we hope to enhance the value of each of these accounts by assigning them to a position on the grid of our space-time matrix. Examined through the lens of 'ecology', these books, and other references used, automatically acquire connections to other works that weren't obvious before. As these associations branch out, new meanings emerge. Each reference work elucidates one branch of the tree of an alternative Japanese architectural genealogy—one inspired by an ecological perspective. In this respect, the fact that most of the case studies in this book do not belong to the classic examples discussed in other surveys on modern architecture in Japan testifies to the original and creative interaction between the present 'ecological' perspective and the sources listed above.

Dialogue on Projected Futures

After rediscovering the past, a fictional dialogue is staged combining quotes of nature's spokesmen in society: architects and scientists. Projected futures of the past are confronted with the visions of today's leading actors to examine how the four ecologies have a latent presence in contemporary debates. These dialogues intend to reveal a historical depth and complexity to environmental issues as, unfortunately, the more ecology has to be accepted as a new paradigm for society, the more it is being applied as a narrow-minded, politically correct or purely technical project. Contemporary ecological architecture can be very boring as a result of these standard practices and assumptions. Ecology in architecture has become a de facto requirement with prepared solutions, an extra layer of insulation or photovoltaic cells on top of existing models. Or worse, a layer of natural materials and greenery used to dress up a building in a 'green' fashion. In a way, the pressing concerns around climate change might be preventing architecture from going deep, in order to go fast.

As the dialogue shows, the danger of a superficial transformation is that society will be prone to repeating old mistakes. Rather than transforming our way of life, the cultural revolution of the sixties ended up as a branding instrument to sell more clothes, cars, music, and other 'stuff'. The pressure to stop debating because it is now time for action bodes well for the absorption of ecology into marketing logics, dragging us back into a consumerist system, which is by nature anti-ecological. Today, a good example of this would be the contradictory idea to host the world's first 'green' Olympics in Tokyo, an event that will in any case be extremely wasteful. While environmental concerns had recently returned to the centre of attention in Japan following the disaster at the Fukushima nuclear plant in 2011, the nation seemed eager to celebrate overcoming this ecological and economical challenge by hosting the Olympic Games less than a decade later. Mega events such as the Olympics are always justified as a lever for investment, but the question remains: where this capital is flowing to? With the Northern region of Tōhoku still far from recovery, the Games would most likely have furthered the imbalance between the Japanese capital and the peripheral regions. Meanwhile, natural disaster has struck again, this time in the form of a global pandemic.

The games have been postponed to 2021 but as of now, there is no guarantee that they will in fact take place. Stressing the importance of developing drugs and a vaccine, Shinzō Abe posed in parliament that 'The Olympic Games must be held in a way that shows the world has won its battle against the coronavirus pandemic.'[25] This brings us back to Toyo Itō's insight post-3/11, claiming that us humans 'cannot win a fight against nature'. Isn't rushing our way to a vaccine in order to be able to hold the Olympics comparable to building ever higher concrete barricades to the tsunami in order to postpone making inevitable changes to an inherently unnatural lifestyle? What is the alternative? The outbreak of the coronavirus has exacerbated the inconsistency between environmental logics and mega-events such as the Olympics. The global lockdown has

D
Dialogue

Architects
+
Scientists

'Strong architecture has failed the people'

'It is the duty of Japan to export design and technique'

'The Japanese must still remove his shoes at the doorway'

'I am not a scientist (anymore)'

'Construction is the hope of twentieth-century man'

'A gigantic monster on the brink of extinction'

'I refuse to play the role of the Japanese architect'

'We are not in the century of construction anymore'

forced a worldwide reckoning, a shared experience bringing the distinction between the essential and the superfluous into focus. Tokyo originally won the Olympic bid by promising compact, no-nonsense games and yet in light of the pandemic, the organizing committee has uncovered much potential for further shrinking: 'We are looking into every possible area' says committee CEO Toshiro Muto. 'It's time for all of us to review what are the essential things for the games. What are the must-have items?'[26] But are the Olympics a must-have to begin with? Isn't the responsible solution to have no Games at all? Or could Japan, perhaps building on its traditions, be radical enough to successfully reinvent the way we organize these events? 'I think we might come up with a new Olympic and Paralympic Games, something that is unique to Tokyo', says Muto.

Looking back in the midst of the pandemic, our discussion will depart here, in the tension field between the disastrous events of 2011 and the prospect of celebrations in 2020, polarizing the contemporary Japanese architectural scene as the disaster of March 2011 seems to have ushered in a new era for Japanese architecture. Two heavyweights of the profession have taken the lead in formulating the guiding principles of a new architecture. In 2011, Kengo Kuma published *The Principles of Place*, in which he details what he terms 'post-earthquake and post-tsunami architectural tenets', and in 2012, Toyo Itō followed suit with a book entitled *Great Transformation of Architecture*, co-authored with anthropologist Shinichi Nakazawa. Contending that 'Strong architecture has failed the people', together they condemn the concrete architecture of twentieth-century 'modernist thinking' and advocate a return to 'smallness' and organic materials, thereby pulling the rug out from under concrete master Tadao Andō, Japan's most esteemed architect at the onset of the twenty-first century.

As a jury member for the international competition for a New National Stadium in view of the Tokyo Olympics, Andō supported a scheme by Zaha Hadid Architects. The latter designed a neo-futuristic concrete mastodon, which, while imposing, was not all that different from Kenzō Tange's 1964 stadium in spirit. Yet the new stadium design immediately faced a surprising amount of opposition by many of Japan's most esteemed architects. Fumihiko Maki gathered a group of designers including Toyo Itō, Sou Fujimoto, and Riken Yamamoto to oppose ZHA's 2020 stadium in a symposium entitled 'Re-thinking the New National Olympic stadium in the historical context of Gaien'. Two years later, the Japanese government officially decommissioned Zaha Hadid Architects on the grounds of not respecting the budgets. The protests are taken into account in the selection of a replacement as 'Consideration of Japaneseness' becomes an explicit part of the criteria.[27] When Kengo Kuma and Toyo Itō make their own proposals for the landmark stadium it becomes clear what their alternative vision is for the future of architecture in Japan. While navigating through the four ecologies, we will deconstruct Itō's and Kuma's new design philosophies as the staged discussion alternates with, and reacts to, historical episodes.

As a story on the spokesmen of nature—architects and scientists—it includes two moments of self-reflection of the professionals in an intermezzo entitled: 'I am not a scientist (anymore)', and a concluding text: 'I refuse to play the role of the Japanese architect.' The first expresses the disappointment of Kinji Imanishi, an ecologist, anthropologist, and the founder of Japanese primatology, at the Western view of nature pervading modern science. To Imanishi, who sees nature as inherently harmonious, species fit together in an ecological whole, adjusting to each other, each finding its own niche. In an article for *New Scientist* magazine pleading for more cultural diversity in science, fellow primatologist Frans De Waal relates how this 'rather un-Darwinian view' led to intercultural disputes. The British palaeontologist Beverly Halstead travelled all the way to Kyoto to confront Imanishi with a document translated into Japanese containing statements such as 'Imanishi's evolution theory is Japanese in its unreality'.[28] Yet even if Imanishi's ecological and evolutionary ideas are problematic, De Waal brings our attention to the fact that his ideas have contributed to fundamental changes in the study of animal behaviour. He reminds us that while Western scientists have extensively adopted Eastern concepts and approaches over the past few decades, they have often appropriated them without being aware of their sources[29].

The question of how cultural views of nature shape science and technology arises in the works of other authors, though in different forms. Watsuji Tetsurō believed that Japan could not have developed its own science in the past because science is inherently a product of the European climate: 'There is a link between the lenience and rationality of nature, for where she is lenient man readily discovers order in nature...Thus, Europe's natural science was clearly the true product of Europe's meadow climate.'[30] Coming back from his travels, Watsuji notes that the cultural discrepancy resulting from the import of foreign technology shows not only by comparison with the past, but even more so in comparison with the adoption of modern technology in Europe itself. 'When I came back to Japan and looked at the cars or the trams in the streets, I did indeed feel that I was watching a wild boar rampaging through the fields. . .. But in Europe these means of communication are dwarfed by the houses; they are treated as means of communication, as retainers in the service of city or individual, and their appearance fits their status perfectly.'[31]

In his 1933 essay 'In praise of Shadows', writer Jun'ichirō Tanizaki blames the degradation of aesthetics in his everyday environment on this lack of an indigenous science: '. . . I always think how different everything would be if in the Orient we had developed our own science. Suppose for instance that we had developed our own physics and chemistry: would not the techniques and industries based on them have taken a different form, would not our myriads of everyday gadgets, our medicines, the products of our industrial art—would they not have suited our national temper better than they do?'[32] As opposed to Watsuji, Tanizaki has an intuition that 'the Orient quite conceivably could have opened up a world of technology entirely of its own.'[33] An intuition which by now has been validated, to the point that Asian claims on the technological future are causing anxiety in the West. Since Japan's rise to industrial and economic dominance in the

1970s, visions of high-tech or even post-apocalyptic futures technically, culturally, and politically dominated by Japan and then by China have become familiar, prompting the Japanese cultural critic Toshiya Ueno to coin the term 'Techno-Orientalism'.[34]

No wonder then, that the over-emphasis on a 'national temper' and 'Japanese aesthetics' turn out to be a burden on Japanese architects building across the globe. The concluding chapter of the dialogue is entitled 'I refuse to play the role of the Japanese architect' and explores the desire of contemporary architects not to be overly associated with their country and its tradition in order to avoid caricatures of their work. Why do SANAA Architects insist that they don't see their work as particularly Japanese even though it is a prime example of a modern translation of traditional Japanese aesthetics?[35] Arata Isozaki, who considers himself a citizen of the world with a Japanese passport[36], addresses the pitfalls of being labelled a Japanese architect in conversation with Jörg Gleiter: 'Almost everywhere in today's so-called globalized world people want to pin me down to a representative of Japanese architects. It is always the same stereotypical questions I am asked: Why as a Japanese I want to come to a foreign country and do a project there?'[37]

A lot has changed since the 1930s of Watsuji and Tanizaki. We now live in a thoroughly globalized world sharing the same technology, information, and resources—even facing a shared environmental challenge—yet Japan is still thought of as the arena of an alternative modernity. 68 years after Watsuji's return from Europe to Tokyo, Atelier Bow-Wow's *Made in Tokyo*[38] opens with a similar comparison: 'I'm often surprised, says Yoshiharu Tsukamoto, when returning to Tokyo, especially when returning from Europe. Roads and tramlines run over buildings, expressways wind themselves over rivers, cars can drive up ramps to the rooftop of a six-story building . . . How have we managed to arrive at such a different place to European modernity despite being equipped with the same building technology?'[39]

This question lies at the heart of this book. If Japan had not ended up at a different place, it would not make sense to turn to Japan for inspiration. The essays show that, arriving in Japan, everything is somehow different indeed. Even convenience stores, probably the most generic spaces one could imagine, a model simply copy-pasted from the US, acquires its own meanings and operational logic in Japan. It is tempting to conclude then and there that Japan is indeed living in a different modernity. But the immersion into Japanese architectural history books has added an important nuance. As the history section finds developments in Japanese architecture and urbanity at the junction of an evolving construction industry embedded in a global market economy, a century and a half of thrilling scientific discovery, and shifting geopolitical ambitions, we cannot speak of an isolated Japanese modernity. As a nation embedded in a global process of modernization, Japan can inspire, not with a different modernity, but with a different story of modernity. Retrieving this story from the mouths of its protagonists, the dialogue, finally, calls for nothing other than an ecological vision with more depth, and more diversity.

1 Deep ecology is an ecological and environmental philosophy promoting the inherent worth of living beings regardless of their instrumental utility to human needs, plus a radical restructuring of modern human societies in accordance.

2 R. Reitan, 'Ecology and Japanese History: Reactionary Environmentalism's Troubled Relationship with the Past', *The Asia Pacific Journal* 15 (2017), 1-2.

3 Vivian Blaxell discusses how the simultaneous spread of syncretic architectural styles of public buildings and wet rice fields helped shape the perception of Hokkaidō, originally home to the Ainu people, from a 'wild and foreign place' to a 'productive and naturalized unit of the Japanese state'. V. Blaxell, 'Designs of Power: The "Japanization" of Urban and Rural Space in Colonial Hokkaidō', *The Asia Pacific Journal* 7 (2009) 1-17.

4 S. Abe, Policy Speech to the 166th Session of the Diet (2007), https://japan.kantei.go.jp/abespeech/2007/01/26speech_e.html

5 Shinzō Abe has repeated his pledge in the context of the 'Green' Olympics Games to be held in Tokyo in 2020. In the run-up to the tournament the Prime Minister had scheduled a revision of the Peace Constitution targeting article 9, which prohibits Japan of controlling a military force (Japan does have so-called 'self-defense' troops) and has been a major thorn in the eye of the political right-wing for decades now. Much to his regret, Abe has missed his goal of introducing this first ever amendment to the Japan's pacifist constitution by 2020.

6 See, for example, Jin Baek, *Fūdo: An East-Asian notion of Sustainability*, Umehara Takeshi, *Mori no Shishō* or Steve Odin, *Environmental Ethics*.

7 See, for example, Richard Reitan, 'Ecology and Japanese History: Reactionary Environmentalism's Troubled Relationship with the Past' or Alexander MacNeill, 'From Nature to Nation: shizen and the Japanese national imaginary'.

8 A. MacNeill, 'From Nature to Nation: shizen and the Japanese national imaginary', *Contingent Horizons* 3 (2017), 3.

9 The English title in Geoffrey Bownas' 1961 translation is *A Climate: A Philosophical Study*

10 J. Day, R. Banham, *Los Angeles: The Architecture of Four Ecologies* (Berkeley: University of California Press), foreword.

11 T. Watsuji, *A Climate: A Philosophical Study,* trans. Geoffrey Bownas (Tokyo: Ministry of Education Printing Bureau, 1961), 7.

12 Ibid., preface.

13 R. Banham, *Los Angeles:The Architecture of Four Ecologies* (London: Penguin Press, 1971), foreword.

14 T. Watsuji, op.cit., 1.

15 J.Day, R. Banham, op.cit., foreword.

16 P. Plagens, 'Los Angeles: The Ecology of Evil', *Artforum* 11 (1972), 67-76.

17 J.Day, R. Banham, op. cit., foreword.

18 J. Baek, 'Fūdo: An East Asian Notion of Climate and Sustainability', *Buildings* 3 (2013), 590.

19 Ibid.

20 T. Watsuji, op. cit., 8.

21 Ibid., 10.

22 Translated from 'Interview: Korekara-no kenchiku (Interview with Architect Ito Toyo: Architecture for the Future),' *Asahi Shimbun*, 15 September, 2016, 13.

23 Tatami mats are a typical flooring material made of rice straw used in traditional Japanese houses. The mats cover the surface of the room, interlocking in modular rectangles of about 0.9 by 1.8 meters, depending on the region.

24 On the Northern island of Hokkaidō, where the climate is closer to that of Western Europe, houses do use thermal insulation.

25 Sean Ingle, 'Tokyo Olympics in 2021 at risk of cancellation admits Japan's PM', *Guardian*, April 29, 2020, https://www.theguardian.com/sport/2020/apr/29/tokyo-olympics-not-reliant-on-covid-19-vaccine-senior-ioc-member

26 Stephen Wade, 'Tokyo Olympic CEO: Games next year may not be 'conventional", *abc news*, May 15, 2020, https://abcnews.go.com/Sports/wireStory/tokyo-olympic-ceo-games-year-conventional

27 Jonathan Soble, 'Japan Selects New Plan for 2020 Olympic Stadium in Tokyo', *New York Times,* December 22, 2015, https://www.nytimes.com/2015/12/23/world/asia/tokyo-2020-olympics-stadium

28 F. De Waal, 'Without Walls', *New Scientist* 172 (2001), 46.

29 Ibid.

30 T. Watsuji, op. cit., 74.

31 Ibid., 158.

32 J. Tanizaki, *In Praise of Shadows,* trans. Thomas J. Harper and Edward G. Seidensticker (Stony Creek: Leete Island Books, 1977), 7.

33 Ibid.

34 D. Beynon, 'So Flat, So Cute! Robots, super flatness and Asian architectural futures', *History in Practice: 25th International Congress of the Society of Architectural Historians Australia and New Zealand* (2008), 7.

35 Jonathan Glancey, 'Sanaa's summer pavilion brings sunshine to the Serpentine', *Guardian*, July 8, 2009, https://www.theguardian.com/artanddesign/2009/jul/08/sanaa-summer-pavilion-serpentine

36 Jörg Gleiter and Arata Isozaki, 'Comments on the Production of International Architecture'. In R. Baumeister and S. Lee, *The Domestic and the Foreign in Architecture* (Rotterdam: 010 publishers, 2007), 280.

37 Ibid., 281.

38 *Made in Tokyo* is a guidebook depicting the Tokyo metropolis as a laboratory for its inventive techno-cute, shameless, semi-architectural constructions.

39 J. Kuroda, M. Kaijima, Y. Tsukamoto, *Made in Tokyo* (Tokyo: Kajima Institute, 2001), 8.

Earthquake Ecology

Earthquake Ecology

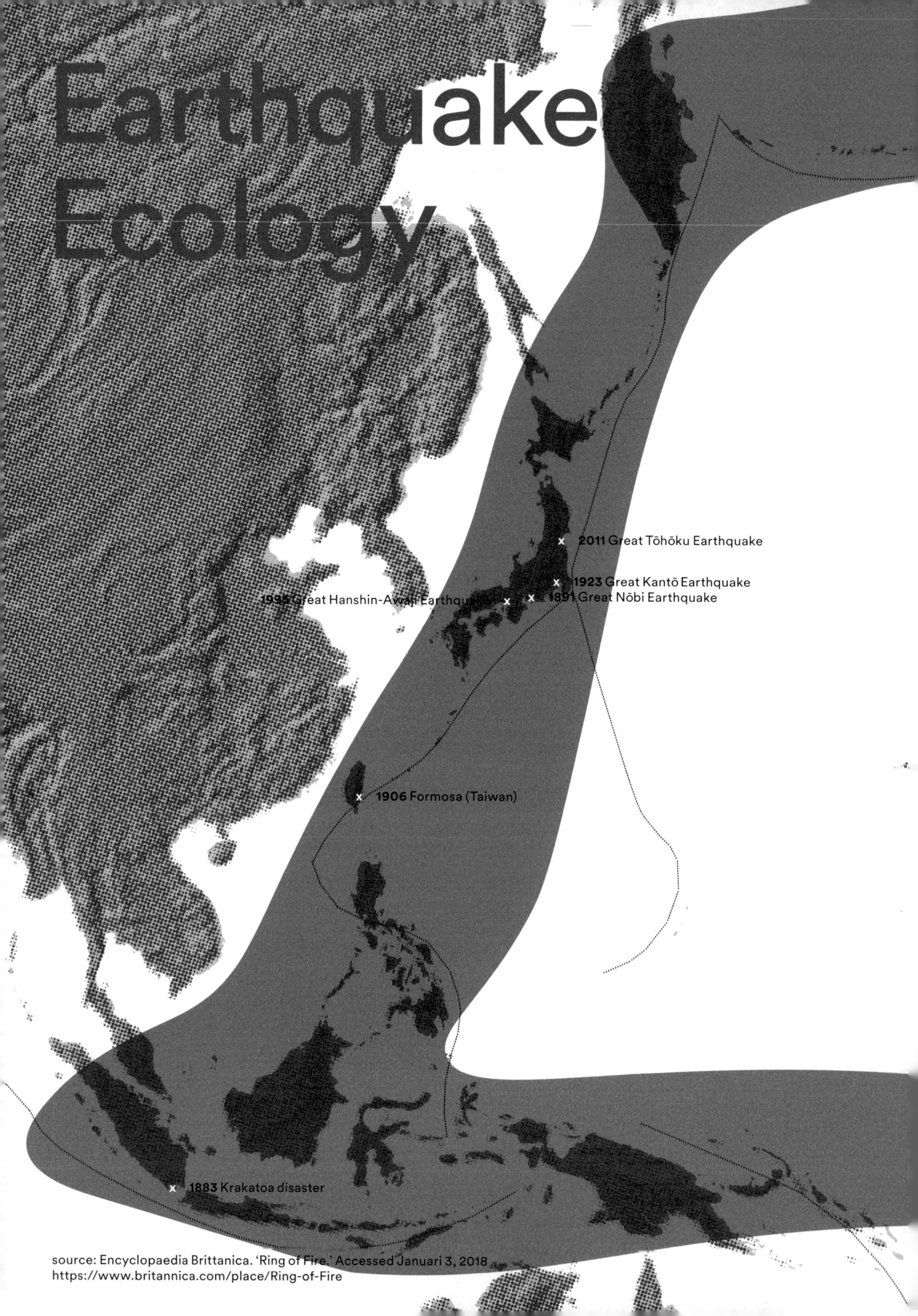

source: Encyclopaedia Brittanica. 'Ring of Fire.' Accessed Januari 3, 2018
https://www.britannica.com/place/Ring-of-Fire

Seismology was the first modern science developed on non-Western soil. Well-funded by a bourgeoning nation aspiring to become a modern power in its own right, the study of earthquakes became entangled in a set of decolonizing as well as colonizing practices. Beating the West at its own game, Japanese scholars were able to scientifically prove the technical inferiority of imported construction methods while legitimizing Japanese influence in other earthquake ecologies, especially around the Ring of Fire where seismic activity peaks around the turn of the century. Branding Japan an 'earthquake nation' in control of its own nature opened a new door to territorial expansion.

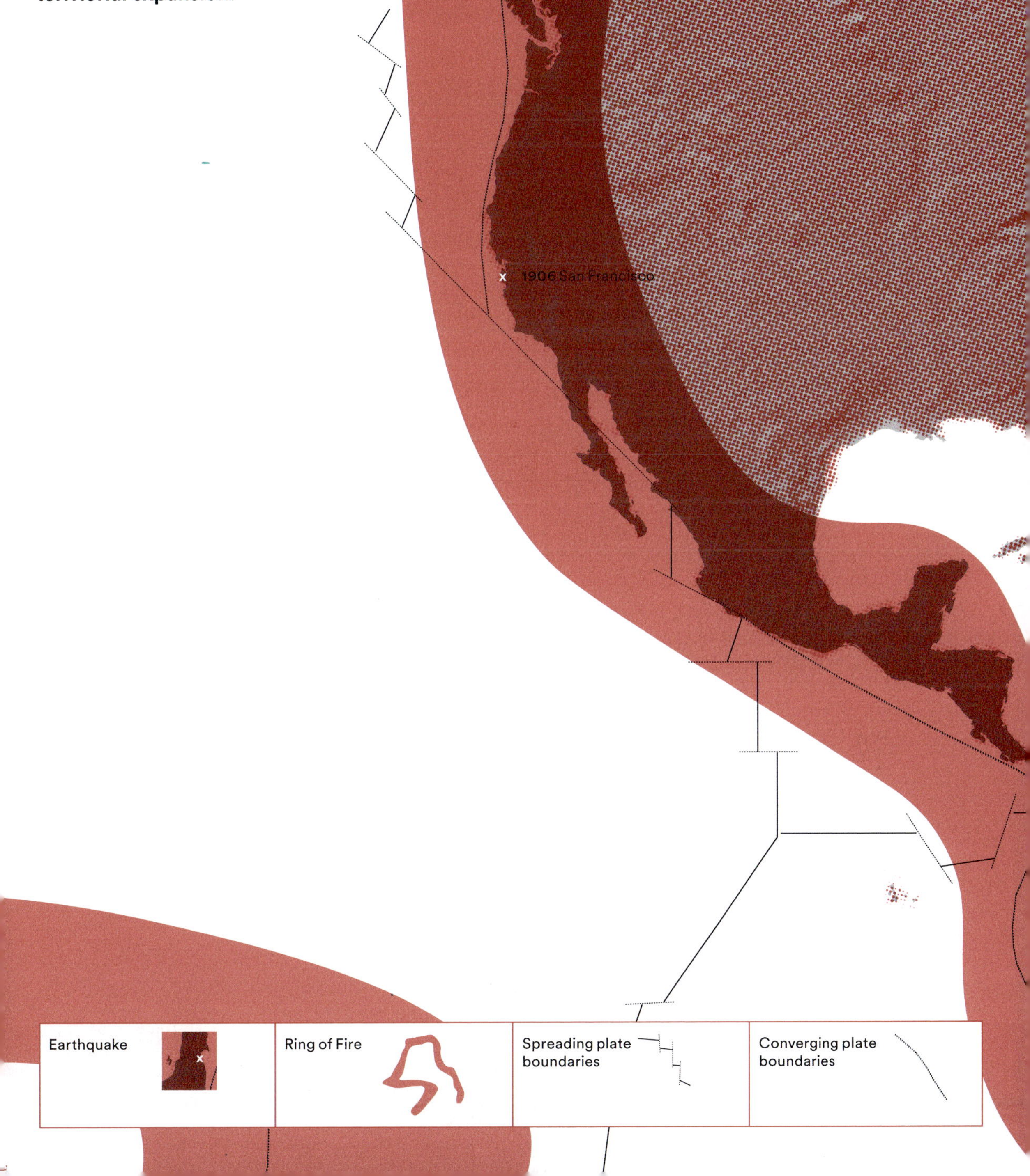

E

無常

Mujō

‘If nature offends your ego, then transcend your ego by becoming one with nature.’[1]

—Matsuo Bashō, haiku poet, seventeenth century

Mujō

To become one with nature is challenging when nature itself shows two faces. While the expectation of cherry blossom petals dancing in the wind takes the mind of the imminent threat of typhoons and earthquakes, Japan's streams, flanked by cherry blossom trees, remain trapped in their concrete embankments. Will modern Japan ever transcend its highly ambivalent relationship with nature? Traditionally, the contradiction of nature's beauty and mercilessness is resolved in *mujō*, the concept of ephemerality promoted by Zen Buddhism. Zen spread into mainstream culture during the seventeenth century. *Mujō*, which combines nothing (mu) and permanence (jō), relates the foreseeable cycle of the seasons to unpredictable eruptions of natural disasters within this single concept. The theory of mujō is derived from the fundamental Buddhist teaching that life has to be accepted as transient and full of suffering in order to find enlightenment. Arriving in Japan through China and Korea as of the sixth century, the archipelago's shaking ground proved fertile for these Buddhist teachings, as they provided a philosophical perspective on destruction. In traditional buildings, the innate impermanence of building components such as wooden joinery and paper screens, which can readily be dismantled and replaced, appeared to provide the best defences against ensured ruin.

Floating World

During the Edo period (1603-1868), *mujō* acquired secular meanings through the arts. The popular woodblock prints that depict premodern Japan in a flat axonometric style are considered a typical expression of *mujō*. In Japanese they are called *ukiyō-e*, literally: floating world. Although the ephemeral world depicted in *ukiyō-e* has indeed disappeared, I sense that the world that has replaced it remains afloat. Earthquakes used to wake me up at the dormitory in Yokohama. The first time, I mumbled half asleep: 'Huh what... who's that pulling my bed back and forth? Stop that.' The sensation was not alarming. It felt like being on a ship, gently rocking on the waves of the ocean. The back-and-forth was always so soothing that I usually went back to sleep as the ground was still shaking.

I should not have been surprised that our building was equipped with earthquake-proof engineering. In its 27-year old life, it must have withstood far greater shocks then I experienced during my one-year visit. But I remember being amazed by its structural flexibility able to smoothly absorb the shocks, a technique I previously associated with sturdy, high-tech buildings as opposed to our three-story dormitory, an ugly concrete building lacking any sort of architectural quality or finesse. It appeared to be put together as quickly and cheaply as possible. The same applies to the surrounding houses, and in fact to the great majority of buildings I encountered in Japan. While all this construction must have an exceptionally strong and resilient structure thanks to local construction knowledge and the appliance of strict safety regulations, this self-evidence seems contradicted by the feeble tectonics of the bulk of Japanese construction. Owners have to take into account the fact that even though their house or building will probably survive most earthquakes without major damage, the government can always enforce stricter legislation, making it hard to sell or lease the property to a next generation.[2] As the building will most likely have almost no resale value after a mere two decades, the foreseen impermanence of the building is naturally translated into cheap and light construction materials. In the street nothing is fixed, any building could be replaced tomorrow.

Civil law also requires all buildings to keep a minimal distance of 50 cm from neighbouring buildings on all sides. Coincidently, this allows for maximum flexibility between structures on this shaking ground. The detachment adds to the airy, floating quality of the Japanese streetscape. Rather than focusing on harmonious scenery in accordance with the historical surroundings like in many European cities, Japanese urbanist regulations are forced to address advanced earthquake- and fireproofing above all else. And since the urban residue of the past has been erased by previous earthquakes and fires anyway, the result is an unfinished, continuously recycled cityscape rather than an accumulated 'oeuvre'. Following the reasonings above, one ultimately starts to see the whole Japanese urban landscape as a result of an invisible 'earthquake ecology'. But the question remains whether *mujō* is still a useful concept to analyse, design, and transform this impermanent living environment. The resulting ugliness of a modern technocratic approach probably still has more to do with 'egos offended by nature' than 'transcended egos becoming one with nature'.

Walking through the streets of central Tokyo in Shibuya or Shinjuku we can observe how the impermanent character of the earthquake city contributes to its vitality. In the dynamic urban space of metropolitan centres, the mechanisms of impermanence have been hijacked by the demands of intense capitalist competition. It is one thing for continual rebuilding to go hand in hand with a lucrative system of real estate speculation. But in commercial centres the facades of these buildings will be subject to renovations of even shorter cycles, and these will in turn be covered in signs and billboards that might not even last for more than a couple of weeks.[3] Businesses move in and out, and must be quick to adapt if they want to stand out.

Shibaura House

In the floating world of Tokyo's frantic competition, one company has harnessed the power of *mujō* to outsmart the market in a contemporary and sustainable way. The Shibaura House is an office building for Kohkoku Seihan Incorporated, a local management company that works in the design and advertising industry and is based in Shibaura, a landfill in Tokyo Bay.[4] Shibaura, originally an industrial landscape of warehouses, has evolved into a business district for offices. Most recently, numerous apartment blocks are being built in the neighbourhood and young families are moving in. Because cross-overs between the residents who live there and businessmen who come to work are still scarce, Kohkoku Seihan decided to rebuild their premises in 2011 as a 'house' that they could share with local people.[5]

The company president, Masaru Itō, reports having a hard time directly after the earthquake of March 2011 when they had no work at all. The company tried to shift from his father's business model with big corporate clients towards a more dynamic and flexible approach. 'In fact', he says, 'many companies that have been running for a long time in the same industry are closing down.'[16]

This is where the architecture comes in to play its part. Itō commissioned SANAA to design an office that could simultaneously serve as a public space. The result is a dynamic landscape that works as a vertical, indoor park where anyone is free to come work, play, learn, or teach. The space draws different crowds at different times of the day. Freelancers come to enjoy the coffee in the morning, at lunch businessmen from around the corner drop in to eat their *bentō*[7], and in the afternoon you might find mothers gathering their kids to play while discussing their projects together. In the evening, a lecture or event takes place upstairs. For a company that was working with a very limited selection of clients and existing management resources, the building brings a lot of potential in terms of relationships being made on a business level, but also as a public agent. The Shibaura House shelters, and feeds on the cycle of local life.

Company president Itō envisions that the architecture brings the company such resilience that even if they were to lose the kind of work they have been dealing with in the past, the Shibaura house would offer possibilities in moving forward by altering the form of the company.[8] Now SANAA's work is easily associated with mujō because its light, transparent design aesthetic already expresses a taste for the ephemeral. Their architecture believes in dissolving and blurring boundaries as a way to enhance the safety and resilience of communities, inviting flux as an ingredient to make life more colourful and resilient. This particular case however is unique, because the ephemeral aspirations were a direct result of management and business considerations rather than architectural ethics and style. Out of the post-earthquake economic crisis mujō emerged as a business model. It reconciles the risk of earthquakes and other hazards with the everyday cycle of life. It reproduces the poetic aspects of Tokyo's floating world by fully accepting the harshness of its competitive arena. With this building, the company effectively transcended its ego by becoming one with the nature of Tokyo.

When there was an earthquake disaster three, four years ago, it was impossible to foresee the future. We didn't know whether we could find tenants even if we would have turned the building into office rental space. With that prospect, I chose the path that I would be least likely to regret later - doing something that I wanted to do to start with. Still, trial and error never end. In a way our management style is unfixed … I don't even have a table now (Laughter). I decide where to work as I wish, following the warmth of the sunlight in winter.[9]

-Masaru Itō, president of Kohkoku Seihan Inc.

大勝
居酒屋
浩司
居酒屋
七十里
貸しおしぼり
アルプス商事

1 Roy Starrs, 'Zen, Japan and the art of democracy.', New Statesman, July 7, 2011, https://www.newstatesman.com/asia/2011/07/japan-essay-nature-earthquake

2 B. Bognar, 'What Goes Up, Must Come Down', *Harvard Design Magazine* 3 (1997), 1-13.

3 Ibid.

4 'Concept & Story', *Shibaura House,* http://www.shibaurahouse.jp/en/about/concept_story

5 Ibid.

6 'Conversation: Between Kazuyo Sejima and Masaru Ito', *Shibaura House,* http://www.shibaurahouse.jp/en/about/architecture

7 A bentō is a typical Japanese lunchbox.

8 'Conversation:...', ibid.

9 Ibid.

H

Auto-colonisation (1868-1889)

'Revere the Emperor, expel the barbarians'

Sonnō jōi, or 'Revere the Emperor, expel the barbarians' is the slogan that united the revolutionary forces against the *bakufu*[1] establishment during the civil war that would mark the beginning of Japan's modern era. For more than two centuries the *shōgun*'s[2] *bakufu* in Edo[3] had successfully managed to keep Japan relatively isolated from the outside world. The period of feudal rule between 1603 and 1868, known as the Tokugawa era, was characterized by economic growth, a strict social order, isolationist foreign policies, a stable population with 'no more wars', and popular enjoyment of arts and culture. Despite its isolationism, Tokugawa rule laid the foundation for an easy transition to modernity. Most Western books were forbidden from 1640 onwards, but from 1720 this ban was relaxed. This started an influx of Dutch books and their translations into Japanese with book details including microscopes, hot air balloons, Western hospitals, techniques for painting and printing, and updated geographical knowledge.

Around the time Japan started manufacturing its first Western-style bricks, Commodore Matthew C. Perry sailed into Tokyo harbour on behalf of the U.S. government to force Japan into trade with his nation. In 1853 and again in 1854, Perry arrived as the commander of a modern fleet, to demand a treaty permitting trade and the opening of Japanese ports to US merchant ships. Russia, Britain, France, and Holland soon followed suit. The *bakufu* recognized that the foreign powers could not be contained any longer and chose compromise over a suicidal war.[4] But the involuntary decision of the shōgunate to open up the country to international trade and influences was unpopular and spurred a revolutionary momentum. The ensuing civil war, also known as the Japanese Revolution, was fought between forces of the ruling Tokugawa and the many nobles seeking to return political power to the imperial court in response to the shōgunate's weak handling of foreigners following the opening of Japan during the prior decade. However, once the revolutionary forces took control of the country and emperor Meiji was 'restored' as the head of state, the latter had to face the same facts.

Ironically, the men who conquered Japan vowing to 'expel the barbarians' were now embarking the country on an adventure of fast and thorough Westernization. While the process of modernization had been ongoing for two centuries in Japan, both through (limited) exchanges with the outside and by internal processes[5], the period from 1868 until 1889 was characterized by an avid desire to assimilate the nation to Western models of imperialism and industrialism. In contrast with the critical reception of foreign culture during the preceding and subsequent eras, the early Meiji period may be described as an exercise in 'auto-colonization', an auto-pilot set to escape the threat of being colonized by others. Faced with the task of matching images of the West, Japan became self-aware[6], its buildings self-conscious. In absence of classical palazzos, the tatami floors of *daimyō*[7] feudal headquarters were promptly disguised with carpets, tables, and chairs.[8]

'Civilization and enlightenment'

An Imperial Charter Oath was promulgated at the enthronement of Emperor Meiji of Japan on April 7, 1868. The Oath set the legal stage for Japan's modernization and accelerates a process of urbanization as people of all classes were now free to change jobs and move to the city for better work. In 1870, the Government started to hire foreign experts called *yatoi*. The *yatoi* staff technical positions in the new ministries, most of them in the ministry of construction. But they also taught at the *Kōbudaigaku*, the new College of Technology.

The official slogan of the Meiji rule became *Bunei kaika*, or 'Civilization and enlightenment', reflecting a spirit diametrically opposed to *Sonnō jōi*.[9] Foreign knowledge was idealized and the ways of Western man were deemed superior. Eager to join the league of great nations, emperor Meiji inaugurated Japan's first constitution in a Western style throne room in 1889, thus proving Japan's cultural enlightenment to the world.[10] But civilization and enlightenment brought more than arrangements on paper, they also implied an infrastructural transformation. To promote an industrial revolution, Japan steadily acquired a modern market economy: monopolies and caste differences were abolished by law, and people were now free to own land, and buy or sell their property.[11] In *Inventing Japan*, Ian Buruma points out that this liberalization was not free from state interference.[12] After all, the goal of modernization was to build a strong and powerful nation. The Meiji period's other popular slogan could not be clearer: 'Rich country, strong army.'

Wooden Japan

In the Meiji era, Japanese architecture was considered a nation-building project like the Japanese army, the Japanese constitution, or Japanese science. In his doctoral dissertation, Gregory Clancey tells us how initially, all architects were brought to Japan as employees of the state, that educatesd them, and provided all the major commissions. Before the Meiji restoration, architecture as a design profession separate from the act of building itself did not exist in Japan.[13] Traditionally the building process was orchestrated by a master-carpenter or *daiku*, an art passed on from father to son. But the architects of the young nation-state did not come from these *daiku* families. They were originally from samurai families, the former ruling class, and taught in a British architectural tradition.[14] In the Edō era, Japan was an overwhelmingly wooden country. Under the auto-colonization premise, it is decided that this wooden Japan was to be be rebuilt in brick and stone. Clancey relates how, according to British impressions, the wooden constructions clearly show that Japanese people were defenceless before a destructive nature with earthquakes and fires.[15] As wooden traditional architecture became an object of denigration, expressing strength—the dominant metaphor of the new regime—became the focal point of Japan's modern architecture.

Tsukiji Hotel

Completion: 1868

Although the Meiji era was unmistakably an era of construction, the number of actually licensed architects in Japan was very limited at first. In 1897 there were still only 45, in all.[16] Their task was to design monumental ministries and the public facilities of modern cities, including post offices and train stations.

The Tsukiji Hotel of 1868 is built with a Japanese timber frame covered in a terracotta finish.[20] Japanese style roofs are topped with a Western-style belvedere featuring a wrought-iron weather vane.

In *Architecture and Authority in Japan*, William Coaldrake argues that the foremost concern of this building campaign was to redefine the image Japan displays to the world, as the initial motivation for Westernization was survival against encroachment of foreign powers.[17] Therefore, the first Meiji building to adopt a Western style was an official guesthouse for international travellers in the port district of Tsukiji, not far from the imperial palace.

Despite the building's terracotta tile cladding, already in use during the Edo period to protect buildings against fire[18], the building burned down a mere four years after construction was completed. The fire of 1872 destroyed a large area of downtown Tokyo, which provided a golden opportunity for the Meiji government to produce a state-of-the art urban plan, worthy of the capital of a modern empire. In this plan, remodelled streets would connect the foreign concession in Tsukiji all the way to Shimbashi station[19], a major hub in the heart of the capital.

Ginza Bricktown

Architect: Thomas Waters
Completion: 1870s

The opportunity of reconstruction in the wake of the great fire of 1872 unleashed the wild ambitions of Japan's visionary elite. The *Daijō-kan* (Council of State) instructs the Tokyo government that 'not only the burned section, but the entire city ought to be rebuilt in brick and stone', according to the European fashion.[21]

Gregory Clancey explains that wooden Japan had appeared a 'mysterious paradox' to the foreign eye, 'the trace of an ancient culture that is not permanently inscribed in the landscape'.[22] Following the remarks of European architects regarding the alleged fragility of wooden Japanese construction, a new material was chosen to realize Japan's first indestructible city. Brick was the preferred material because it was the quickest to build with.[23] In a hurry to build an eternal city, the government devised a plan for Japan's modern streetscape that was as paradoxical as the ancient one.

Ultimately, the Ginza district was realized on a very modest scale.[24] Managing all the investments in Japan's profound transformation, the Meiji government was facing bankruptcy. Interestingly, this did not impair the country's industrial revolution.[25] In fact, the moment when the government was forced to sell off its infrastructure to private entrepreneurs is the moment the industrial economy of Japan really started thriving.

'No matter how much it costs, we have to do it for the sake of our honour', said oligarch Saigō Takamori.[26] Indeed, the Meiji government's architectural fantasy could well be described as realizing the Ginza Bricktown on a national scale.

Akasaka Detached Palace

Architect: Tōkuma Katayama
Completion: 1909

Thanks to the limitless demand for Western-style buildings at the onset of the Meiji era, Japan mastered the European architectural vocabulary even before the nation had a constitution. In *Architecture and Authority in Japan* William Coaldrake argues that these buildings were more than imitations; they were state-of-the-art.[27] The stone-clad Akasaka Palace is his best example of Japan's cutting-edge construction technology. To build the palace, architect Tōkuma Katayama spent eleven months in Germany studying palace architectures.[28] During the design phase he took one more trip to Europe, and one to the United States to investigate the technical aspects of air-conditioning, central heating, and detailing of the interior. He also arranged the import of 3000 tonnes of steel from Pittsburgh along with two American engineers for the erection of the steel frame of the building. The use of structural steel for the project was the first occasion for this new technology to be applied in a seismic environment. Nevertheless, Katayama criticized the American steel frame model and with his team, made amendments for earthquake-proofing.[29] After a couple of decades, Japan's 'auto-colonization' had produced a generation of Japanese architects confidently rivalling their foreign teachers.

'We were aware from studying recent cases of earthquakes (in Japan) ... that, although steel frame structures had been used, these were not really safe and caused a lot of problems. At the Bureau for the Construction of the Eastern Palace we therefore thoroughly considered this defect in the American system and have been careful to give thorough consideration to the problem.'[30] – Tōkuma Katayama

Deer Cry Pavilion
Architect: Josiah Conder
Completion: 1883

Katayama's defying attitude towards the foreign 'architecture masters' followed a general trend-break in Japanese politics. The late 1880s witnessed a rise of nationalism and self-confidence of the nation in its own power. It was in this context that the government decided to sell the emblem of Japan's attempts at assimilation: the Deer Cry pavilion. In *Inventing Japan* Ian Buruma describes the *Rokumeikan* or 'Deer Cry pavilion' as a club where elites interacted in a Western manner, conceived as a stage for 'Europeanized posturing' of Japanese rulers aiming to impress foreign associates in business and government.[31] It was designed by Katayama's mentor Josiah Conder, now known as 'the father of Japanese architecture'.

Although the *Rokumeikan* was just a place for ballroom dancing, playing whist, and smoking Havana cigars, the intentions behind the masquerade were dead serious.[32] By adhering to Western customs, Prime Minister Inoue and his 'dancing cabinet' were looking to be accepted as equals by their European and American counterparts in the hope of finally abolishing unequal treaties. As the years went by it became clear that this was not going to happen and in 1889 the pavilion was sold off. With the failure of the dancing cabinet came a backlash against Europeanization in Japan, which was replaced by the idea that 'colonial conquest would be the ultimate sign of greatness and modernity'.[33]

Josiah Conder established the course on European architectural styles at the Kō budaigaku, where he changed the initial Japanese emphasis on utilitarian engineering to doctrinaire architectural style.[34] For the Deer Cry pavilion he designed a building that mixed French second empire style with Palladio and high Victorian.[35]

1 *Bakufu* is the term used for the *shōgun*'s government. Originally, *bakufu* meant 'tent government' or 'field headquarters', referring to the quarters of a general on the battlefield, implying the temporary nature of such an administration.

2 *Shōgun* originally refers to a military rank equivalent to 'general', the highest officer in an army. However, from the twelfth century onwards, Japan's *shōgun* held de facto power over the country while the emperor remained in place as *de nomine* head of state.

3 Edo is the name of what became Tokyo in the modern era. The city was rebaptized after it became the new imperial capital in 1868.

4 I. Buruma, *Inventing Japan: 1853-1964* (London: Weidenfeld & Nicholson, 2003), 13-14.

5 During the isolationist period or *sakōku*, lasting from 1633 to 1853, the Japanese had regular exchanges with the Dutch, who provided access to the latest scientific, medicinal, and military developments in the Western world. Furthermore, historians have highlighted that developments occurring during the Edo period, such as the advent of a money economy, urbanization, and a rising literacy rate prepared Japan exceptionally well for the era of modernization after 'the advent of the West'. Robert Oxnam, H. Paul Valery and Carol Gluck, 'Tokugawa Japan: Path to Modernization', *Asian Topics*, http://afe.easia.columbia.edu/at/tokugawa/tj02.html

6 W. Coaldrake, *Architecture and Authority in Japan* (Hove: Psychology Press, 1996), 208.

7 *Daimyō* were Japan's most powerful feudal lords. The name consists of *dai* (大), 'large', and *myō*, short for *myōden* (名田), meaning private land.

8 W. Coaldrake, *Architecture and Authority in Japan* (Hove: Psychology Press, 1996), 208.

9 I. Buruma, op.cit., 35.

10 Ibid., 35-36.

11 Ibid., 36.

12 Ibid., 35.

13 G. Clancey, 'Foreign Knowledge or Art Nation, Earthquake Nation: Architecture, Seismology, Carpentry, The West, and Japan, 1876-1923', PhD diss., Massachusetts Institute of Technology, (1999), 15-17.

14 Ibid.,79.

15 Ibid., 47.

16 Ibid., 25.

17 W. Coaldrake, op. cit., 209.

18 Ibid., 216.

19 T. Grunow, 'Empire by Design: Railways, Architecture, and Urban planning in Tokyo, Taipei, and Seoul,' PhD diss. University of Oregon (2014), 48.

20 W. Coaldrake, op. cit., 216.

21 T. Grunow, op. cit., 26.

22 G.Clancey, op. cit., 22.

23 W. Coaldrake, op. cit., 212.

24 The project comprised only a couple of streets which remained largely unoccupied at first due to the high rent.

25 I. Buruma, op. cit., 40-41.

26 G. Clancey, op. cit., 16.

27 W. Coaldrake, op.cit., 217-219.

28 Ibid., 219.

29 Ibid., 220.

30 Ibid.

31 I. Buruma, op. cit., 46.

32 Ibid., 47.

33 Ibid..

34 W. Coaldrake, op. cit., 217.

35 I. Buruma, op.cit., 46.

D

‘Strong architecture has failed the people’

Kengo Kuma, paraphrased from *The Japan Times,* ‘Born of disaster.’

Beachgoers enter through a hole in the concrete seawall.
Odawara, 14 August 2020

Cyclic Renewal

After a destructive earthquake, there are two possible attitudes. A disaster of a critical scale is an opportunity to rebuild a shinier, more modern version of society, as we have seen in the case of the 1972 fire, inviting a complete remodelling of the Ginza area and, by extension, the rest of the capital.[1] Conversely, it can cause a generalized questioning of modernity's foundations. It can feed the longing for a return to the way things were before, or even to a fictional natural state. After the Tōhoku catastrophe of March 2011, the governor of Tokyo, Shintarō Ishihara, caused outrage by declaring that the earthquake was 'divine punishment' for Japan's present-day materialism.[2] Similar comments were made after the Great Kantō earthquake of 1923, by an older member of Japan's National Diet[3] who linked the 'divine punishment' to the frivolous and luxurious lifestyles of Tokyo's younger generations.[4] These statements harked back to a premodern belief that human behaviour directly affects earthquakes. In mythology, the cause of the earthquakes is represented as a giant catfish, shaking the earth whenever history takes a wrong turn. Despite bringing damage and death, this *Namazu* is venerated as a heavenly messenger because the creature's wake-up call reveals the ills of society and pushes for its improvement.[5] Among other things, the earthquake, tsunami, and nuclear meltdown of March 2011 revealed the vulnerability of modern infrastructure causing Japanese architects to reconsider the country's most recent course of history.

> The reported scene of a fishing village in Sanriku devoured in seconds struck me and made me wonder what Japan's sixty years of modernization was all about.[6]
>
> –Toyo Itō, architect

It is clear that if in addition to their material impact disasters assume prophetic meanings, they will invite big change. Remodelling an entire city after a fire in a single district 'for the sake of our honour' as happened in Ginza after the 1872 fire, may seem exaggerated. But knowing that after a major disaster traditional rulers took extreme measures like moving the capital, puts things into perspective.[7] Earthquakes are a catalyst for change in Japan, and their cycles of destruction and renewal are deeply engrained in the country's general belief system.[8] While modern science tells us that the shaking of the earth is inevitable and is unrelated to human behaviour, the distinction between natural and man-made disasters is still ambiguous. Tall buildings and dense cities are an earthquake's deadly weapon. Since it is only when man inhabits the planet in such unnatural ways that natural phenomena become destructive and dangerous to humankind. There are, strictly speaking, no purely natural disasters. Acknowledging the compliance of architects in the construction of what is, potentially, a deadly environment, Toyo Itō came to question collective efforts geared at 'modernization' altogether. The events of March 2011, in Itō's view, warned us that what is achieved by what we call 'progress', is destined to collapse. And not just one day, in the distant future. Tokyo, home to a quarter of Japan's population, too, could be wiped out any day.

> I am amazed by the fragile state of things despite all the economic and technological 'strength' Japan has been so proud of. If the disaster happened in Tokyo, the situation would no doubt be even more devastating. Was our achievement of the past several decades a house of cards?'[9]
>
> –Toyo Itō, architect

Natural Order

Now that we can see how modern modes of production and consumption directly affect the climate, with catastrophes multiplying worldwide, questions of social guilt in the face of earthquakes and tsunamis resonate with the general ecological concerns of our time. Like governments, in these times of crisis architects and urban planners bear a double responsibility: to accept both the blame for the present failure and the task of reimagining a safer future. For visionaries it is tempting to see a disaster as a clear indication of what is the right way to go and a point of argument in discussions with those who oppose it. But this deterministic temptation can be misleading. Although earthquakes have proved to be a game changer in architecture, they ultimately accelerate changes already underway, which are not necessarily related to earthquakes as such. In 1891 for example, the Great Nōbi earthquake coincided with a rise in Japanese nationalism and a desire for emancipation from Western influences. In his account of the earthquake's social impact, Gregory Clancey shows that accordingly, the crumbling of brick factories and steel bridges was contrasted with the resilience of pagodas in Buddhist temples.[10] Before Nōbi, the replacement of wood with 'stronger' stone materials was considered an essential step on Japan's path of progress, as an anonymous Japanese author clearly expressed in the architectural journal *Kenchiku Zasshi* in 1888:

> Gradually, we should make every building in Japan completely brick or stone. Academically trained people should be in charge of this, and architectural regulations should be set. This is the basis of a strong nation.[11]

The Nōbi earthquake that brought down the modern infrastructure imported from the West was portrayed in a social determinist perspective as mother nature's call for a return to the 'natural order', which in this case was interpreted to be a return to traditional materials or construction techniques. Interestingly, the narrative emerging from the discussions after the March 2011 earthquake is in many ways reminiscent of what happened in architecture after Nōbi. Here too, in response to the disaster, a new era is being defined in architecture. The protagonists of the movement are Toyo Itō and Kengo Kuma, united in a rebellion against what most people generally consider 'modern'.

> The 'strong architecture' that humans, employing the fruits of modern science, rationally planned and rationally erected, crumbled without the least resistance before the power of nature . . . The 'strength' of architecture is not a physical 'strength' built into the individual unit. The total thing we call 'place' surrounding architecture is the strength that affords blessings to humans and gives them real security.[12]
>
> –Kengo Kuma, architect

Kuma classifies materials such as concrete and steel as products of an urban-centric culture to be overcome.[13] Our urban-centric culture, says Kuma, has produced 'monumental objects', concrete monoliths that may look strong, but in the end 'real strength' is to be found in human-scaled 'places'. What is needed now, according to the architect, is a sense of place in each region, preserved through the use of local architectural styles, traditional construction techniques, and local materials, as they were prior to the twentieth century.

> I want to go beyond the era of concrete. What people want is soft, warm and humane architecture.[14]
>
> –Kengo Kuma, architect

This architecture is presented as 'anti-object,' in a book with that very title: *Anti-Object: The Dissolution and Disintegration of Architecture*. The reaction is aimed at the 'new-empire architecture' of 'the twentieth-century's most modern culture', the American way, which has imposed itself on Japan. As the recipient of the collateral damage, Tadao Andō, for a long time the most esteemed voice in Japanese architecture, was indirectly put under pressure for his bare concrete fetish. Ironically, his concrete buildings in Kobe received a lot of praise after flawlessly withstanding the Great Hanshin-Awaji earthquake that devastated the region in 1995. Furthermore, his concrete, although untraditional, has been widely associated with an aura of 'Zen' and 'Japan-ness'. However, the March 2011 Tōhoku earthquake, tsunami, and nuclear power meltdown 'abruptly washed away supposedly invincible modern architecture', making Andō and his concrete a thing of the past.

> I'm well aware of what Kuma says about me and all my concrete. I got all hot under the collar when I first heard it, but after some thought I realized that he may have a point. Unlike us, Kuma lives in a totally new age.[15]
>
> –Tadao Andō, architect

Tokyo Governor Ishihara denouncing Japan's present-day materialism and architects calling out inhumane concrete architecture did not just coincide with the Tōhoku earthquake, but also with a broader questioning of American leadership and models. The clearest political expression of this trend is the revision, due for 2020, of the American imposed Peace Constitution of 1947. We can see that the changes promoted in the wake of disaster have more to do with pre-existing trends in society than with the natural disaster per se. The surprising amount of attention which the post-earthquake architectural discussions bring to their building material of choice is symptomatic of the fact that disasters serve as catalysts, accelerating broader trends occurring on a social and political level. It strikes us that, looking back over the various periods, stone, wood, steel, and concrete can in fact all be made to absorb the shocks of earthquakes. These different materials do not bear within themselves inherent qualities of strength or weakness. They bear associations with different identities, each suited for a different political climate. Indeed, when the Great Kantō earthquake occured during the more liberal Taishō era[16], 32 years after Nōbi had put wood back on track, reinforced concrete emerged as the winner, and an American design ended up as the icon of resilience: Frank Lloyd Wright's Imperial Hotel.

1 G. Clancey, 'Foreign Knowledge or Art Nation, Earthquake Nation: Architecture, Seismology, Carpentry, The West, and Japan, 1876-1923,' PhD diss., Massachusetts Institute of Technology, 1999, 18-19.

2 Roy Starrs, 'Zen, Japan and the art of democracy', *New Statesman*, July 7, 2011, https://www.newstatesman.com/asia/2011/07/japan-essay-nature-earthquake

3 The Diet (*Kokkai*) is Japan's bicameral legislature.

4 E. Oguma, *A Genealogy of 'Japanese' Self-Images*, trans. David Askew (Melbourne: Trans Pacific Press, 2002), 189.

5 G. Weisenfeld, *Imaging Disaster: Tokyo and the Visual Culture of Japan's Great Earthquake of 1923* (Berkeley: University of California Press, 2012), 22-23.

6 R. Koolhaas and H.U. Obrist, *Project Japan: Metabolism talks* (Köln: TASCHEN, 2011), 697.

7 G. Weisenfeld, op. cit., 15.

8 Ibid., 13.

9 R. Koolhaas and H.U. Obrist, op. cit., 697.

10 G. Clancey, op. cit., 11.

11 Ibid., 23.

12 Roger Pulvers, 'Born of disaster, modern architecture is itself now an ongoing disaster', *Japan Times*, May 13, 2012, https://www.japantimes.co.jp/opinion/2012/05/13/commentary/born-of-disaster-modern-architecture-is-itself-now-an-ongoing-disaster/

13 Ibid.

14 Aya Takada and Katsuyo Kuwako, 'Olympics Architect Wants to Bring Wood Back to Tokyo's Concrete Jungle', *Bloomberg*, May 24, 2017, https://www.bloomberg.com/news/articles/2017-05-23/olympic-architect-sees-wood-as-answer-to-tokyo-s-concrete-legacy

15 R. Pulvers, 'Architect Kuma Kengo: "a product of place",' *Asia-Pacific Journal* 2 (2013), 2.

16 The Taishō era (1912-1926) is the period coinciding with the reign of the Emperor Taishō, characterized by what is now called 'Taishō democracy', a liberalization and democratization of the political sphere coupled with a liberal attitude towards foreign culture

H

Discovery of Wooden Japan (1891-1923)

Stone vs. Seismic Science

Continuing to construct Japan in wood was out of the question for early Meiji Japan's architects and planners. *In Foreign Knowledge or Art Nation, Earthquake Nation* Gregory Clancey quotes architect Itō Tamekichi saying 'buildings of today are chemical inventions as opposed to traditional buildings', to illustrate how, in keeping with the European prejudice[1], stone architecture was equated with science and progress.[2] But the bricks are damp in Japan's humid climate and when a big earthquake hit the Nōbi plain close to Nagoya in 1891, brand new brick and steel factories, post offices, and bridges came crashing down.[3] With a surface wave magnitude of 8.0, the Great Nōbi Earthquake was the strongest inland earthquake to have ever occurred in the Japanese archipelago. It struck at a time when Japan was transforming into an industrial nation and it advanced its scientific understanding in many fields.

Clancey argues that the shock of the earthquake motivated Japanese architects and engineers to start questioning imported knowledge. They started reappraising the wooden temples and pagodas, many of which survived the big quake with little to no harm. But even though Japanese architects rediscovered traditional timber frames, now used to strengthen brick buildings, the nation did not turn its back on modern science. On the contrary, Clancey relates how the 'big bang' became a big break for the national project of 'Japanese science' as seismology became the first modern science to develop in non-Western territory.[4] At the turn of the century, only European seismology rivalled Japanese research while the latter claimed a monopoly over the Pacific Rim. The 'Ring of Fire', an earthquake-prone zone around the Pacific plate boundary, witnessed an unusual amount of shaking at the time, culminating in the big San Francisco earthquake in 1906.[5]

Inventing Nationalism

The post-Nōbi generation of architects took on the task of adapting foreign knowledge to Japanese nature. The study of carpentry made a comeback in parallel with the discoveries of seismologists who sometimes became architecture critics.[6] While the move away from foreign authority counted as a progressive factor, the ensuing vacuum posed the need to invent a local style, making Japan look back to the past. Clancey highlights the fact that the Nōbi earthquake crushed foreign construction at a moment of rising nationalism in Japan, when Westernization was being questioned in different areas. In *Inventing Japan* Ian Buruma identifies the late 1880s as the time when ballroom diplomacy was abandoned in favour of military force.[7] In 1889, Japan inaugurated its first constitution. A year later, the Meiji government enforced the 1890 Imperial rescript on education. This rescript revolved around the notion that Japan's unique system of government or *kokutai* was based on a historic bond between benevolent rulers and loyal subjects, and that the purpose of education was in the first place to cultivate virtues, especially loyalty and filial piety. National education thus became a military education, followed by setting up a conscript army.[8]

Ian Buruma tracks the 'invention' of Japan, as popular nostalgia for the good old wooden days was exploited by rulers who 're-established' Japanese 'traditions' and 'ancient duties' like Emperor worship, which were in fact modern fabrications.[9] The break with Westernization was only superficial since culture and religion were politicized after the model of the contemporary German style of ethnic nationalism. The nationalistic and militaristic General Yamagata, who dominated the 1890s as Japan's Prime Minister, was still eager for modernity and learning from the West, so long as access to new ideas did not 'confuse people and make them rebellious'.[10] The outbreak of the First Sino-Japanese War in 1894 also marked the emergence of Japan as a major world power. The war grew out of a conflict for supremacy in Korea where natural resources of coal and iron attracted Japanese interest. In the Russo-Japanese War of a decade later, Japan became the first Asian nation in modern times to defeat a European power.

Niche

In spite of heated debates on wood's reconsidered status as a construction material, the prestigious projects characteristic of Meiji power did not change right away. Structural wood joinery was used in some projects, but this was also the case before the discussions triggered by the Nōbi earthquake. A good example analysed by William Coaldrake is the *Sōgakudō*, a music Hall for the Tokyo University that was completed in 1890.[11] The question of realignment with wooden Japan posed itself more prominently in niches of architectural activity and experimentation that appeared in the periphery of the government's official architecture. As the number of Japanese architects grew, in the 1910s architects began to build small private residences and write books on house design.[12] Their Western-inspired public buildings, Coaldrake notes, are set apart by the history books from other typologies built by the same experts but showing no Western influences, including houses, shrines, and stores. Shrines and other pre-modern heritage had been overlooked during the early period of frantic modernization. However, as Japan sought to reinstate national identity, there was a renewed concern for preservation. In 1897 the first laws for preservation of traditional buildings were issued under the direction of architect Chūta Itō. Finally, wooden Japan presented as a natural product of an earthquake ecology played a role in criticizing the Western colonial project but also in legitimizing Japanese colonial rule in earthquake-prone territory.

Shinko Sub-Prefectural Office

Reporter: Fusakichi Omori
Publication: 1906

In 1906, a strong earthquake hit Formosa (Taiwan), a Japanese colonial conquest of the recent Sino-Japanese war. Fusakichi Omori, Japan's leading seismologist, visited the island and reported on the damage to local construction. The scientist reported a high number of casualties due to 'the structural weakness of native dwelling houses'.[13] Omori further stated that Japanese buildings on the island 'received no particular damage' except for superficial details. In the town of Dabyo, he noted, the only building still standing was the new Japanese Sub-Prefectural Office. Gregory Clancey makes the argument that, 'in setting the earthquake in the chronology of Japanese shocks'[14], Omori made the seismological map and the imperial political map converge into a single earthquake ecology. Contrasted with the architecture of its Asian rivals, Japan's technical proficiency demonstrated that its culture was well-suited for earthquake country Formosa.[15] The report was addressed to the international seismological community, in other words, mainly for European readers. Clancey shows how these were put in the position of judging the architectures of different Asian peoples as Omori 'justifies the Japanese colonial project on scientific grounds'.[16]

The report includes a photo of the wood-framed Sub-Prefectural Office in the town of Shinko next to a photo of a destroyed Chinese wood and masonry temple, for comparison. While the Japanese structure appeared to have suffered no harm apart from cracks in the plaster, the 'ant-infested' Chinese temple was reduced to rubble.[17]

Daibutsuden

Technical director: Yorinaka Tsumaki, Chūta Itō (ass.), Tadashi Sekino (ass.)
Completion: 1913

As Japanese architects and engineers started questioning foreign knowledge for the first time after a long period of deliberately neglecting native construction, the art of the master carpenter was almost forgotten. The first laws for the preservation of art and architecture heritage ('Law for the Preservation of Old Temples and Shrines') appeared in 1897 under the guidance of architect Itō Chūta.[18] In 1906, the Ministry of the Interior started one of the major projects of the Meiji era within the framework of the new legislation. The Daibutsuden, Hall of the Great Buddha, at Tōdaiji in Nara was in urgent need of repair and reconstruction. Coaldrake explains that the repair of the great hall had long been put off because the building radically differed from the projects that the state usually sponsored in terms of religious affiliation[19] and political meaning.[20] However, now that Japan is looking to reinstate a sense of national identity, the investment made more sense.

Crumbling under 2000 tonnes of roof tiles, the hall needed to be completely dismantled and reconstructed with earthquake-resistant structural reinforcements.[21]

The specialists in charge of the reconstruction were trained in Western architecture and engineering. Their solution compromised the traditional structure with a modern box truss of Sheldon steel over the Buddha's head, concealed behind a suspended ceiling, and added diagonal bracing in the roof structure.[22] It seems like the solution was only concerned with preserving a Japanese appearance, dismissing the value of preserving the original craft. Coaldrake notes however that a previous attempt at repair with conventional means in 1882 had been unsuccessful.[23] At the turn of the century most master-carpenters capable of building on this scale had passed away, and there had been no projects of the sort for a long time.

Memorial for the Great Kantō Earthquake

Architect: Itō Chūta
Completion: 1930

In 1923, another great earthquake hit the Tokyo-Yokohama region, then home to about four million inhabitants. A year later, there was an effort to erect a memorial for the victims of this Great Kantō earthquake. Style and construction method were of great importance as they potentially set the tone for the architecture in which the capital would rise from its ashes. By this time, the debate on wood seemed to have lost its relevance. In her survey of responses to the big earthquake, Gennifer Weisenfeld explains that by 1923, reinforced concrete technology had reached widespread use, and was now a reliable and cheap way to build.[24]

The earthquake memorial appears as a belated embodiment of the early Meiji slogan: 'Eastern ethics and Western science (*Tōyō no Dōtoku, Seiyō no Gakugei*)' or retrospectively, an early attempt to materialize wartime Japan's ambition of 'overcoming modernity'.

Initial plans for the memorial were abandoned due to widespread demand for a public competition.[25] The government conceded and the competition for a fire-retardant and anti-seismic memorial received 220 entries, in styles ranging from modernist to classical and Japanese traditional. The first prize went to a young modern architect, but after a public outcry from petition groups of local residents it was decided to change the design once again. The Allied Buddhist Association[26] too felt that the scheme was 'too modern, too Western to express the national and spiritual nature of the tragedy'.[27] Jury member and historicist Itō Chūta, who was previously involved in heritage preservation[28] and was by now renowned as the first Japanese architectural historian, was asked to produce a new design. His pan-Asian style proposal, promoted as 'Japanese', used a fire-proof reinforced concrete structure that emulated the architecture of wooden temples. His idea that this kind of East-West eclecticism could still express 'national taste' proved to be popular, as Itō was later commissioned to do many variations of this pan-Asian style on memorials for war casualties as the empire expanded.[29]

1 The Americans, who live in a country full of wooden cabins themselves, do not necessarily hold the same prejudice.

2 G. Clancey, 'Foreign Knowledge or Art Nation, Earthquake Nation: Architecture, Seismology, Carpentry, The West, and Japan, 1876-1923,' PhD diss., Massachusetts Institute of Technology, 1999, 32.

3 Ibid., 9.

4 Ibid., 145.

5 American seismology begins 15 later than in Japan, after the big San Francisco earthquake of 1906.

6 G. Clancey, op. cit., 10.

7 I. Buruma, *Inventing Japan: 1853-1964* (London: Weidenfeld & Nicholson, 2003), 50-51.

8 Enlisting commoners for the army was a novelty as traditionally, war-waging was reserved to members of the upper class.

9 I. Buruma, op. cit., 55-56.

10 Ibid., 54.

11 W. Coaldrake, *Architecture and Authority in Japan* (Hove: Psychology Press, 1996), 243.

12 J. Sand, *House and Home in Modern Japan: Architecture, Domestic Space, and Bourgeois Culture, 1880-1930* (Cambridge Massachusetts: Harvard University Asia Centre, 2003), 95.

13 G. Clancey, op. cit., 153.

14 Ibid., 153.

15 Ibid., 155.

16 Ibid.

17 F. Omori, 'Preliminary Note on the Formosa Earthquake of March 17, 1906', *Bulletin of the Imperial EIC* 2 (1907), 62.

18 W. Coaldrake, op. cit., 248.

19 The temple in Nara belongs to the Buddhist tradition while the religious affiliation then promoted by the government is state Shintō.

20 W. Coaldrake, op. cit., 248.

21 Ibid., 244.

22 Ibid., 245.

23 Ibid., 247.

24 G. Weisenfeld, *Imaging Disaster: Tokyo and the Visual Culture of Japan's Great Earthquake of 1923* (Berkeley: University of California Press, 2012).

25 Ibid., 269.

26 Memorial association members estimated that roughly ¥1 million would be needed for construction costs. half of which would be provided by the Tokyo municipality. Memorial Association members hoped to enlist the support of Buddhist associations throughout Japan to raise the remaining ¥500,000. J.C. Schencking, *The Great Kanto Earthquake and the Chimera of National Reconstruction in Japan* (New York: Columbia University Press, 2013), 294-295.

27 G. Weisenfeld, op. cit., 274.

28 Besides his involvement in the restoration of the Daibutsuden, Itō helped formulate the Ancient Temples and Shrines Preservation Law of 1897, an early measure to protect the cultural properties of Japan.

29 G. Weisenfeld, op. cit., 275.

D

‘It is the duty of Japan to export design and technique.’

Kenzō Tange, quoted in Koolhaas and Obrist, *Project Japan*, 603.

The Tokyo Skytree seen from Sensōji Temple.
Asakusa, Tokyo, 9 January 2017

'Why fight the quake?'

The alleged failure of Western construction technology during the Great Nōbi earthquake of 1891 caused the first generation of Japanese architects to seriously question imported technology. In doing so, they realized that like Japan has learned from the West, Japanese architecture had its own lessons to teach the world. While the story of Nōbi remained virtually unknown outside of Japan[1], the view of Japanese architecture as a model that could benefit the making of a contemporary architecture was later adopted by some of the most influential architects of the modern movement, including Walter Gropius, Bruno Taut, and Frank Lloyd Wright. When Wright built in Japan, however, he emphasized the fact that modern architecture can liberate Japan from obvious flaws in its traditional construction methods. Like many foreign architects preceding him, he found that traditional construction methods were not adapted to the danger of earthquakes. As he discussed the construction of his Imperial Hotel in Tokyo, he comments:

> Roof tiles of Japanese buildings have murdered countless thousands of Japanese in upheavals, so a light hand-worked copper roof was planned. Why kill more?[2]
>
> –Frank Lloyd Wright, architect

As a pioneer of modern architecture, Wright was aware that building in an earthquake-prone country was an opportunity for him to discover new creative principles for modern architecture, which he felt should be grounded in the principles of nature itself. Therefore, even though Wright hired a Japanese structural engineer to build his hotel, he disregarded the latter's calculations for the design of concrete elements, used his own innovative foundation system, and took overall responsibility for the building's structure.[3] He came up with a new aseismic structural system which he compared to a waiter carrying his tray:

> A construction was needed where floors would not be carried between walls, because subterranean disturbances might move the walls and drop the floors. Why not then carry the floors as a waiter carries his tray on upraised arm and fingers at the centre—balancing the load. All supports centred under the floor slabs like that instead of resting the slabs on the walls at their edges as is usually the case?[4]
>
> –Frank Lloyd Wright, architect

For Wright, flexibility was the key concept that would harmonize his architecture with Japan's shaky nature. Apparently, he did not take notice of the post-Nōbi generation of Japanese architects who had come to similar conclusions by observing ancient pagodas and ceremonial halls where flexibility was integrated by using intricate wood joinery.[5] For the post-Nōbi critics of foreign knowledge, the emphasis on flexibility countered the image of a fragile wooden Japan projected by comparing it with the imported stone architecture of Europeans. A culture in touch with nature, they implied, can see that real strength is flexible, not rigid. For Wright, neither the Japanese nor the classical Western buildings were adapted to nature. Attuning architecture to nature was the project of (his own) modern architecture.

> We solved the problem of the menace of the quake by concluding that rigidity couldn't be the answer, and that flexibility and resilience must be the answer... Why fight the quake? Why not sympathize with it and outwit it?[6]
>
> –Frank Lloyd Wright, architect

Today, we seem to have entered a modern world in which mobility and agility are indeed generally valued over sturdiness and stability; where editability is valued over rigidity. But as we can see, those 'new' values meant to keep us resilient in this fast-changing world have been an ongoing concern. After yet another wave of destruction in World War II, the post-war avant-garde group of Metabolism also advocated rebuilding Japan with futuristic designs immune to natural and manmade disaster by inscribing resilience and editability into the 'DNA' of their architecture. Each time a disaster strikes however, modern thinking itself is found to be the core of the problem.

> I can't help sensing a more fundamental disruption between our norm and the reality. I think we design things in a mechanical manner as a 'complete machine', complying with nature defined in quantities or abstract definitions. . . I think our task now is to rethink how we 'assume' design conditions, rather than reviewing the conditions. We need to start by questioning the way we relate to nature. . . And we architects should find it an invaluable opportunity to work on such a proposal for tackling this issue, where we can question the norm of modernism that is so embedded in us.[7]
>
> –Toyo Itō, architect

Earthquake Nation

There is a paradox in the double advantage of creating architecture in an earthquake ecology, which partly explains these ambivalent attitudes towards modernity. The devastating effects of earthquakes led to periods of critical introspection and a perpetual necessity to reinvent technique as man is defeated by nature time after time. But in the intervals, periods of self-assurance as a modern earthquake country in control of its own nature enabled a turn towards expansion, as the Japanese could promote this technology when an earthquake hit abroad. Internationally active architects such as Shigeru Ban, who specializes in aseismic buildings and disaster relief projects made of 'Japanese' construction materials such as wood and paper, still rely on Japan's identity as an earthquake country to build across the globe.

Back in 1965, this Japanese expertise and projected identity enabled non-Western architects to rebuild a European capital into a modern city for the first time in history, at a time when Japan was viewed in Europe as a third world country.[8] It is after an earthquake destroyed 65 percent of Skopje, capital of Macedonia, that the Japanese team of Kenzō Tange won a UN competition to rebuild the city. Tange, who seized this chance to become an international architect, was interviewed by the *Asahi Shimbun* newspaper a decade later. By then, he had completed numerous high-profile projects abroad, many of them in developing countries. With ecological concerns in mind, the interviewer argued that as we begin to question our optimistic aspirations for the progress of industry and technology, we might want to be careful as we export this lifestyle abroad.[9]

> Q: Would it really benefit the happiness of developing countries to sympathize and provide them with design based on industrialization?
>
> A: We are beginning to criticize progress and growth as they result in the destruction of our environment. But that is a luxurious problem of developed countries... developing countries do need growth and technology in order to undo technical, economic and cultural imbalance, and to redistribute wealth. Thanks to the progress of technology, I think we can manage to create a development model free of pollution.[10]
>
> –Kenzō Tange, architect

In Tange's mind, taking care of the environment and economic development were separate challenges, although he said they might converge in the future. This schism is precisely where Toyo Itō sees a problem when he talks about the disruption between our 'norm of modernity' and reality. But unlike Itō, Tange did not in his mind's eye envision Japan's modern infrastructure washed away by a tsunami. He saw a decolonizing Africa and a modernizing Middle East. In these countries, emancipating from Western dominance in the sixties and seventies, Tange could present himself as an ambassador and advisor from the country who did it first: Japan.

> I think it is the duty of Japan, who already has industrialized know-how in energy conservation, to export design and technique.[11]
>
> –Kenzō Tange, architect

Without questioning his good intentions or even the fact that what he said may well be true, Tange's portrayal of developing countries as defenceless and dependent on Japan's cutting-edge technology is reminiscent of earlier Western portrayals of Japan as a fragile, feminine, and irrational country as they imported their modernity to the archipelago. This orientalist point of view reappeared in the discourse of the Japanese themselves as they offered science and technology to their less modern neighbours. An identical standpoint was taken in 1892, when Japanese architects, engineers and scientists first came together to form the Imperial Earthquake Investigation Committee.[12] Sensitive to the unique opportunity of Japanese scientists producing knowledge for an international audience, this Earthquake Investigation Committee's interest in strengthening Japan's infrastructure became entangled with geopolitical interests. They saw that Japanese seismology was capable of maintaining visibility in the international scientific community, because Japan was now universally recognized to be an earthquake country.[13] In *Foreign Knowledge* Gregory Clancey writes that as a result of the international attention, seismology became 'big science' in Japan; 'increasingly well-funded and institutionalized, and capable of attracting patronage on the highest levels'.[14] In 1904, the same year Japan defeated a European nation (Russia) in war, the secretary of the Earthquake Investigation Committee, confidently declared:

> Organized scientific investigation connected with seismology is a duty that Japan owes to the scientific world.[15]
>
> –Baron Kikuchi Dairoku, Secretary of the Earthquake Investigation Committee

Subsequently, Japanese seismology embarked on overseas expeditions following the example of the European sciences. In 1905, Japan's leading seismologist, Omori Fusakichi, led a group of scientists and architects to India to record the after-shocks of the Great Earthquake in Assam and in 1906 he travelled to devastated San Francisco[16], and to Formosa, one of Japan's colonial conquests.[17] The Earthquake Investigation Committee's pan-Asian and pan-Pacific knowledge-producing ambitions implied a certain authority over this territory, which potentially included the whole 'ring of fire' on the Pacific Rim. By characterizing the recently conquered Formosa (Taiwan) as an earthquake country in a report on the 1906 quake addressed to a Western audience, Omori justified the Japanese colonial project by explicitly mapping Formosa within Japan's earthquake ecology.

> The island of Formosa is pre-eminently an earthquake country, having suffered eighteen severe shocks between the mid-seventeenth century and the present.[18] The quake of March 17, 1906 is as far as the loss of life is concerned (and) among the recent Japanese shocks, only second to the great Mino-Owari (Nōbi) catastrophe of 1891.[19]
>
> –Fusakichi Omori, seismologist

Pendulum

Clancey writes that Japanese Seismology's scientific community not only acted as a representative of the Japanese state towards the international public, but also had to cover for the state at home whenever an earthquake threatened to unleash discord among its own people. Omori, an expert on aftershocks took on the task of 'calming the people's nerves', by predicting earthquakes. After two shocks in the Tokyo region in 1922 and a third in 1923 he declared:

> Tokyo may be assumed to be free in future from the visitation of a violent earthquake like that of 1855, as the latter shock originated right under the city, and as destructive earthquakes do not repeat from one and the same origin at least not in the course of 1000 or 1500 years.[20]
>
> –Fusakichi Omori, seismologist

That same year, Tokyo was ravaged by the famous Great Kantō Earthquake. Omori died not long after the event and his school of seismology was discredited. Images of the imperial capital in ruins were widely published in worldwide media, which cast serious doubt over Japan's ongoing project of modernity, both abroad and at home. Amongst the local population, dark tourism and fire ruin sight-seeing even became popular activities in the destroyed metropolis.[21] Japan discovered that identification as an 'earthquake nation' had a flip side: It now appeared as if nature itself sentenced Japan to stay out of reach of modernity, forever unable to match the level of civilization and enlightenment of its world peers. This posed a threat to the general confidence in the nation's efforts to jump-start reconstruction, which was magnified in architecture by the image of Frank Lloyd Wright's Imperial Hotel standing tall in a sea of Japanese ruin.

> Hotel stands undamaged as monument of your genius. Hundreds of homeless provided by perfectly maintained service. Congratulations, Okura.[22]
>
> –Telegram to Frank Lloyd Wright

The publication of this telegram in the newspapers started a widely believed myth that the Imperial Hotel was the only building in Tokyo still standing, an image that was in fact far from the truth. Not only was the building listed in the category of second-best performance out of five categories (light damage) by insurance companies, it was also located in the second most intense category out of four on the seismic intensity map of Tokyo.[23] In his seismic re-evaluation of the Hotel, Robert Reitherman notes that Tokyo buildings designed by architect Tachu Naitō[24] performed better. Furthermore, Naitō's aseismic techniques were, unlike Wright's, still part of the lineage that led to contemporary aseismic construction techniques.[25] With regard to the impact on architectural history, however, Wright's hotel was unrivalled. Now speaking from a position of authority, Frank Lloyd Wright expresses concern for Japan's future. On 26 September 1923, in a letter about the miraculous survival of his major Tokyo project, he wrote to his teacher Louis Sullivan:

> The Yankee skyscrapers are some of them standing badly wrecked and some with the top floors shaken down—all visibly seriously damaged, probably murdering thousands trapped in them—unable to get out. Several are completely gutted by fire also. Of course it is impossible to tell how the strain has really affected the connections still hidden by whatever of 'architecture' is left clinging to their bones. People die of panic and fright and elevators don't run

> in an earthquake. You can imagine the piles of dead on the stair landings—stairs four feet wide—ten stories high—half flights. And this congestion on the basis of eight or ten stories, where it was already too great for safety or comfort on the basis of three stories, was a crime, but a tribute to Yankee salesmanship.[26]
>
> –Frank Lloyd Wright, architect

During the construction of the hotel, Wright had pointed at the inadequacy of Japanese roof tiles as a frequent cause of death in earthquakes. This time, Wright framed the failure of Tokyo as a crime of the Yankees who sold to Japan a metropolis that never really took account of Japan's natural constraints. But although the architect now blamed his own countrymen, he implicitly criticized Japan for its efforts to become more like the West.

> I am opposed to the tall building from now on, in the Pacific Basin, even if the human scale of things and safety and convenience are to be sacrificed to the ubiquitous American Landlord. I have written something outlining these views which will appear somewhere perhaps, and I am sending it to Tokyo to try and head off the propaganda which will try to rebuild Tokyo as a modern American city.[27]
>
> –Frank Lloyd Wright, architect

Here, rather than a self-assigned duty to export modernity as a licensed expert, identification as an earthquake nation took on a radically opposed meaning. It virtually became a banishment from modernity. The image of the Japanese as a people in control of their own nature, carefully developed by Omori and his colleagues in the preceding decades, seemed erased overnight along with Japan's modern capital. The characterization of Japan as an 'earthquake nation', which supported faith in Japanese science internationally, became a source of humility or even embarrassment for the scientists.[28] During an American lecture tour, Omori's successor as president of the Imperial Earthquake Investigation Committee opposed Wright's interpretation of the earthquake on every level, as he aimed to re-establish Japan as a country on the path of modernization. The new EIC president, naval architect Suyehiro Kyōji, presented a rationale that was equally a clear departure from Omori's apologetic discourse of wooden Japan. Kyōji started by praising the accomplishments of the imported ferro-concrete regime while making no excuses for the destruction of parts of Tokyo built in traditional wooden materials. Then, he attempted to revise Japan's identity as an 'earthquake nation':

> I wish to call to your attention to the fact that my country, Japan, is generally believed to be one of the most seismic countries in the world. The late professor J. Milne, a famous British seismologist, said in a joke that we have earthquakes for breakfast, dinner, supper, and earthquakes to sleep upon. Needless to say, this is merely a joke and is far from the truth. As a matter of fact, seismicity in my country is somewhat exaggerated.[29]
>
> –Suyehiro Kyōji, naval architect

If architects in Japan had followed the stipulations of Frank Lloyd Wright, nature would have been obeyed and Tokyo would not have been rebuilt as the high-rise metropolis that it is today. Wright's rhetoric came close to Itō and Kuma's 'post-tsunami' architectural tenets discussed in 'Strong architecture has failed the people'. Indeed, from the perspective of the contemporary environmental crisis, the idea to confine architecture's aspirations to the laws of its natural space seemed perfectly valid. However, overemphasis on the demands of 'space' arguably implied a gradual 'freeze in time' of Japanese society and its way of life. History shows that Japanese architects have made the opposite out of their earthquake ecology: over and again, earthquakes have been the springboard for dynamic leaps in time, with architecture swinging back and forth between retrospective introversion and future-oriented extroversion. When the Asakusa Twelve Stories, a skyscraper only slightly shorter than the world's tallest tower in New York when it was built, was decapitated by the Great Kantō earthquake of 1923, inhabitants and the media turned to the prominent Buddhist temple Sensōji31. Just a couple of blocks from the Twelve Stories, this ancient wooden structure famously survived both the shaking and the fire. Since 2012, the Asakusa district is crowned once again with the worlds' second tallest tower. Symbolically, the 600-meter Tokyo Skytree is a successor of the Twelve Stories as a monument to Japan's inexhaustible status as a beacon of modernity. But its earthquake-resistant structure is actually modelled after traditional pagodas, with a counterbalancing mast at its core, just like the one in Sensōji.

1 G. Clancey, 'Foreign Knowledge or Art Nation, Earthquake Nation: Architecture, Seismology, Carpentry, The West, and Japan, 1876-1923,' PhD diss., Massachusetts Institute of Technology, 1999, 10-11.

2 R. Reitherman, 'Frank Lloyd Wright's Imperial Hotel: A Seismic Re-evaluation', *NISEE – National Information Service for Earthquake Engineering*, 150.

3 Ibid., 149.

4 Ibid., 148.

5 The rediscovery of traditional wooden architecture following the Great Nōbi Earthquake is related in detail in professor Gregory Clancey's book *Earthquake Nation*.

6 R. Reitherman, op. cit., 150.

7 R. Koolhaas and H.U. Obrist, *Project Japan: Metabolism talks* (Köln: TASCHEN, 2011), 697.

8 Ibid., 44.

9 Ibid., 603.

10 Ibid.

11 Ibid.

12 The EIC monopolized knowledge production in seismology and aseismic construction until the Great Kantō earthquake of 1923.

13 G. Clancey, op. cit., 141.

14 Ibid., 140.

15 Ibid., 141.

16 San Francisco was then recognized by European as well as Japanese seismologists as belonging in Omori's sphere of research.

17 G. Clancey, op. cit., 144.

18 Ibid., 153.

19 Ibid., 144.

20 Ibid., 160.

21 For a detailed description of the Great Earthquake of 1923 in visual media, see Gennifer Weisenfeld's book *Imaging Disaster.*

22 R. Reitherman, op. cit., 145-146.

23 Ibid.

24 Tachu Naitō is known as the father of earthquake-proof design in Japan and built many broadcasting and observation towers, including the Tokyo Tower, modelled after the Eiffel Tower.

25 R. Reitherman, op. cit., 145-146.

26 G. Weisenfeld, *Imaging Disaster: Tokyo and the Visual Culture of Japan's Great Earthquake of 1923* (Berkeley: University of California Press, 2012), 148-149.

27 Ibid.

28 G. Clancey, op. cit., 196.

29 G. Weisenfeld, op. cit., 112-115.

TIMELINE
Earthquake Ecology

1603: Start Tokugawa era/Edo period
1720: Relaxation of ban on Western books
1854: Commodore Perry ends Japanese isolationism
1857: First iron foundry in Japan
1868-1869: Civil war/Japanese Revolution
1868: Start Meiji era
1868: Tsukiji Hotel
1872: Great fire burns down central Tokyo
1872: Ginza Bricktown Project by Thomas Waters
1872: First Western-style brick factory in Japan
1872: First railway line in Japan
1880: First academic society of seismology established in Japan
1883: Krakatoa disaster
1883: Deer Cry Pavilion by Josiah Conder
1889: First Japanese constitution enacted
1889: Bandai volcano eruption
1889-1991: General Yamagata Prime Minister
1890: Imperial rescript on education mandates cultivating virtues of loyalty and filial piety
1891: Great Nōbi Earthquake
1894-1895: First Sino-Japanese War fought over supremacy in Korea, rich in industrial resources coal and iron
1897: First laws for preservation of traditional buildings
1898-1900: General Yamagata Prime Minister
1904-1905: Russo-Japanese War fought over imperial ambitions in Manchuria
1906: San Francisco Earthquake
1906: Formosa Earthquake
1912: Start Taishō era
1909: Akasaka Detached Palace by Tōkuma Katayama
1906-1913: Repair and reconstruction Daibutsuden by Yorinaka Tsumaki, Chūta Itō, Tadashi Sekino
1919: Imperial Hotel Tokyo by Frank Lloyd Wright
1923: Great Kantō Earthquake
1926: Start Shōwa era
1930: Memorial for the Great Kantō Earthquake by Chūta Itō

Monsoon Ecology

source: J. Li, and Q. Zeng, 'Geographical Extent of the Global Surface Monsoons,' Accessed February 14, 2018 http://www.lasg.ac.cn/staff/ljp/monsoon/

As Western modernity crosses over the confines of public space into the intimate space of the household, the proliferation of a 'cosmopolitan' lifestyle quickly reaches a saturation point. Rediscovering the remains of their country's own 'unique' culture as the product of a monsoon climate, Japanese intellectuals enquire into the possibility of formulating an alternative, East-Asian rationale. The environmental determinism placing climate at the source of a fundamentally different view of nature buttresses the Japanese territorial claim over the Greater East-Asia Co-Prosperity Sphere. That monsoon climates are in fact not homogeneous phenomena, is either overlooked or used to underline the uniqueness of Japan although even on the archipelago itself, climates vary substantially. Meanwhile, the expansion of the Japanese empire does largely coincide with the monsoon zones, due to the fact that both the monsoon climate and the imperial navy come from the sea. . .

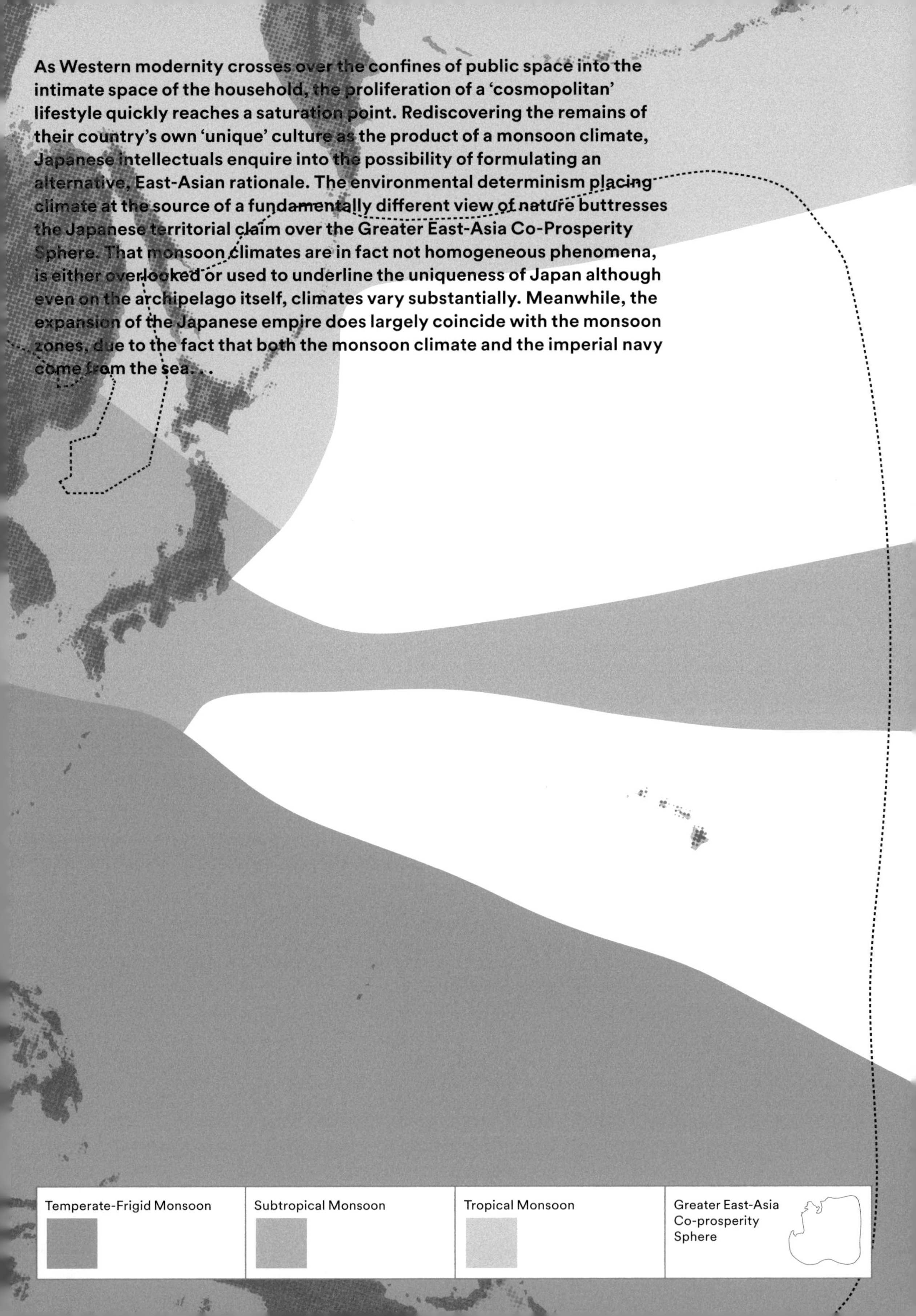

E

風土
Fūdo

Japanese who have travelled to the West think that if they only put into practice the external forms of factories, governments or anything else, then they can make a fine civilisation with that alone. If they just bring back the form, then what good is that without the substance?[1]

-Narrator of Kichōsha no Nikki (Journal of a Returnee), by author Nagai Kafū, 1909

Fūdo

Literally, it signifies wind and earth. *Fūdo* has origins in the ancient concept of *sui-do*, or water and earth, harking back to the notion that nature is made up of four elements (water, wind, fire, and earth).[2] The concept was elaborated in the 1930s by Tetsurō Watsuji (1889-1960), an ethics professor at Kyoto University, who conceived it as a primal experience of the environment, before the observer and the observed were split into separate abstractions by the mind.[3] Simply arguing that since time as a concept is abstracted from the initial experience of temporality, like space is an abstraction of the concrete experience of spaces, he found that there had to be a deeper reality that conditioned our being in this world.[4] According to Watsuji, before we speak of nature, understood as an abstract framework of space and time, we experience *fūdo*.

In the 1920s and 1930s, European philosophy was popular among Japanese scholars, particularly German philosophy.[5] Watsuji himself travelled to Berlin to study with Martin Heidegger and it was on his way from Japan to Germany, and back, that he acquired an awareness of the *fūdo*, or 'climate'[6] of his own country.[7] He later used the observations made on his voyage to develop the concept of *fūdo* as an adjustment to Heidegger's phenomenology, whom, despite criticizing 'the Western tradition's over-emphasis on the individual subject', was still 'shackled by individualism' according to Watsuji.[8] Indeed, Watsuji's writings and subsequent studies of *fūdo* have served as a basis to criticize Western thought and underline the 'uniqueness' of Japanese culture resulting from the influence of climate on peoples. The contemporary *shinfūdoron*, or 'new theories on climate', made up a significant category of *nihonjinron*, a popular genre of texts that focused on issues of Japanese national and cultural identity following a narrative of homogeneous cultural community.[9]

Despite the common association of *fūdo* with a typically 'Japanese view of nature', it has its counterparts in European science. For instance, *fūdoron* is comparable to mesology[10], the science of *milieux* studying the mutual interrelationships between the living creatures and their biological, social, and environmental surroundings. In particular, the semiotic theories of Jakob von Uexküll and Thomas A. Sebeok, distinguishing *umwelt*, the environment as experienced by the observer, from *umgebung*, the objectively measurable description of the environment, correspond to Watsuji's distinction between *fūdo* and nature.[11]

In essence, the concept offers an alternative to the cartesian definition of space. Cartesian geometry renders space as an endless and featureless framework existing outside the consciousness of the observer. Whereas in *fūdo*, space becomes something tangible with specific characteristics, of which the perceiver becomes an integral part. As such, space can impose its specific features on man, which then produces culture: 'It is in our relationship with the tyranny of nature that we first come to ourselves in joint measures to secure early protection from such tyranny.'[12] Watsuji contends that it is in climate that 'man apprehends himself', both as an individual and as a social being.[13] The self is described in Watsuji's book as the capacity to be imbued by a climatic phenomenon. This derives from an East-Asian notion of defining the self as empty.[14] And since climatic phenomena are shared by a society, the self is located between the individual and the group.[15]

The concept of *fūdo* is still popular among Japanese architects, albeit not as an existential philosophy. At least, this is what my supervisor at Yasui Architects told me. Mentioning a design Yasui Architects made for a project in Turkey, where they took account of routines like the five daily prayers, Kumagai-san described a conception of *fūdo* as an environmental philosophy considering climatic features in synergy with social customs, and behaviours. As such, I believe *fūdo* can offer an interesting perspective on the omnipresence of informal (and illegal) street gardens in Tokyo. I had never seen such a thing before, and while their originality and casual charm often caught my attention, the reason for their popularity remains a mystery to me. Apparently, I am not alone in this. Interviewed by a researcher a local lady is asked why she keeps her little garden. 'Because everybody does', she answers, and, after some thought, because her mother did so too.[16]

Street Gardens

The idea of Tokyo may conjure up images of soaring towers and hybrid blocks but statistically, it remains a surprisingly low-rise city, overwhelmingly composed of small detached houses.[17] I remember walking through one of these residential neighbourhoods, thinking of Le Corbusier's famous dictum: 'un rêve fois un million égale un cauchemar' (a dream times a million equals a nightmare). In it, the modernist master was pointing out the irony of the suburban dream. Replicated a million times, the ideal of the detached house with a private garden, intended to bring one closer to nature after a working day in the metropolitan centre, would in effect end up consuming the natural surroundings of the city, leaving commuters in a dull, sterile environment.

Tokyo equals a dream times thirty million and, due to the high value of land, coupled with high inheritance taxes, building lots have been pixelized over the past generations, squeezing detached homes ever closer to one another. In many cases, the private backyard has gradually been cancelled out of the equation. And yet I have to admit that in most places, it isn't so bad. Statistically speaking, Tokyo isn't a green city either.[18] But walking through the city's narrow residential streets, especially during the summer, one is overwhelmed with the vitality of a lush greenery squeezed into every nook and cranny. Best of all, this greenery does not have to be maintained with taxpayer's money.

In a proposal to transform the interstices in Tokyo's porous residential clusters into a continuous network of green space, architect Koh Kitayama related this spatial form of narrow, green alleys to Tokyo's humid, temperate monsoon climate so that 'an unexpected breeze blows through the gaps, and a comfortable space in which gentle sunlight passes through the trees emerges'.[19] The closing gaps between the houses have led inhabitants to place their garden on the sidewalk, which is now a stage for man and community to come together 'in climate'. The street garden, as an 'in-between space' mediating the public and the private realm, mirrors Watsuji's *fūdo* operating as an atmosphere that embraces, permeates, and unites different individuals.

Then again, as Anna Berkhof remarks in her master's dissertation on the street gardens, the division of the private and the public is a Western notion and in this case the Japanese distinction between *uchi* and *soto* seems more adequate.[20] These Japanese notions were introduced in academic literature by psychoanalyst Takeo Doi who attracted wide acclaim but also controversy for stressing the importance of such constructs in understanding the Japanese psyche. Just like *fūdo*, the concepts of *uchi* and *soto* are seen as enriching Western science by some, while others dismiss it as another way to promote the myth of Japanese uniqueness.[21]

Inside, Outside

Uchi versus *soto* metaphorically opposes 'inside' and 'outside'.[22] *Uchi*, literally meaning 'home', can signify a number of concentric circles ranging from the family, the community, up to the nation.[23] As Watsuji explains at length in his *Fūdo*, the Japanese house with its open plan is characterized by 'an internal fusion', but at the same time, it is clearly sealed off from the outside. Although many contemporary designs by Japanese architects suggest the opposite[24], Watsuji's observation remains true, as one can almost never get even a glimpse of a house's interior from the street.

But while the *uchi* of the house is clearly demarcated from the *soto* of the street, the street garden offers a platform for a wider circle of *uchi*, from where one can interact with the neighbours. By greeting the people watering their plants on your way to work in the morning it is possible to develop a sense of belonging, domesticity, and identity in the middle of an otherwise confusing and hurried metropolis. Indeed, while the houses' facades typically look clumsy and often lack proper maintenance, and even the pots of the plants often look rather random, the plants themselves are in general meticulously taken care of.

The apparent lack of 'architecture' is symptomatic of public space in general in Japan and often seems restr cted to transit hubs and commercial spaces. Traditionally, the Japanese public realm would take place in events rather than in dedicated spaces. In *Japan-ness in Architecture*, architect Arata Isozaki speaks of Japanese public space as *kaiwai*, an 'ambiguous demarcation' of temporary and amorphous communal events.[25] Likewise, this example shows that the house in itself, as a static entity or image, is not important. What counts is the ephemeral performance of the different *uchi*s in- and outside of the house.

1 E. Schulz, 'Nagai Kafu's Reflections on Urban Beauty in Hiyorigeta', *Review of Asian and Pacific Studies* 36 (2011), 148.

2 T. Watsuji, *A Climate: A Philosophical Study,* trans. Geoffrey Bownas (Tokyo: Ministry of Education Printing Bureau, 1961), 1.

3 Ibid., 1-8.

4 J. Baek, 'Fūdo: An East Asian Notion of Climate and Sustainability', *Buildings* 3 (2013), 590.

5 I. Buruma, *Inventing Japan: 1853-1964* (London: Weidenfeld & Nicholson, 2003), 76-77.

6 *Fūdo* is commonly translated as 'climate'.

7 J. Baek, op. cit., 589.

8 T. Watsuji, op. cit., 3-4.

9 R. Reitan, 'Ecology and Japanese History: Reactionary Environmentalism's Troubled Relationship with the Past', *The Asia Pacific Journal* 15 (2017), 2.

10 Mesology is a former term for the science of ecology. Louis-Adolphe Bertillon derived the concept from the French expression, with the same meaning, 'Science des milieux' (science of environments).

11 A. Berque, 'Peut-on rationnellement parler de 'science naturante'', *Scripta Philosophiae Naturalis*, December 30, 2014, https://scriptaphilosophiaenaturalis.wordpress.com/2014/12/30/peut-on-parler-rationnellement-de-science-naturante-shizengaku-自然学/

12 T. Watsuji, op. cit., 6.

13 Ibid., 8.

14 J. Baek, *Architecture as the Ethics of Climate* (New York: Routledge, 2016), 22.

15 T. Watsuji, op. cit., 8-9.

16 M. Jonas, 'Private use of public open space in Tokyo. A study of the hybrid landscape of Tokyo's informal gardens', *Journal of landscape architecture* 2 (2007), 26.

17 K. Kitayama, et al., *Tokyo Metabolizing* (Tokyo: TOTO, 2010), 38.

18 Tokyo officially has less than 4 per cent of green space compared with 40 per cent for London, Rio de Janeiro, and Hong Kong.

19 K. Kitayama, et al., op. cit., 21.

20 A. Berkhof, 'Notion and appearance of home and nature in Tokyo street gardens', Masters diss., University of Groningen (2014), 93.

21 For a critique of Takeo Doi's views, see P. Dale, *The Myth of Japanese Uniqueness* (1986), 116-175.

22 A. Berkhof, 'Feeling at home in Tokyo'. In C. Fruneaux and E. Gardner, *Tokyo Totem: A Guide to Tokyo* (Tokyo: Flick Studio, 2015), 239-240.

23 Psychoanalyst Takeo Doi discusses the concepts of *uchi* and *soto* in 'The Anatomy of Self: the individual versus society' (1986), along with *honne* and *tatemae* (inner feelings vs public display) and *omote* (front) and *ura* (rear)

24 A typical example would be Sou Fujimoto's House NA (see last photograph of this essay).

25 A. Isozaki, *Japan-ness in Architecture* (Cambridge Massachusetts: MIT Press, 2006), 66.

H

Domesti-city (1918-1930)

A Housing Problem

From the nineteenth century to the first quarter of the twentieth, architecture in Japan had mainly been concerned with the design of public buildings and infrastructure. But the expansion of heavy industry following the sudden decline of European industrial production during World War I attracted workers to Japan's major cities in unprecedented numbers, causing the nation's first housing crisis. In 1918, the so-called 'rice riots' erupted as a series of popular upheavals from July to September when rice prices peaked due to post-war inflation. Unparalleled in size, these demonstrations showed that urban masses were henceforth a national force to be reckoned with. The same year, the government hastily issued a new Town Planning Law, an Urban Building Law, and a Tuberculosis Prevention Law to get a grip on accelerating urbanization.

The overcrowding in industrial areas made large cities such as Tokyo and Osaka prone to fires and disease as public investments in social welfare and infrastructure were outgrown by the population increase.[1] In *The Great Kantō Earthquake and the Chimera of National Reconstruction in Japan*, Charles Schencking explains how in the early Taishō era[2] Tokyo came to be seen as a hotbed of physical and mental dysfunction by commentators and bureaucratic elites who saw it as a place of 'temptations and hedonistic excesses' and also as one of 'social ills, disease, and potential unrest'. Focusing on the middle class, Jordan Sand explains that this social unrest was not confined to the slums and the working class, as post-war inflation caused a doubling of commodity prices while wages for the white-collar workforce remained constant.[3]

In *House and Home in Modern Japan*, Sand discusses how the shaping of domestic life through architecture and urbanism became an extension of Japan's nation-building exercise in its continuing effort to modernize the country. In Japan, he says, 'the mass market in print and images of a modern lifestyle comes in advance of a mass market in these commodities themselves'.[4] But the transition from a relatively distant dream of cosmopolitan culture to its intrusion into the heart of private life was accelerated in just a couple of years with the coincidence of an economic boom, housing policy reform, and reconstruction of the capital after the earthquake of 1923.

Everyday Life Reform

As relief of the middle class became an issue of public policy, architects began to discuss the topics of housing reform and urban planning. The house was seen as an educational device for criticizing and amending those aspects of the Japanese way of life deemed out of line with Japan's contemporary aspirations. In architecture journals, the 'maleficient effects' of *tatami* mats and overattention to guest reception in Japanese homes were discussed alongside translations of European planning laws.[5] To illustrate this point, Sand draws our attention to an article entitled 'The reconstruction of dwelling architecture from the perspective of the nation's economy', by Motono Seigo of the Kansai Architecture Association.[6] The latter advocated taking position between viewing dwellings as 'boxes inhabited by machines'—the 'pure materialist' mechanistic worldview of the West—and viewing them as 'extremely subtle vessels for harbouring the spirit', the 'pure spiritualist' interpretation of the Japanese. He claimed that the Japanese way of dwelling was leading to waste: waste of time, labour, and money.

In 1922, the term 'culture house' was coined in reference to the Western-style reformist architecture that housed an aspiring cosmopolitan middle class. A 'Culture Village' (*Bunka Mura*) was erected in the Ueno district of Tokyo for the Peace Memorial Exposition the same year. Observing the fast modernization taking place worldwide after the war, the more radical architects demanded the 'globalization' of Japanese habits of life, and the abandonment of all national distinctions in everyday life.[7] The 'Everyday Life Reform League', uniting architects, social policy makers, and domestic ideologues, promoted 'culture life' by displaying houses and amenities at various exhibitions.

At such an occasion, Junkichi Tanabe, one of their architects, presented a three-step plan for converting a typical rented house in Tokyo into a house suitable for modern middle-class citizens.[8] In his discussion of the exhibition, Sand goes on to explain how the exhibition posters clarified Tanabe's argument in favour of conversion. Modern living, says Sand, was portrayed as emancipating in contrast to the 'master-centred' traditional house.[9] Rather than 'tinkering with antiques', men were now encouraged to engage in 'family gathering'. Meanwhile, the housewife could work standing upright in a bright kitchen with modern appliances rather than on the dirty floor of a dark and smoky traditional kitchen. In sum, Western rooms were presented as an appropriate setting fostering health and togetherness.

Alienation and Anxiety

Such top-down didactic efforts at 'popular education' were probably relatively small-scale in proportion to the total population of Tokyo. In 'Tokyo as an Idea', Henry Smith cites the lingering effects of Edo era neo-confucian morals and the rise of popular religious movements as factors supporting the view that in fact, 'far more moralizing came spontaneously from within the lower and particularly middle levels of Tokyo culture than the Home and Education Ministries could ever hope to infuse from above'.[10] From the 1920s, however, the ideal of the so-called 'culture life', initially promoted by bureaucratic reformers, became a popular name for a generalized cosmopolitan dream of modernity fully absorbed by the market. Sand argues that the intrusion of modern life in the house, 'bringing into question distinctions that previously seemed natural', triggered a reaction against the 'culture life' by those who felt left behind.[11]

A widespread anxiety took hold of Japanese urbanites, among male intellectuals in particular, fearing Japan's colonization by Western products. The colonial metaphor held special relevance since many of the urban reforms were tested in Japan's colonies. There, planning successes were guaranteed by 'the absence of political and landowner opposition, a talented pool of bureaucrats and staff, and noninterference from political elites', according to Shinpei Gotō, former Mayor of Tokyo and Home Minister during the 1923 reconstruction.[12] In 1919 Japan joined the Paris Peace Conference as one of the 'Big Five' military and industrial powers, and Japan was granted a permanent seat on the Council of the League of Nations. The fact that Japan was now established as a colonizing rather than a semi-colonized country diminished the threat of cultural subjugation to the West, and made it easier to embrace foreign culture for the time being.[13]

Electric Home

Architect: Yamamoto Setsurō
Completion: 1921

In most cases, the small-sized developers of Japan's suburbia built cheap, low-quality wooden houses, which were not too different from the houses built in the Edo period.[14] In contrast, Architect Yamamoto Setsurō's first 'electric house', designed for his brother Tadaoki, who wanted to promote his appliance store, cost an extravagant sum[15] of 60,000 yen (including the electric equipment).[16] Yet the Yamamotos tried to convince the public that since the electric house saved the household 35 yen a month on other expenses such as paying a maid, the price was not really that unreasonable. Shibusawa Hideo built a second electric house in 1924 and opened it to the public as a promotional event for the new suburb it was built in.[17] In twenty days, 12,000 people visited it. At the time, many new suburbs were constructed by railway companies that were in a position to buy cheap land around their new hub stations.[18] These rail-integrated communities were complemented with amusement parks and retail stores, embedding the 'reformed' life in an ecology of consumption.

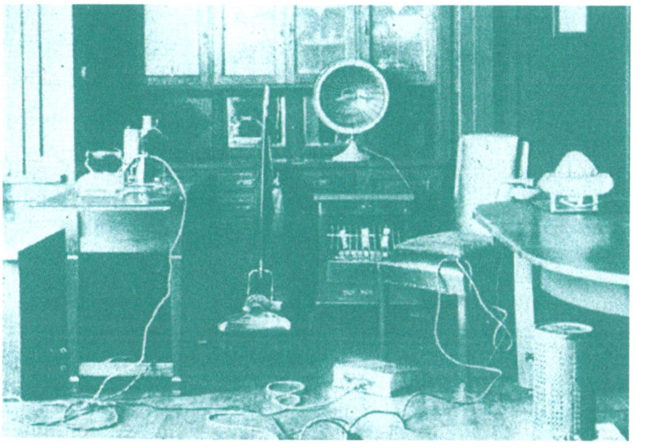

The electric home featured all kinds of novelties such as radiating electric heaters, guests' chairs with electric cushions and foot warmers, percolators in each room, and an electric milk-warmer in the nursery. Electrification promised to reduce the wasted time that burdened households 'economically and in family terms'.[19]

Experimental Houses

Architect: Fujii Kōji
Completion: 1920-1930

In response to the dismissal of traditional ways of life based on the scientific analysis and statistics of reformers, architect Fujii Kōji, instructor of 'dwelling studies' at the Kyoto College of Arts and Engineering, went on a personal mission to demonstrate the scientific validity of traditional homes.[20] He explored the possibilities of *sukiyaki* aesthetics as a suitable concrete embodiment of this tradition. Since the beginning of the 1920s, Kōji and like-minded architects such as Yamada Jun or Horiguchi Sutemi conducted detailed studies of the relation of Japanese dwellings to climate. Kōji performed his experiments on traditional houses of his own design which he built on his suburban estate near Kyoto. Unsurprisingly, he was able to conclude that the Japanese dwellings were well adapted to the Japanese range of temperatures and humidity, a climate characterized by hot and humid summers.[21]

Jordan Sand underlines the fact that the architecture of Kōji's experimental houses was not a pure imitation of traditional construction, nor a Western architecture applying 'Japanese taste'. Kōji's exercise was to recompose the traditional *sukiya* house on the basis of a Western-style training. By building upon the foundation of scientific experiment, Kōji suggested the possibility to design houses in a way that was both truly Japanese and truly modern. The *sukiyaki* style reached international audiences when Horiguchi Sutemi designed the critically acclaimed Japan Pavilion at the 1954 Centennial Exposition in São Paolo.[22]

The result is an unmistakably 'Japanese' house that nevertheless stands out from surrounding buildings as it features glass[23] in its sliding doors and a 'designed' roof with gentler slopes than the vernacular ones. Inside, Kōji combines chairs, tables, and benches with *tatami* rooms in a harmonious composition.

Housing reform project in Northern Japan

Architect: Wajiro Kon
Commission: 1934

Following the experiments of Jun, Kōji and Horiguchi, university-trained architects pursued the quest for a truly Japanese architecture by further experimenting with material, style, and proportion while writing tracts about Japanese space. Rural houses started to be reappraised and some were even transplanted from the countryside to the urban estates of wealthy connoisseurs.[24] The foundational work in the new field of rural house studies became *Nihon no Minka* (People's Dwellings of Japan) by Wajiro Kon, a young assistant at Waseda University who travelled across the country to study the *minka*.[25] Published in 1922, *Nihon no Minka* showed a renewed appreciation for the houses and lifestyles of rural Japan in an ethnographical survey conceived as a historical record of a culture in disappearance.

The *minka*, for Kon, held wisdom on how to dwell in the world, which he wanted to apply to the reform of urban architecture. Indeed, there is much to be learned from the Japanese way of dwelling. In *The Origins of Japanese Planning Culture*, Kuniko Shibata explains that since in Japanese neighbourhoods human waste is systematically collected to be used as fertilizer, neighbours share the cleaning of streets and traditional wooden houses have more ventilation than Western brick houses, the improvement of working-class living conditions is not as urgent in Japan as it is in the West.[26]

In 1933 the League for Lifestyle Reform joined the Bureau for Economic Reform and reoriented itself towards the improvement of rural living conditions.[27] Although Kon was a formal member of the league he did not agree with the idea of lifestyle reform as inspired by European rationalism.[28] A year later, Kon was commissioned to propose designs for collaborative workshop space, community storage, and a new model for peasant housing in Northern Japan, which had recently been hit by a number of climatic disasters.[29] In *Domesticating Others' Space* Izumi Kuroishi presents Kon's design research as exceptional as he integrated an array of topics related to traditional social systems, the area's climate, and geographical conditions in his proposals. Kon presented 68 housing types, an impressive number of possible choices determined by individual lifestyles and regional conditions rather than just applying a standard according to the number of family members. Due to the complexity of his design parameters however, they could not be adapted to government policy.

In Nihon no Minka, Wajiro Kon shows the rural dwelling not as a relic of the past, but as a building type in constant transformation, reacting to a rapidly changing environment.

Karuizawa summer house and studio

Architect: Antonín Raymond
Completion: 1935

Antonín Raymond arrived in Japan in 1919 as a staff member working on Frank Lloyd Wright's Imperial Hotel, after which he established his own office in the country. While working on the Imperial Hotel, he already showed strong interest in the use of natural materials adapted to the Japanese climate, to the point where it became a cause of problems in his association with Wright.[30] Although at the time, Japan was open to a full-on modernization of its building stock, Raymond made a deliberate effort to bring back elements such as *shōji* (sliding paper screens), *engawa* (a sunroom mediating between in- and outside), *amado* (storm shutters) or *ranma* (opening in a lintel beam for lighting and ventilation) as valid components of a modern architecture.

With its blend of modern and traditional elements, the *minka*-inspired house Raymond built in Karuizawa looked similar to Fujii Kōji's experimental houses, but it was in fact the result of an opposite approach. While Kōji departed from the *minka* and then introduced modern elements to adjust it to a modern taste and lifestyle, Raymond started by drawing a copy of a house in the International Style by Le Corbusier, then applied local materials and vernacular building elements to adapt it to local conditions.[31] After publication, the 'stolen' design for the Karuizawa house, which bears a striking resemblance to one of Le Corbusier's unbuilt projects, the Mattias Errazuris House in Chile (1929-1930), became the subject of debate on intellectual property.[32] In a letter to Raymond, the Swiss master reassured him: 'I am often copied, but very badly or clumsily or stupidly. So that it is at this point that my compliment comes in. Your interpretation of my plans is entirely spiritual and this compliment is sincere.' Raymond reiterated this view in response to criticism from an American reviewer: 'I feel that you lay too much stress on the question of the influence of Frank Lloyd Wright and Corbusier on my work at the expense of those vital qualities which make it valuable. Even to speak of the Japanese influence in my work is to see the truth only from a superficial angle. There is a strong Japanese influence in my work, but it is one of spirit and not of form'.[33]

Like Fujii Kōji, Czech-American architect Antonín Raymond experimented with a rural retreat, a summer house and studio for him and his life and work partner Noémi. Here, adaptation to climate was a feature of the site itself since Karuizawa was a popular resort for those who could afford to escape the heat and humidity of summer in Tokyo. As such the mountain town has been, and still is, a laboratory for architectural invention.

1 J.C. Schencking, *The Great Kanto Earthquake and the Chimera of National Reconstruction in Japan* (New York: Columbia University Press, 2013), 159.

2 The Taishō era (1912-1926) is the period coinciding with the reign of the Emperor Taishō, characterized by what is now called 'Taishō democracy', a liberalization and democratization of the political sphere coinciding with a liberal attitude towards foreign culture.

3 J. Sand, *House and Home in Modern Japan: Architecture, Domestic Space, and Bourgeois Culture, 1880-1930* (Cambridge Massachusetts: Harvard University Asia Centre, 2003), 171.

4 Ibid., 14.

5 Ibid., 176.

6 Ibid., 177.

7 Ibid., 177.

8 Ibid., 178.

9 Ibid., 182.

10 H. Smith, 'Tokyo as an idea: An exploration of Japanese Urban Thought until 1945', *Journal of Japanese Studies* 1 (1978), 65-66.

11 J. Sand, op. cit., 217.

12 J.C. Schencking, op. cit., 161.

13 J. Sand, op. cit., 217.

14 K. Shibata, 'The Origins of Japanese Planning Culture: Building a Nation-State, 1868-1945', *Research Papers in Environmental and Spatial Analysis* 128 (2008), 15.

15 For comparison: Junkichi Tanabe's 'affordable houses' cost between 3.000 and 4.000 yen.

16 J. Sand, op. cit., 246.

17 Ibid., 247.

18 K. Shibata, op. cit., 14.

19 J. Sand, op. cit., 248.

20 Ibid., 314-315.

21 Ibid.

22 H. Cho, 'Competing Futures: War Narratives in Post-war Japanese Architecture 1945-1970' PhD diss., University of Southern California (2011), 63.

23 The commonly used material in sliding partitions was rice paper.

24 J. Sand, op. cit., 315.

25 Ibid., 316.

26 K. Shibata, op. cit., 15.

27 I. Kuroishi, 'Domesticating Other's Space: Surveys and Reforms of Housing in Chosen and Japan by Wajiro Kon'. In I. Kuroishi, *Constructing the Colonized Land: Entwined Perspectives of East Asia around WWII* (Surrey: Ashgate Publishing Ltd., 2014), 234.

28 Ibid., 238.

29 Ibid., 236-237.

30 J. M. Cabeza Lainez and J.R. Jimenez Verdejo, 'The Japanese Experience of Environmental Architecture', *JAABE* 1 (2007), 36.

31 H. Čapková, 'Influence of Spirit and not of Form: Antonín Raymond, Le Corbusier, and Architectural Piracy in the Transwar Era'. In S. Inaga, *A Pirate's View of World History: A Reversed Perception of the Order of Things from a Global Perspective* (International Research Center for Japanese Studies, 2017), 86-88.

32 Ibid.

33 Ibid., 93.

D

'The Japanese must still remove his shoes at the doorway.'

Tetsurō Watsuji, quote from Watsuji, *A Climate*, 167

Entrance to a home in a small town on the West coast.
Naoetsu, 24 July 2015

Architecture of Everyday

Destroying large swaths of Tokyo's older districts, the Great Kantō earthquake of 1923 supported the proliferation of a modern, globalized, and consumption-oriented lifestyle, much like the triple disaster of March 2011 appears to contribute to a reverse course.[1] The events in the Tōhoku region have strengthened the contemporary reconsideration of consumerism and reanimated a desire to ground architecture in regional features. Until now, steadily rebuilding the urban landscape in concrete has been the default government policy in Japan. In Kengo Kuma's view, this departure from traditional construction materials was involuntary, a decision made out of fear for urban fires. But now that advanced technology produces fire-resistant lumbers he argues, the Japanese can finally be freed from their concrete enclosures.

> Wooden construction is now a major trend on the international building scene. In Japan people were traumatized by the Great Kantō earthquake of 1923, when fire consumed the wood-built capital of Tokyo. But major technological strides in the past two decades have given rise to wooden materials that are just about as fire-resistant as concrete. This has made it practical to put up large buildings made of wood.[2]
>
> –Kengo Kuma, architect

Kuma fails to mention that while the disaster of 1923 did accelerate the globalization (or Westernization) of the housing stock, the gradual transformation of Tokyo into a metropolis of concrete was already an ongoing project at the time. It was first implemented as a bureaucratic solution, seeking to remedy housing shortages and poor sanitary conditions in industrializing urban centres. Later, the promotion of modern housing was absorbed by the real estate market, which advertised cosmopolitan 'culture' houses as a must-have for the progressive middle class. Abandoning traditional wood-built construction was not just a preventive measure, but also an ideological choice. It is telling that in the 1920s, the term 'culture', *bunka* in Japanese, would refer to a modern, globally shared, cosmopolitan culture, as opposed to Japan's folklore.[3] But the ensuing transformation of the cityscape has been a cultural loss according to Kuma, who expresses nostalgia for anterior times, when people realized their 'own unique landscapes' by means of local construction techniques and materials.[4]

> All of this was destroyed by concrete and steel in the twentieth century. The tragedy of 3/11 was a consequence of this huge and lamentable course of history.[5]
>
> –Kengo Kuma, architect

The architect likes to wrap his buildings in local materials, like *washi*, the paper used in traditional partitions before the first plate-glass factory in Japan opened in 1906.[6] When lecturing overseas, he is often asked whether this kind of building is sustainable, if the materials last and if there isn't a lack of insulation. Part of the answer is that the building's performance should be assessed in the context of the regional climate.

> In a place such as Japan, this kind of 'paper house' uses methods of directly heating the body, such as with a *kotatsu* [charcoal brazier in a floor well] or an *irori* [sunken hearth]. People can get through a winter without using [modern] energy sources. And in the summer, when it's hot and humid, a 'paper house' is delightfully comfortable. Can't we have a varied sustainability for varied locales?[7]
>
> –Kengo Kuma, architect

In Kuma's description, the building itself does not offer a self-sufficient solution, since the system heavily relies on the occupant's behaviour and lifestyle. In other words, the building's performance results from the users' 'performance of the building'. In this case, this performance equally relies on a regional context of customs and traditions. Nowadays however, it is hard to imagine that many people would like to be forced to spend a winter around the sunken hearth. Already in the 1930s, the exiled modernist architect Bruno Taut, who greatly admired the Japanese vernacular, thought it unreasonable to expect such a lifestyle from his contemporaries.

> The modern Japanese have in their houses a quite right point; the traditional Japanese house can no longer be inhabited by the current people of Japan... people who sit in chairs and tables will no more stay crouched under the *kotatsu* wearing several layers of kimonos or remain trembling in the house while the cold winter winds whistle through the rattling *shōji*.[8]
>
> –Bruno Taut, architect

The kind of sustainability Kuma proposes differs significantly from the 'high-tech' version of sustainability his audience probably had in mind. Since everyone agrees that we need to do something about climate change—but nobody wants to change the way they live—we generally try to engineer houses with new equipment such as solar panels and thermal insulation, allowing the user to turn on the air conditioning and watch television, while being 'green' at the same time. This approach is understandable, but to have an architecture that encourages us to change our ways might be desirable as well. However, the idea of an architecture that conditions the thoughts and behaviours of its inhabitant may seem out of line with our liberal values. Can architects really expect their clients to transform their way of life and value system in order for the home to function? Interestingly, the generation of the Everyday Life Reform did not just approve of using architecture as a means to amend entrenched behaviours[9], they did so in order to teach Japanese people these values of freedom and independence. At the time, Japan just witnessed a second industrial boom due to World War I. If Japan was to remain competitive, Japanese architects of the 1920s believed, the Japanese way of life needed to be reformed. Tatami life was considered unhygienic and wasteful.[10] By housing people in modern dwellings with tables and chairs, the Japanese would automatically acquire modern, liberal values. This, in turn, would align Japanese people with the nation's progressive aspirations and simultaneously turn them into consumers of its modern industry. One of the founders of the league stated in 1921:

> We started this movement with the thought to touch upon the practical problems of our so-called 'everyday life', and from there proceed naturally to our spiritual problems.[11]
>
> –Norisugi Kaju, Everyday Life Reform League

Inevitably, this idealism was met with a great deal of scepticism. Writing in 1924, a year after the Great Kantō earthquake gave an impetus to the modernization of the Japanese capital, novelist Jun'ichirō Tanizaki gained popular acclaim with a story satirizing the pitfalls of the cosmopolitan lifestyle.[12] In 'Naomi: A Fool's Love' his main character Jōji falls for a young Japanese waitress who reminds him of the American actress Mary Pickford. Jōji is obsessed with all things Western, and moves Naomi into his home to make her into his perfect modern wife. Tanizaki forces us to reflect on the agency of architecture as he describes how the couple's modern commodities and the Western-style house itself play a key role in perverting their relationship.[13] Although they are married, Jōji ends up sleeping in a separate bedroom, while Naomi, who is now a modern and 'independent' woman, entertains Western visitors in another room.

Paper House

Tetsurō Watsuji, who befriended Tanizaki in Tokyo[14], wrote his *Fūdo* ten years later, as part of a general backlash against the frantic modernization of the previous decade. Watsuji's view of domestic architecture relates the conflicts arising from the adoption of Western houses, as exposed in 'A Fool's Love', to his discourse on climate. European buildings need thick walls to keep out the cold. The resulting separation of the rooms, Watsuji claims, has produced a society based on individualism.

> A house in Europe is partitioned into individual and independent rooms which are separated by thick walls and stout doors... to go out of a room in Europe has the same significance as to go out of a house in Japan.[15]
>
> –Tetsurō Watsuji, Fūdo

Watsuji discussed vernacular housing types as evidence that showed how architecture bridged the gap between a cultural value system and climate. The house regarded as 'a structure of human relations', he claimed, was clearly reflected in the layout of a house 'simply as a building'.[16] So even though by 1930 many Japanese living in the city own a Western-style house, Tetsurō Watsuji believed that due to their cultural baggage, a Japanese 'performance' of the house would always stay part of their internal nature.

> One is tempted to ask, 'Is there anything of Japan left? ... Is not this house even, a building on Western models?', it may well be asked. Externally, it is. But it has a gate, a fence, and a hallway; and after all, funnily enough, the Japanese must still remove his shoes at the doorway. Here not one of the qualifications of the Japanese house has been lost.[17]
>
> –Tetsurō Watsuji, *Fūdo*

By posing regional climate as the decisive factor in the development of architecture, Watsuji reverses the common idea that society, with its knowledge, values and norms produces a certain architecture. Here architecture, a pure response to climate, is viewed as the mould that gives shape to society. For instance, in Japan, there is a monsoon climate[18], so that architecture has to deal with hot and humid summers. This has led to an open plan with sliding partitions that enable cross-ventilation. Since the plan consists only of adjoining rooms (no corridor), there is no wind unless a 'collective tuning' takes place.[19] If one family member keeps his room closed, there will be no ventilation for the others. Thus, the architecture, in turn, must rely on a social norm that enables the family to live together as a single entity rather than as a gathering of individuals.

> Even if there is a partitioning by *shōji* [sliding doors] of *fusuma* [screens] this is a division within a unity of mutual trust ... their removal is in itself a show of a completely unbarred selfless openness.[20]
>
> –Tetsurō Watsuji, *Fūdo*

This logic is questionable, as one could ask, for example, why the Japanese house could not simply include a corridor for ventilation instead of imposing this 'selfless openness' on all rooms. Doesn't the choice not to include a corridor point to the fact that there had to be pre-existing social norms that favoured an open plan? Nevertheless, Watsuji's point of view still provides an interesting perspective on the interaction between social systems and architecture. Architectural theorist Jin Baek has written that Watsuji's *Fūdo* could provide an ethical basis for an 'East-Asian Notion of Sustainability'.[21] The vernacular

Japanese house, he says, is 'a paradigmatic image of the social dimension of sustainability' as it simultaneously addresses the relationship between human and available resources, and between human and human. We tend to think of technology, architecture included, as objects instrumentalized by us subjects. Living in the belief that these tools give us freedom we do not consider how they in turn condition our behaviour. But what is remarkable in the description of the 'collective tuning' necessary for the house to function, is that a certain way of life is inseparably linked to the sustainable response to climate. The Japanese house is not the inhabitant's device, used in free will. It is a delicate ecosystem that demands the constant adjustment of the architecture, the family and the natural environment to each other.

Geographer Augustin Berque has pointed out that while the subject-object dualism seems natural to us in the West, the Japanese rejection of this paradigm in favour of a worldview defining the self as an intertwined existence is derived from, or at least supported by the grammatical structure of the Japanese language.[22] In fact, the notions of subject (*shugo*) and personal pronouns (*ninshō daimeishi*) were only introduced in Japan during the Meiji era in order to try and fit Japan in one of the European grammatical categories as part of the modernization and nation-building efforts.[23] Based on the Japanese premise viewing the subject-object dualism as illusory, robot engineer and professor Masahiro Mori articulates an alternative approach to technology in his book *The Buddha in the Robot*.[24] Rather than dualistic, our relationship with robots (or architecture) might better be described as inter-subjective.[25]

> The Buddha said that 'all things' have the buddha-nature, and 'all things' clearly means not only all living beings, but the rocks, the trees, the rivers, the mountains as well... There must also be buddha-nature in the machines and robots that my colleagues and I make.[26]
>
> –Masahiro Mori, robot engineer

To illustrate his point, Mori takes the example of a car, which is considerably simpler than a robot:

> Depending on how you look at it, I could be regarded as managing the automobile, or it could be regarded as managing me. To control, in effect, is to be controlled: by driving the car properly I enable it to play a safe and useful role in life; but by controlling me, the automobile enables me to be a reliable and effective driver. The same relationship links human beings with all machines. They don't do what you want them to do unless you do what they force you to do.[27]
>
> –Masahiro Mori, robot engineer

We can see now that Kuma's idea of a regional sustainability suggests a renewed awareness of our inter-subjective relationship with architecture. To make an analogy with Mori's example, the 'high-tech' sustainable architecture is like a self-driving car: it might get you where you need to go and it is definitely more convenient, but it will not make you a better driver. However, admitting that we need to change the underlying premise of a system that relies on consumerism for perpetual growth, it is evident that contemporary society needs a new value system as much as an upgrade of its infrastructure. In other words, if we all need to become better drivers, the performance-based sustainability of the Japanese paper house may have something to teach us. In the 1920s, Le Corbusier famously described the modern house as a 'machine for living', while comparing his architecture to new car models in his manifesto 'Towards a New Architecture'.[28] But since the house is 'managing me, as much as I am managing it', as Professor Mori would say, maybe we should start viewing houses as living machines instead. Based on a similar hypothesis, Atelier Bow-Wow published a study of their work in 2010 entitled 'Behaviorology'.[29]

> Behaviorology is not only about the human being who behaves around architecture, it is also about natural elements like wind, heat, and lights, because they also behave and some parametric design is also dealing with these natural elements, simulating and then trying to graph them into resources to design... The relevant thing is ecology, how this natural behaviour, human behaviour and objects behaviour create a kind of sustainable ecology where all of these different actors can allow an actor to perform in a better way.[30]
>
> –Yoshiharu Tsukamoto of Atelier Bow-Wow, architect

Rather than placing humans at the centre of architecture, human users of the building are placed on the same level as the natural elements who also 'behave' inside the house. Together they form a small ecosystem that keeps itself in balance. By emphasizing the totality of the system, rather than just focusing on the comfort of the user, the subject-object dualism is overcome.

> Behaviorology brings about an immediate shift in subjectivity, inviting many different elements together and calling into question who or what may be the main protagonist of a space. Through this ecological approach our imagination follows the principles of nature and experiences space from a variety of perspectives. When one is surrounded by and synchronized to the liveable rhythms embedded in different behaviours – there is no experience quite so delightful.[31]
>
> –Yoshiharu Tsukamoto of Atelier Bow-Wow, architect

From this perspective, their idea of an architecture that promotes an intimate bond between the human body, the building and the natural environment appears as an embodiment of the principles of the traditional 'paper house'. However, it can also be understood as an argument in favour of 'smart house' architecture, the pinnacle of high-tech, in which a computer-controlled house manages the synergy of all parameters, including the behaviour of the user. At the 2013 House Vision exhibition in Tokyo, an event showcasing visions for the Japanese house of the future, curator Kenya Hara suggested that the high-tech house and the traditional house could actually be complementary.

> Here is a good example of taking advantage of Japanese traditional housing [while still moving forward]; take the habit of taking off [one's] shoes at the entrance [of a house]. 'The high-tech entrance' could possibly manage our physical data, such as pulse, blood pressure, temperature, and weight. The bed and carpet capture these data and send them to the hospital for the purpose of health control. This illustrates the possibility of the 'future-style house', in which [even] the intelligent 'bed' could directly dialogize with the human body.[32]
>
> –Kenya Hara, Curator House Vision

Typical Japanese behaviours, such as taking off one's shoes at the entrance, Hara speculates, are a potential resource for the future. Atelier Bow-Wow, Kengo Kuma, and some of Japan's most renowned architects also participated in House Vision in cooperation with industrial giants like Toyota, Panasonic, and Muji. The idea behind the House Vision (2013) and House Vision 2 (2016) exhibitions was that Japan's 'superior electronic appliances and technologies' could be integrated in the house, and merged with traditions and past housing typologies.[33] But rather than aiming to activate an inter-subjective bond between user and architecture, the smart house described by Hara, it could be argued, only reverses the roles of subject and object. The 'smart' house is seen as the subject, taking care of everything, while the user takes on a passive role, repeating mechanical behaviours. In this view, despite his efforts to emphasize Japan-ness, Hara's description of how Japanese features could be integrated appears rather superficial.

Here we must ask whether the revived desire to ground architecture in regional features, emerging as part of general reconsiderations of consumerism in the wake the Tōhoku disaster, are not serving an opposite purpose. This desire, manifest in the designs for the House Vision exhibition, when simply applied as a fashion, serves marketing interests rather than the commitment to a different lifestyle. As we have seen, the Japanese house can be an inspirational model in exploring the synergy between house, humans, and environment. But the implication that the user of the building would have a greater responsibility, and would have to give up a degree of comfort that goes with the high-tech approach, cannot be avoided if this architecture is to have an emancipating function. Using the house as an educational device, designed to reform its users' way of life is questionable on an ethical level. However, the fact that a certain architecture will condition its inhabitants' behaviour is inevitable. The high-tech approach to sustainability, while giving the user an illusion of freedom, actually only strengthens the role of the inhabitants as passive consumers of their environment.

1 I. Kuroishi and J. Traganou, *Design and Disaster: Kon Wajiro's Modernologio* (New York: Parsons The New School for Design, 2014), 2-5.

2 Y. Kiyono, 'Architect Kuma Kengo Shares His Thinking Behind Japan's New National Stadium Design', *Nippon*, June 30, 2016, https://www.nippon.com/en/people/e00101/

3 J. Sand, *House and Home in Modern Japan: Architecture, Domestic Space, and Bourgeois Culture, 1880-1930* (Cambridge Massachusetts: Harvard University Asia Centre, 2003), 228.

4 Roger Pulvers, 'Born of disaster, modern architecture is itself now an ongoing disaster', *Japan Times*, May 13, 2012, https://www.japantimes.co.jp/opinion/2012/05/13/commentary/born-of-disaster-modern-architecture-is-itself-now-an-ongoing-disaster/

5 Ibid.

6 The Takayanagi Community Centre in Niigata Prefecture uses washi and wood to create a confluence of indoor and outdoor light.

7 Roger Pulvers, op. cit.

8 J. M. Cabeza Lainez and J.R. Jimenez Verdejo, 'The Japanese Experience of Environmental Architecture', *JAABE* 1 (2007), 35.

9 J. Sand, op, cit., 181-184.

10 Ibid., 176.

11 Ibid., 183.

12 Ibid., 218.

13 Ibid.

14 E. Oguma, *A Genealogy of 'Japanese' Self-Images*, trans. David Askew (Melbourne: Trans Pacific Press, 2002), 261.

15 T. Watsuji, *A Climate: a Philosophical Study*, trans. Geoffrey Bownas (Tokyo: Ministry of Education Printing Bureau, 1961), 146.

16 Ibid., 145.

17 Ibid., 167.

18 Ibid., 146.

19 J. Baek, 'Fūdo: An East Asian Notion of Climate and Sustainability', *Buildings* 3 (2013), 594-595.

20 T. Watsuji, op. cit., 145.

21 J. Baek, 'Fūdo: An East Asian Notion of Climate and Sustainability', *Buildings* 3 (2013), 594-595.

22 A. Berque, 'Peut-on rationnellement parler de 'science naturante'', *Scripta Philosophiae Naturalis*, December 30, 2014, https://scriptaphilosophiaenaturalis.wordpress.com/2014/12/30/peut-on-parler-rationnellement-de-science-naturante-shizengaku-自然学/

23 Ibid.

24 The Buddha in the Robot was first published in 1974.

25 L.C. Pope and T. Metzler, 'Has a Robotic Dog the Buddha-nature? Mu!', *Technical report WS-08-05 23-26* (Menlo Park, California: AAAI Press, 2008), 23-27.

26 Ibid., 24.

27 Ibid.

28 Vers une architecture (1923), commonly known as Towards a New Architecture after the 1927 translation by Frederick Etchells, is a collection of essays written by Le Corbusier, advocating for and exploring the concept of modern architecture.

29 Y. Tsukamoto and M. Kaijima, *The Architectures of Atelier Bow-Wow: Behaviorology* (Milan: Rizzoli Libri, 2010)

30 J. P. Urrutia, Juan Pablo. 'Yoshiharu Tsukamoto: We have to avoid treating people just like numbers', *Materia Arquitectura* 12 (2015), 22.

31 Y. Tsukamoto and M. Kaijima, *The Architectures of Atelier Bow-Wow: Behaviorology* (Milan: Rizzoli, 2010), 15.

32 B. Porada, 'House Vision 2013 Exhibition Hits Tokyo', *ArchDaily*, 2013, https://www.archdaily.com/345209/house-vision-2013-exhibition-hits-tokyo

33 Ibid.

H

Climate and Colonial Architecture (1930-1945)

Beyond Modernity

The modernization of Japan, which was led by a liberal 'Western dream' after the first World War and during the 1920s, was reinvented in the 1930s as a search for a new Japanese identity that transcended modernity as defined by the West. The political climate was restless as two Prime Ministers were assassinated for their efforts to keep Japan out of a total war, which Japan moved into anyway as the military gradually took control of the nation.[1] In 1931, the Japanese staged the 'Manchurian Incident' as a pretext for the annexation of Northeastern China. In 1932, Prime Minister Inukai Tsuyoshi was murdered by a group of naval officers also known as the 'blood pledge society' in an attempted coup, after he tried to keep radical military factions from going to war with China. From then until the end of the war in 1945, only four out of fourteen prime ministers would be civilians, the others were military leaders.

In this context, the ideal of 'overcoming modernity' emerged out of disenchantment with modernization's effects and ramifications of the past decade, and anxiety and confusion about the future.[2] The project of overcoming modernity was used as an intellectualization and legitimation of Japan's pan-Asian colonial project bearing the name of 'Greater East-Asian Co-Prosperity Sphere'.[3] To support the establishment of an ultra-nationalist regime, philosophy, science, art, and architecture were solicited in search of a 'national essence'.[4] Most notably, a group of intellectuals from Kyoto University later called the 'Kyoto School philosophers' laid out the basic principles of a specifically Japanese way of being in the world. These principles inspired the *kokutai no hongi* (Principles of the national body, 1937), a propaganda pamphlet published by the Ministry of Education. This vulgarized version of the Kyoto School's conception of Japan's historical evolution ties the 'national character' to the physical environment.

Monsoon Climate

Watsuji Tetsurō, also a professor at Kyoto University[5], was part of the team that masterminded the pamphlet. As an established figure in Japanese ethical studies, his most influential work may be *Fūdo* (A Climate: A Philosophical study, 1935), in which he divides the world into three main climatic zones.[6] Japan fell into the category of the monsoon climate of East-Asia but, as Watsuji explains in a separate chapter, the climate of Japan has a unique character compared to its Asian neighbours. In *A Genealogy of 'Japanese' Self-Images* Eiji Oguma relates this 'uniqueness', which combines characteristics found in different parts of Asia to Watsuji's earlier theory of the Japanese as a people of 'mixed blood', showing characteristics of the 'emotional' Indians and 'intellectual' Chinese.[7] Captured by the theories of German philosophers such as Nietzsche and Heidegger who announced an impasse reached by Western rationalism, Watsuji entertained the idea of the Japanese, synthesizing emotion and intellect, as a people 'beyond good and evil'[8], able to overcome modernity. During the war, 'Overcoming Modernity' was chosen as the overarching theme of a 1942 colloquium gathering prominent artists and intellectuals in Tokyo in a joint effort to define the Japanese counterpart to 'Western modernity'.

Critique

Watsuji conceived his study of *fūdo* as a critique of the German philosopher Martin Heidegger's ontology, which, according to the former, failed to properly take environmental factors into account.[9] The study draws inspiration from *Principles of Human Geography* by French geographer Paul Vidal de la Blache, published posthumously in 1918. Human geography analyzes the development of society through interaction with the 'milieu' (environment) and, in Vidal's case, places the world's societies in an evolutionary order, topped by the European Mediterranean civilization.[10] In the spirit of the human geographic tradition, Watsuji discusses architecture as primary evidence of the interaction of humans and their environment. Environment, or *kankyō*, and climate became key concepts in the search for a non-Western monumental expression in architecture. But as *kankyō* was applied as an emblem of national identity rather than a generator of spatial planning, the discourse on climate took a largely passive role in the construction of the colonized land.

In an article discussing its 'uses and abuses', Patricia Morton concludes that Vidal's human geography has given architectural history a highly ambivalent heritage.[11] Architecture and geography have long traditions of 'representing geographically located difference as historically immutable', she says, by fixing hierarchical social differences as a naturalized product of climatic and environmental differences. Meanwhile, Morton regards the theorization and documentation of cultural and regional differences as strategic in the development of post-independence national cultures and the conception of postcolonial spatiality. In Japan, we find that both aspects coincide since the search for an environmentally determined national essence was instrumental in the liberation from Western cultural domination as well as in the legitimation of colonial practices. Watsuji himself considered it the duty of Japan to liberate other Asian peoples, but also opposed assimilationist practices.[12] However, since in Watsuji's view it is the regions that enjoy the same climate that need to remain independent in order to avoid racial discrimination, it is not a big leap from *Fūdo*'s environmental determinism to the idea of uniting the children of the East-Asian monsoon climate under the leadership of a 'unique Japan'.

Special Report to the Governor-General of Korea

Architect: Wajiro Kon
Publication: 1924

Before the rise of ultranationalism, and through the newly developed scientific disciplines of ethnography, anthropology, geography, and sociology in consideration of differences that need to be understood in order to rule the colonies effectively and peacefully[13], architects such as Wajiro Kon had the opportunity to appreciate and defend the sociocultural and historical heritage of indigenous peoples. After publishing his influential study of Japanese rural dwellings *Nihon no Minka*, architect Wajiro Kon conducted a series of field studies in the villages of Chosen, Korea, and was subsequently commissioned by the Governor-general of Korea to report on his findings. Kon's research led him to propose a critical inquiry into the historiography of the origins of Japanese architecture, in which he would like to stress the effects of cultural diffusionism. Among other things, Kon suggested that the typical Japanese cross-plan could have originated in Korean residential dwellings, instead of in the sacred architecture of Izumi shrine, which was the accepted theory at the time. He did not consider the Korean house inferior to Japanese dwellings, although he found them closer to Western types.[14]

Architectural historian Izumi Kuroishi writes that in addition to his rebuttal of national purism, Kon opposed the positivist approach to architecture history. The architect took a critical stance towards the prevailing nationalistic and modernist prejudices against foreign customs in architecture, by praising traditional features, such as *ondol*[15] floor heating. These were recognized by the Japanese architectural academic society in Korea as old and conservative lifestyles to be eliminated.[16] Just a few years earlier, the Koreans had rebelled against assimilation as second-class Japanese citizens after hearing of the right of national 'self-determination' proclaimed at the 1919 Paris Peace Conference. Kuroishi stresses that openly supporting the historical value of Korean architecture in a Japanese academy was highly audacious at the time.[17] On one occasion, during a speech in the academy in 1923, Kon condemned the policies of the Governor-general of Korea himself, as he had decided to demolish the historical Gwanghwamun gate.[18]

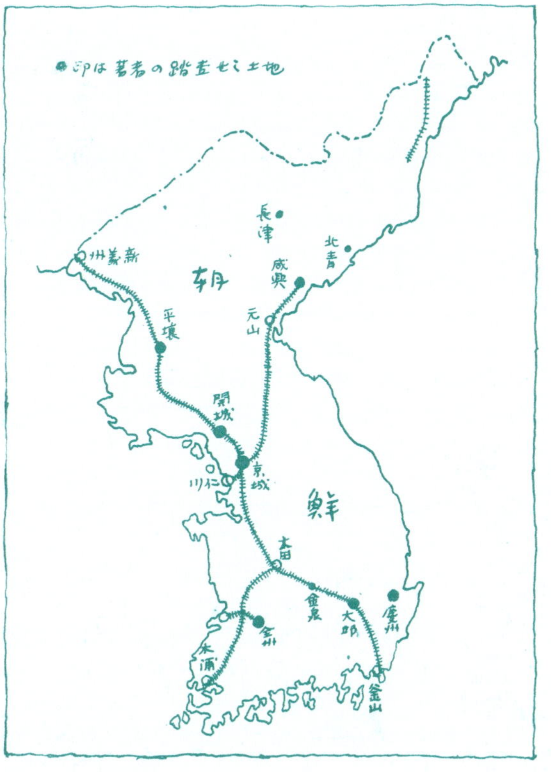

In the third and final chapter of his report on Korean rural dwellings, 'Influence: Chosen residential dwellings and Japanese houses', Kon divides houses across the world into categories, according to climatic and other local factors.[19] He argues that similarities in the historical transformations of climatic adaptations such as heating systems on the Korean peninsula, in Japan, and on the European continent were caused by the transfer of architectural form and technology by migrants. The illustration above shows a self-drawn map of Kon's research travels through Korea as he traced the migration of architectural form and technique.

Japanese Cultural Centre in Bangkok
Architect: Kenzō Tange
Competition: 1943

In 1941, the surprise attack on Pearl Harbor involved Japan—and the US—in a full-fledged global war. In the midst of the action, in 1943, representatives of all parts of Japan's Greater East-Asian Co-Prosperity Sphere gathered for a conference in Tokyo and issued the official statement:

This Great East Asian project is based entirely on justice, and is opposed to the exploitative, aggressive, exclusionary egotism of Britain and America. It will stand as a great lesson that will be revealed to all the peoples of the world.

National architecture competitions of the time illustrated how this discourse translated to the monumental architecture of the empire in the eyes of Japan's leading architects.
Because it could relate the Asian cultures to each other while shutting out alien Western meddling, *kankyō* (environment) became a key word in a Japanese architecture that sought to redefine its traditional roots from a modern perspective. In 1942, the young Kenzō Tange won a national competition for a 'Monument for the Greater East-Asian Co-Prosperity Sphere' with a proposal for a 'holy sanctuary' on the slopes of Mount Fuji.[20] He explained that Western monumentality was characterized by 'ascending forms' that had 'lost contact with nature and territorial realities'. The abstract forms of the pyramid and the tower were the 'Lilliputian symbol of the Occident's thirst for domination'. Conversely, his own scheme suggested a fusion of architecture and nature, with forms reminiscent of Shintō shrines[21] disappearing into a mystical landscape of mountains and fogs. The design remained unmistakably modern nonetheless, because the monument was connected to the Imperial Palace in Tokyo by a new highway, intended as the first line of an infrastructural matrix connecting all sanctuaries to be built across Asia.[22] In a competition for a Japanese cultural centre in Thailand, a year later, Tange repeated the strategy of blending Japanese forms in the landscape as an expression of 'modern Japanese monumentality' with the use of teak wood as the only reference to Thai culture.[23] The young architect received first prize and his mentor Kunio Maekawa second prize. Both stressed the importance of 'environment' and 'climate' as determining factors of their design as an ideological standpoint but without clarifying concrete implications.

In his design statement Tange declared: 'These ethical principles and the Japanese tradition of state planning represent the form of our character, they reveal our reverence to these values. It has nothing to do with the individualistic structure of Western architecture, there is only the Japanese way of planning an environmental order that can help us.'[24]

Golconde Ashram for Sri Aurobindo

Architect: Antonín Raymond
Completion: 1945

While the uniquely Asian challenge for buildings to deal with the heat and humidity of monsoon climates did draw the attention of prominent European modernists, attractive opportunities for experimentation remained scarce in the early twentieth century.[25] Up until the rise of ultra-nationalism, Japan had been the exception among Asian countries in offering realistic opportunities for Western architects to set up a modern architectural practice. And it was thanks to years of experimentation with shading and natural ventilation in Japan that Antonín Raymond was able to construct India's first modern building, now considered one of the earliest embodiments of sustainable modern architecture.

In 1935, Antonín Raymond's architectural office in Tokyo was commissioned by the famous Indian guru Sri Aurobindo to design a modern, state-of-the-art residential dormitory for his ashram in Pondicherry, India. Raymond initially worked on the scheme with Kunio Maekawa, one of Japan's leading modernists and an apprentice of Le Corbusier. But in 1937, the escalating threat of war forced Raymond to leave Japan and give up the office he established in Tokyo twenty years earlier. He continued to work on the project from abroad and sends George Nakashima, a Japanese-American architect who had also worked with Frank Lloyd Wright, and Francois Sammer, a Czech architect who had worked for Le Corbusier, to oversee construction. In the absence of skilled contractors in Pondicherry, the construction team was comprised solely of members of the ashram.[26] Nakashima spent the next two years as both an ashram devotee and a project architect, developing specific construction methods on site.

Informed by his experience in Japan, and to a lesser degree in China and Cambodia, Raymond was keen to carefully manipulate the play of natural elements in his design.[27] The building is shaped as an elongated concrete slab to minimize heat gain on the short facades in the East and the West where the sun hits the building from a low angle. Meanwhile, the architect brought in reflected light using 'horizontal mirrors' on the North and South sides. The large horizontal louvers composing the North and South facades are operable, allowing for the building to respond to prevailing sun and wind conditions. Between the rooms and the corridor, sliding panels reminiscent of Japanese *shōji* screens were specially designed to allow for passive cooling by cross-ventilating while maintaining visual privacy. The corridor in Golconde dormitory appears as a modern interpretation of the Japanese *engawa*. On the outside, the first modern brise-soleil appears in all its magnitude. On the inside, sliding panels made of staggered strips of teak wood allow for the passage of breeze.

The building is shaped as an elongated concrete slab to minimize heat gain on the short facades in the East and the West where the sun hits the building from a low angle. 'Horizontal mirrors' in the North and South facades scoop in reflected light and allow for cross-ventilation.

1 A turning point comes with the ratification of the London Naval Treaty of 1930 which would severely limit Japanese naval power. The treaty is strongly opposed by the military, and is portrayed by the opposition as having been forced upon Japan by a hostile United States, which further sparks anti-foreign sentiment. In 1932, a group of junior naval officers and army cadets assassinate Prime Minister Inukai Tsuyoshi. Although the assassins are put on trial and sentenced to fifteen years' imprisonment, they are seen popularly as patriots and an atmosphere is set where the military is able to act with little restraint. I. Buruma, *Inventing Japan: 1853-1964* (London: Weidenfeld & Nicholson, 2003), 75-76.

2 A. Rieu, 'The syndrome of "overcoming modernity": Learning from Japan about ultra-nationalism', *Journal of Global Cultural Studies* 9 (2014), 2.

3 Ibid., 7-9.

4 Ibid.

5 Although Watsuji is not formally a member, he is usually counted as one of the Kyoto philosophers because of the similarities in his theories.

6 In 1943 Watsuji republishes *Fūdo*, taking this opportunity to eliminate 'traces of leftist theory' in the book.

7 E. Oguma, *A Genealogy of 'Japanese' Self-Images,* trans. David Askew (Melbourne: Trans Pacific Press, 2002), 260-265.

8 Ibid., 270.

9 T. Watsuji, *A Climate: a Philosophical Study,* trans. Geoffrey Bownas (Tokyo: Ministry of Education Printing Bureau, 1961), preface.

10 P. Morton, 'The uses and abuses of human geography', *Journal of Architecture* 6 (2011), 806.

11 Ibid., 805.

12 E. Oguma, op. cit., 282.

13 I. Kuroishi, 'Domesticating Other's Space: Surveys and Reforms of Housing in Chosen and Japan by Wajiro Kon'. In I. Kuroishi, *Constructing the Colonized Land: Entwined Perspectives of East Asia around WWII* (Surrey: Ashgate Publishing Ltd., 2014), 215.

14 Ibid., 227-229.

15 Ondol is a traditional Korean floor heating system, typically incompatible with Japanese tatami floors.

16 I. Kuroishi, op. cit., 230.

17 Ibid., 227-229.

18 The main gate built in 1395 for the Gyeongbokgung Palace is demolished to make space for the Japanese government buildings. The act comes to symbolize the Japanese destruction of Korean culture.

19 I. Kuroishi, op. cit., 227-229.

20 B. Jacquet, 'Compromising Modernity: Japanese Monumentality during World War II', New York University, Institute of Fine Arts (2009), 6.

21 State Shintō is the official religion of the imperialist regime.

22 Linking Japanese shrines as holy national emblems also appears in the Japanese proposal for the Olympic torch relay in preparations for the cancelled 1940 Tokyo Olympics. The Japanese propose that the Olympic flame be carried by an airplane called 'kamikaze' along a South Asian route, avoiding China with which they are at war. Within Japan the fire would be carried by relay from the holy Mount Hyūga in Kyushu, Japan's main Southern island, through the Ise Shrines to Tokyo.

23 B. Jacquet, op. cit., 8.

24 Ibid.

25 J. M. Cabeza Lainez and J.R. Jimenez Verdejo, 'The Japanese Experience of Environmental Architecture', *JAABE* 1 (2007), 34.

26 P.V. Gupta and C. Mueller, 'Golconde: The Introduction of Modernism in India', *AIA Report on University Research*, 2005, 149-151.

27 J. M. Cabeza Lainez and J.R. Jimenez Verdejo, op. cit., 37.

D

I am not a scientist (anymore).

-Kinji Imanishi, paraphrased from Imanishi, 'A proposal for Shizengaku', 358.

Inside a dense forest of giant cypress and cedar trees, the experience of 'total nature' contributes to the monumentality of the architecture.
Ise Jingu Shrine, 19 May 2017

Western Science

> When I speak of nature, I mean nature in its entirety, with flowers blooming, butterflies fluttering, and birds singing. It's not to be found in a laboratory.[1]
>
> -Kinji Imanishi, ecologist

After a pathbreaking career as an ecologist, a primatologist, and an evolutionary biologist, Kinji Imanishi declared he was leaving science for what it was. His first book is *Seibutsu no sekai* (A World of Living Things), written in 1941 as a 'self-portrait' he could leave behind in case he died, which he thought was fairly likely as Japan was at war.[2] The booklet spells out a 'Japanese view of nature' emphasizing a holistic experience at odds with the modern reductionist conceptions of the natural environment. Deploring the cultural fragmentation flowing from the ever more specialized, censorial, and constrictive nature of contemporary art, morality, religion, and science, Imanishi's ultimate concern was to raise awareness for the wholeness of our cultural experience.[3] Imanishi exposed the separation of science from culture as an illusion, showing how science was tainted by cultural views, predominantly Western ones.

> The continuing popularity of Darwinism is, as I expressed my worries shortly before, not just a matter of logic, but that there is something which Westerners find deeply attractive about it. One begins to suspect that this is due to the long-nourished difference in our views of nature.[4]
>
> –Kinji Imanishi, ecologist

According to Imanishi, Western science has given us a flawed view of nature in which humans are at the centre, competing with themselves and with other species.[5] In his own evolutionary theory, Imanishi brings all living creatures on the same level, each finding their own productive niche in a harmonious natural world, fundamentally at odds with Darwin's view of nature as 'a scene of the struggle for survival'. Ignoring the fact that Darwin's competitive worldview was now under heavy attack in the West as well[6], writing in 1984, the 82-year old professor seriously doubted whether the West would ever consider a different point of view.[7]

> It's hard to say whether or not those Westerners can change their way of thinking in fifty years. It seems that they are finally beginning to understand that Christianity isn't the only religion in the world.[8]
>
> –Kinji Imanishi, ecologist

Imanishi traced back Europe's humanist point of view to Christianity, while others pointed to the coincidence of Darwin's theory of natural selection with the spread of capitalism and free market competition.[9] But in 1935 Tetsurō Watsuji already worked out that the roots of the European point of view went much deeper. From its inception, Watsuji claims, science in and of itself was quintessentially a product of the European climate.

> There is a link between the lenience and the rationality of nature, for when she is lenient man readily discovers order in nature. And if in his approaches to nature he takes due account of such order, nature herself becomes even more lenient, and man, in turn, is led further to search for the order in nature. Thus Europe's natural science was clearly the true product of Europe's 'meadow climate'.[10]
>
> –Tetsurō Watsuji, *Fūdo*

Europe's naturally 'docile' environment lent itself to the formulation of the laws governing it, and consequently to the development of technology for it to be governed by man himself.

> It was because nature was docile and hence already in primeval times there was technical control over nature that this realization came; for nature was made man's lackey.[11]
>
> –Tetsurō Watsuji, *Fūdo*

All of this originated in the bright sunshine of ancient Greece where 'Greek nature bright and clear, hiding nothing and well regulated', produced the essence of a European attitude of observation.[12] 'Theoria', Watsuji maintains, 'was something that monsoon or desert area could not produce.'

Oriental Science

Watsuji's depiction of science as non-Japanese was published in the mid-1930s, at a time when Japan was trying once again to define its identity in comparison with and often in opposition to the West. In a contemporary essay entitled 'In praise of Shadows' (1933) by Jun'Ichirō Tanizaki, the novelist describes the erosion of the Japanese cultural aesthetic taking place following foreign technology's invasion of everyday life in the 1920s. He opens the discussion by stating that, compared to the 'very crude and tasteless' idea to expose a white porcelain toilet to excessive illumination, one could rightfully claim that 'of all the elements of Japanese architecture, the toilet is the most aesthetic.'[13]

> Every time I am shown to an old, dimly lit, and, I would add, impeccably clean toilet in a Nara or Kyoto temple, I am impressed with the singular virtues of Japanese architecture. The parlour may have its charms but the Japanese toilet truly is a place of spiritual repose.[14]
>
> –Jun'Ichirō Tanizaki, novelist

Having caught the attention of the reader, Tanizaki goes on to describe the delicate lighting and intimacy of Japan's traditional bathrooms. Nevertheless, he must admit that the everyday benefits of science and technology outweigh the mystical experience of Japanese aesthetics, which begs the question why Japan could not have both.

> There is no denying the impulse to accept the services of a heater if it happens to be there in front of one, no matter how cruel its inelegance may shatter the spell of the day. But it is on occasions like this that I always think how different things would be if we in the Orient had developed our own science.[15]
>
> –Jun'Ichirō Tanizaki, novelist

By identifying Japan as the 'Orient', Tanizaki framed Japan within a Western worldview, and by extension, its historical narrative of progress. Perhaps that is why, as opposed to Watsuji, who demonstrated that science is almost by definition the product of a foreign culture, Tanizaki cannot help but wonder what Japanese science and technology might have looked like.

> Suppose for instance that we had developed our own physics and chemistry: would not the techniques and industries based on them have taken a different form, would not our myriads of everyday gadgets, our medicines, the products of our industrial art—would they not have suited our national temper better than they do?[16]
>
> –Jun'Ichirō Tanizaki, novelist

The quest for this indigenous modernity gained momentum in the early 1940s when Japan engaged in an all-out war against Western imperialism in East Asia. Here, Western 'modernization' was instrumental in the subjugation of indigenous peoples. If Japan wished to justify the construction of a 'Greater East-Asian Co-prosperity Sphere' as a liberation from the West, it could no longer forge this empire with means borrowed from the enemy. Thus, the rise of nationalism and pan-Asian ambitions motivated Japanese intellectuals to formulate a counter-project aiming to 'overcome modernity'.[17] In essence, this slogan referred to an effort to dig out the Western roots of modern thought, and replace them with Japanese metaphysical principles. Most notably, Kitarō Nishida's influential logic of 'place', was guided by the Buddhist notion that nothing is substance, and everything exists as relation.[18]

Total Nature

When René Descartes proposed 'I think, therefore I am' in the 'Discourse on the Method' in 1637, he laid the foundation for the modern scientific paradigm by distinguishing an observing subject (res cogitans) from a surrounding objective world (res extensa). Nishida's logic of *bashō*, or place, which was to be the Japanese counterpart of cartesian logic, reversed this with the Eastern spiritual notion that 'when I don't think, I am'. In other words, the experienced subject-object dualism is viewed here as an illusion concealing the fundamentally intertwined nature of being.

> The various forms, variations, and motions a plant or animal expresses are not mere unions or mechanical movements of insignificant matter; because each has an inseparable relationship to the whole, each should be regarded as a developmental expression of one unifying self.[19]
>
> –Kitarō Nishida, founder of the Kyoto School of philosophy

But just as Descartes later stated that the proof of his own existence in turn proved the existence of God, Nishida, after defining the self as empty, goes on to argue that the divine emperor embodies this central emptiness.[20] Needless to say, this kind of discourse lost its validity after the war. The questioning of scientific objectivism however, continued. Kinji Imanishi pointed to his mountaineering explorations as the transcendental experience that taught him 'the existence of total nature', and helped him to formulate theories of collective, intertwined consciousness.[21] In 1983 Imanishi finally bundled these ideas in a proposal for *Shizengaku* instead of *Shizen Kagaku*, or 'naturing sciences'[22] instead of natural sciences. Today, this may be the closest thing to the kind of 'Oriental' science Tanizaki had in mind. It is presented as complementary to the 'Western' natural sciences.

> In the pursuit of Shizengaku, there is a facet which cannot be attained by using only the methodologies of natural sciences. Within shizengaku we must also incorporate the intuitive and unconscious realms.[23]
>
> –Kinji Imanishi, ecologist

Shizengaku defines itself as the science of 'total nature', as opposed to constituent nature.[24] From the modern scientific point of view, physics is the ideal model, towards which other natural sciences ought to be striving. Since physics follows the principles of cartesian reductionism most closely, it ranks higher than chemistry, and then biology. The latter two, in this view, can be deduced from the former, which describes constituent mechanisms on smaller scales. According to Imanishi, this paradigm has caused twentieth-century scientists to lose track of what nature really is.

> With the study of minute things like genes and DNA, what kind of view of nature will emerge? There are people in the world who have spent their whole life dressed in white smocks, and have never once been out of the laboratory. There are probably even famous scholars who have never once seen animals and plants as they exist in nature. I will not stand for the lumping together of people who have views of nature like that, and people like me, who have shaped their views of nature by spending their lives in the midst of nature.[25]
>
> –Kinji Imanishi, ecologist

Shizengaku essentially reverses the hierarchy of scientific observation. Instead of cutting up our experience of things into ever smaller systems, until we have finally zoomed in on the abstract space of cartesian mathematics, shizengaku zooms out, placing our experience of nature into broader units until we reach the 'grand spectacle' of evolution at the top of the pyramid.

> From our point of view, biological nature is a great, everlasting, immortal behemoth... Whether we call this an absolutely splendorous and brilliant picture scroll, or a great, magnificent drama or romance, this is a phenomenon at which we can but gaze with wide-eyed wonder, and which we cannot comprehend simply.[26]
>
> –Kinji Imanishi, ecologist

While 'constituent science' ultimately lands us on the border with mathematics, on the other end of the spectrum, understanding natural phenomena as part and parcel of ever larger spheres ends up pairing natural science with history.

> . . . evolution happens only once. History, too, happens only once. So, you can see there's this significant similarity to history. . . The British philosopher Popper said that evolution cannot be the object of study by the natural sciences, and I agree with him. So, if one wants to study evolution, one must come from historical philosophy.[27]
>
> –Kinji Imanishi, ecologist

From this perspective, Imanishi agrees with the critics that complain that his views do not lend themselves to scientific debate.[28] Imanishi's view of nature is essentially an ethic of how to relate to and understand nature and, from there, humankind's place in it.[29] Works like Watsuji's and Imanishi's are receiving renewed attention because now that our civilization is heading toward an ecological crisis, we are forced to ask ourselves whether (dualistic) science can really solve the problem it created. Their argument seems to imply that we need to change our way of thinking... maybe even our way of feeling? While some find that this Japanese perspective could complement the natural sciences, and call for an 'East-West Gaia Theory of nature'[30], to others it remains a history of civilization based on nationalistic and unrealistic views of the world.[31] If there is some truth to either one of these reactions, the least it tells us is that science does not exist in a vacuum, but takes shape in a dynamic cultural context.

While in the West modernity is typically defined in contrast to what came before, the questions posed by Watsuji, Tanizaki, Nishida, and Imanishi were formulated at a time when in Japan modernity was defined in contrast to what is not Western, in other words, in contrast to Japan itself.[32] After the war, this point of view shifted, and Japan was placed in the lineage of creators of the modern. In 1957, one of Imanishi's disciples, anthropologist Tadao Umesao, published *An Ecological View of the History of Civilization*, which, like Watsuji's *Fūdo*, divides the world into climatic regions.[33] The 'first tier' countries of 'wet, forested regions', correspond to Western Europe and Japan, both of which built modern civilizations after passing through feudalism. He opposes these to 'dry, continental regions' such as Russia and China, which made a transition from authoritarian empires into socialist states. Using similar reasonings as Watsuji, Umesao arrives at an opposite conclusion. Because Umesao wrote his theory at a time of rapid economic growth and industrial expansion, his Japan finds itself in a natural environment closely resembling Western Europe, explaining why it equally succeeds in modernizing. Furthermore, his dismissal of Russia and China as authoritarian reflects Japan's position as a Western ally in the Cold War. If Japanese views of nature like Watsuji's and Imanishi's are receiving renewed attention today, this should not simply be understood as a sign of their universal validity. It is, in the first place, an indication of the current crisis of faith in the modern paradigm.

1 K. Imanishi, 'A proposal for shizengaku: The conclusion to my study of evolutionary theory', *Journal of Social and Biological Structures* v.14 n.3 (1983), 357.

2 K. Imanishi, *A Japanese View of Nature: The World of Living Things*, trans. P. J. Asquith, H. Kawakatsu, S. Yagi, and H. Takasaki (New York: Routledge, 2002), xi.

3 P. Asquith, 'Imanishi Kinji's Natural Ethic: The Contribution of a Twentieth-Century Japanese Scientist to Ideas of "Being in the World".' In B. James, *Historical Consciousness, Historiography, and Modern Japanese Values* (Kyoto: International Research Center for Japanese Studies, 2006), 202.

4 K. Imanishi, 'A proposal for shizengaku, 366.

5 Ibid., 357.

6 Rick Davis underlines the similarities between Imanishi's theory and the (Western) equilibrium theory. He notes that Imanishi's ignorance on the subject is probably due to the fact that he can no longer do a lot of reading due to bad eyesight.

7 K. Imanishi, 'A proposal for shizengaku, 357-359.

8 Ibid., 359.

9 F. De Waal, 'Without Walls', *New Scientist* 172 (2001), 2.

10 T. Watsuji, *A Climate. A Philosophical Study,* trans. Geoffrey Bownas (Tokyo: Ministry of Education Printing Bureau, 1961), 73.

11 Ibid., 79.

12 Ibid., 89.

13 J. Tanizaki, *In Praise of Shadows,* trans. Thomas J. Harper and Edward G. Seidensticker (Stony Creek: Leete Island Books, 1977), 4.

14 Ibid.,3.

15 Ibid.,7.

16 Ibid.

17 The question of overcoming modernity became official as the theme of a colloquium that took place in Tokyo on 23-24 July 1942.

18 A. Berque, Augustin, 'La logique du lieu dépasse-t-elle la modernité?', *Approches critiques de la pensée japonaise du XXe siècle* (2001), 3.

19 K. Imanishi, *A Japanese View of Nature*, xxxvi.

20 A. Berque, Augustin, op. cit., 7.

21 Imanishi's theory examines the consciousness of living things as a three-tiered structure: the specion (individual), specia (species), and holospecia (collective consciousness of all specia).

22 In French, Augustin Berque translates Shizengaku as 'science naturante'.

23 K. Imanishi, 'A proposal for shizengaku, 367.

24 Ibid.

25 Ibid., 360.

26 Ibid., 363.

27 Ibid., 358.

28 Ibid.

29 P. Asquith, op. cit., 202.

30 Steve Odin links a specifically Japanese concept of nature to the environmental ethics and conservation aesthetics of Aldo Leopold to propose what he calls an East-West Gaia Theory of nature.

31 Imanishi's ideas have been written about in terms of cultural, nationalist or *nihonjinron* genre writings. Some of his main disciples, such as Umesao Tadao, have been accused of writing a history of civilization based on nationalistic and unrealistic views of the world. Pamela Asquith argues that in this case, those who fear right-wing tendencies, see them in Imanishi's work; those who embrace these tendencies also claim to see them in Imanishi.

32 A. Berque, Augustin, op. cit., 1.

33 E. Oguma, 'Post-war Japanese Intellectuals' Changing Perspectives on "Asia" and Modernity', *The Asia-Pacific Journal* 2 (2017), 8-9.

TIMELINE
Monsoon Ecology

1912: Start Taishō era

1914-1918: World War I triggers industrial boom in Japan, accelerates rural exodus

1918: Rice riots demonstrate force of urban masses after post-war inflation

1918: Government issues Town Planning Law, Urban Building Law, and Tuberculosis Prevention Law

1918: *Principles of Human Geography* published by Paul Vidal de la Blache.

1919: Japan joins Paris Peace Conference, granted permanent seat on Council of the League of Nations

1919: Korean rebellion against assimilation as second-class Japanese citizen

1919-1920: Everyday Life Reform exhibition Tokyo

1921: Prime Minister Takashi Hara signs treaty limiting build-up of Japanese battle fleet

1921: Prime Minister Takashi Hara stabbed to death

1922: Term 'culture' house is coined

1922: *Nihon no Minka* published by Wajiro Kon

1922: Hirohito steps in as regent

1923: Great Kantō Earthquake

1923: Men over the age of 25 with a steady income get right to vote

1924: Electric Home byYamamoto Setsurō

1925: Peace Preservation Law outlaws participation in organized opposition to the kokutai (national polity)

1926: Start Shōwa era

1928: Hirohito 'reborn a living God' at Ise Jingu

1928: Experimental House no. 5 by Fujii Kōji

1930: Prime Minister Hamaguchi Osachi signs treaty further limiting Japanese naval build-up

1930: Prime Minister Hamaguchi Osachi survives assassination attempt

1931: Annexation of Manchuria by Japanese army

1932: Prime Minister Inukai Tsuyoshi assassinated after trying to halt war with China

1933: Everyday Life Reform League joins Bureau for Economic Reform

1933: Karuizawa House and Studio by Antonín Raymond

1934: Housing reform project in Northern Japan by Wajiro Kon

1935: *Fūdo* published by Tetsurō Watsuji

1937: *Kokutai no Hongi* (Fundamentals of the National Polity) published by Ministry of Education

1937: China incident/Nanking Massacre

1937-1945: Golconde Dormitory Pondicherry by Antonín Raymond

1940: Cancellation of Olympics planned in Tokyo

1941: Attack on Pearl Harbor involves Japan in World War II

1942: Overcoming Modernity colloquium in Tokyo

1942: Monument for the Greater East-Asian Co-Prosperity Sphere architecture competition

1943: *Fūdo* second edition published by Tetsurō Watsuji, eliminating 'traces of leftist theory'

1943: Japanese Cultural Centre in Bangkok by Kenzō Tange

1945: Imperial Palace hit by bomb in air raid

1945: Japan surrenders after nuclear bombing of Hiroshima and Nagasaki

Post-Nuclear Ecology

Post-Nuclear Ecology

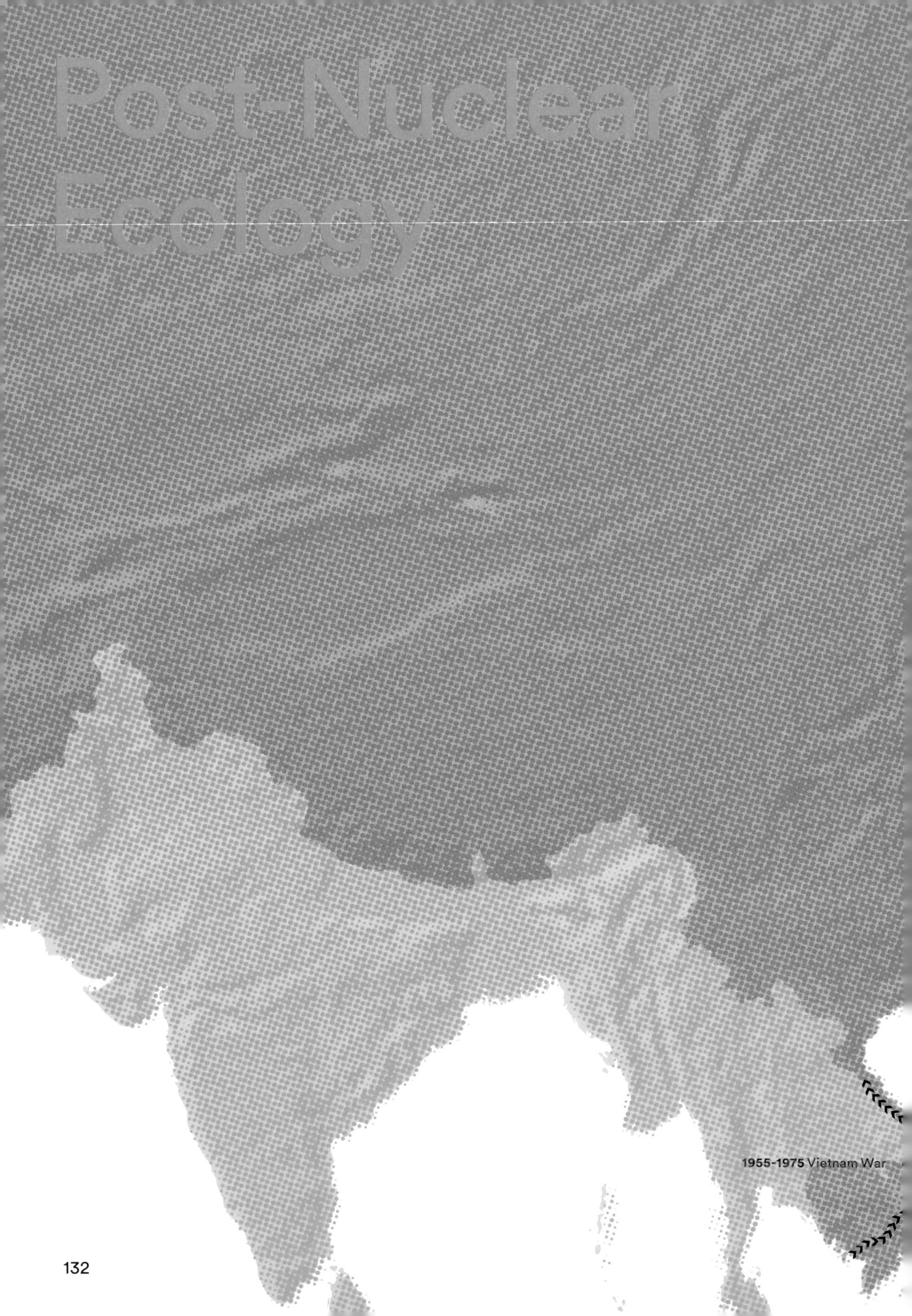

Caught in the crossfire of the Cold War, the world's first pacifist nation was forced to trade an autonomous army for America's nuclear umbrella. Physically and morally ruined after its defeat in World War II, Japan was rebuilt into a bastion of American 'hard power' by offering a platform for American troops in a predominantly communist East-Asia, and an avid consumer of American 'soft power' as multiplying the incomes of the middle class became an effective distraction from political conflicts. The pursuit of affluence and uninhibited consumption justified a pro-nuclear energy campaign in spite of the threat of nuclear warfare present in the back of Japanese minds ever since the bombings of Nagasaki and Hiroshima.

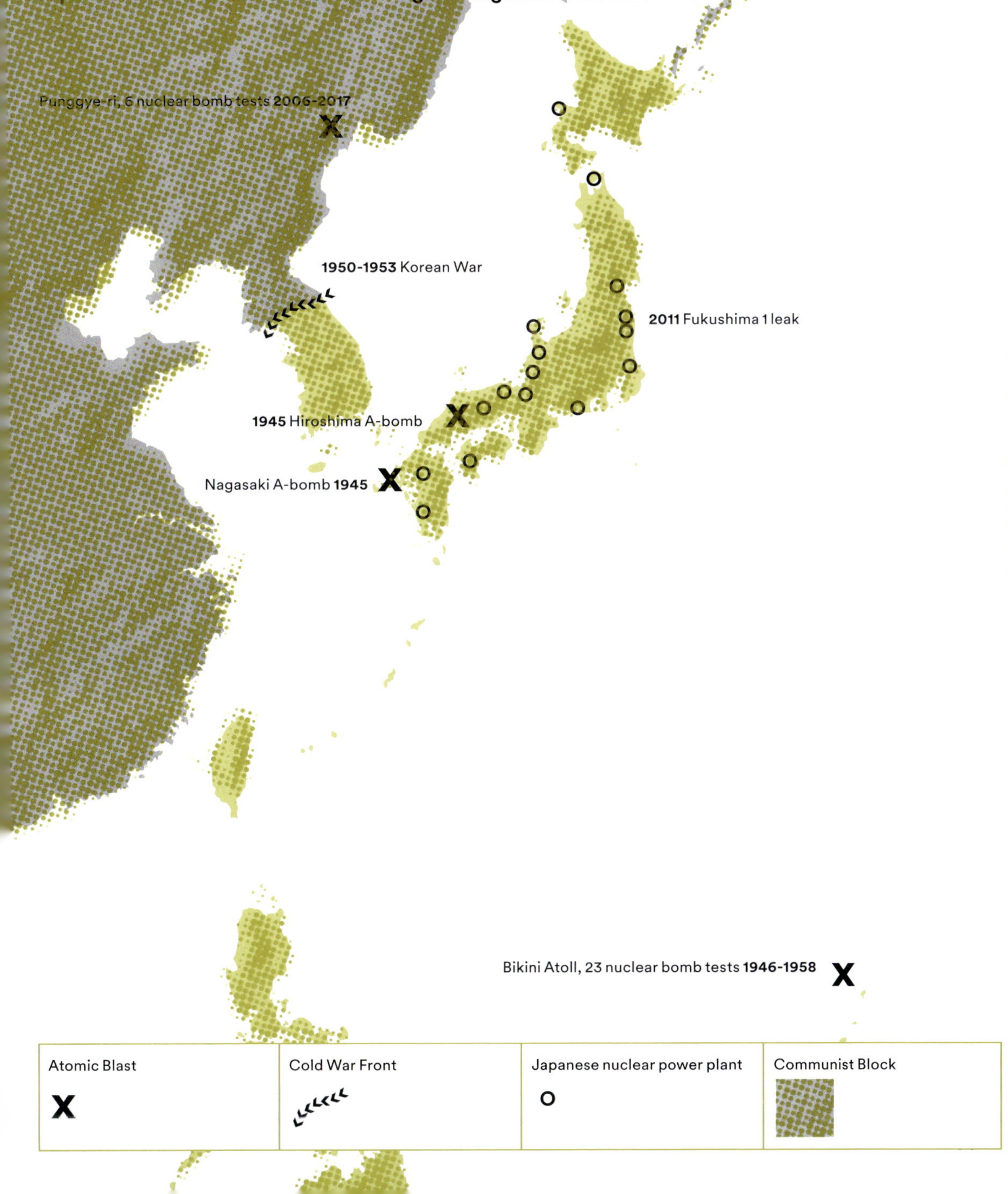

E

共生
Kyōsei

I based my thinking about a new organizational structure for Canon in the 1970s on the organizational design used by one of Japan's most successful seventeenth-century Shōguns. But many are surprised when I tell them that *kyōsei* also has roots in early Japan.[1]

-Ryuzaburo Kaku, company president (Canon), 1997

Kyōsei

Kyōsei, combining *kyō* (together) and *sei* (life), is a scientific term used by biologists and ecologists as a Japanese translation of 'symbiosis', defined as the cooperative living-together of unlike organisms. But since the 1960s, the term is applied in diverse contexts as a popular meta-concept referring to both the co-living of humans and nature and of human beings with other human beings.[2] For example, *kyōsei shakai* (symbiosis society) appeared as a key concept in the political programme of the Democratic Party of Japan, in the political domains of welfare and social justice, or even foreign policy.[3] Small green parties such as Midori no Kaze, meaning 'Green Wind', actively promote the concept of 'symbiosis' as opposed to 'competition', the other evolutionary concept that provides a metaphor for the liberal model of economy and society.[4]

Meanwhile, in an article for the Harvard Business review, Canon Inc.'s company president Ryuzaburo Kaku explained how *kyōsei* could contribute to operations within the paradigm of free-market competition by integrating it as a core principle of his multinational corporation's business credo.[5] He recalled being inspired by kyōsei at the time when Canon first started doing business on a global scale in the late 1960s. A recovering Japan was set to prosper in peaceful trade with the world's nations, something which, according to Kaku, had not happened in four centuries.[6] He compared the liberal post-war Japan to medieval Japan from about 1500 to 1640, when Japan's traders were among the most successful in the world. Kaku attributed this success to *shuchu kiyaku*, a set of guidelines set up by a successful Japanese trader and a famous Confucian scholar, stating that trade must be carried out not just for one's own benefit but also for the benefit of others. The regulations also stated that despite differences in skin colour and culture, trading partners should be considered equals. *Shuchu kiyaku*, in other words, is the precursor of the contemporary *kyōsei*. Besides the biological-ecological discourse and Japan's premodern mercantilism, *kyōsei* has roots in Japanese Buddhist discourse, which contributed to the popularity and growing influence of the concept.[7]

Homo Movens

Architect Kishō Kurokawa, the youngest member of the Metabolist group, an avant-garde movement fusing megastructures with principles of organic and genetic growth, claimed parentage of *kyōsei* as a political concept.[8] Kurokawa began to use the word frequently at the end of the seventies and launched his political career after becoming a popular media figure presenting his views on architecture and urbanism on national television.[9] He founded the New Kyōsei Party, with a programme proposing a symbiosis between economy and culture, town and nature, disabled and non-disabled people, different generations, Tokyo and the provinces, science and art, history and the present, different cultures, and globalism and localism.[10] Kurokawa's *kyōsei* is a design philosophy that learns from the failures of Metabolism's utopia: rather than aiming for a perfect social utopia stressing 'compromise' or 'harmony', *kyōsei* is a form of thinking and acting which views the various antagonisms and contradictions in society as resources to establish 'new creative relations', born from conflicts, contradictions, competition, and tensions. The generalized use of the concept, which, apparently, is capable of expressing the core ethic of planners as well as of environmentalists or multinational corporations, with meanings ranging from 'symbiosis' to plain 'conviviality' appears rather vague and hollow. To what extent then, one may ask, is *kyōsei* still a working concept to read, adapt, or transform our living environment? The key value that *kyōsei* brings to the table is the continuum it implies between human-human and human-nature relations. As the 'greening' of architecture is shifting its emphasis from a techno-scientific approach to a socio-ecological one, it is interesting to look into a concept that imagines social and ecological relations as 'one' rather than a combination of two separate realms. Kurokawa himself envisioned the symbiotic urban future as a decentralized, network-like, 'rhizomatic'[11] structure in which a contemporary *homo movens*, can establish resilient relations with himself and with nature.[12]

This *homo movens* is no science-fiction in Tokyo, where rhythm is everything. Sometimes, the city's thirty million inhabitants seem to merge into a giant clock that tames the concrete jungle with streams of synchronized steps and mechanical manners. The legions that flood the world's most complex urban train network every morning must be exhausted from working overtime, heavy social pressures, and hourlong commutes in packed wagons. Yet they all feel it. The energy, the *ki*, that possesses not the individuals, but the crowd, making you 'go with the flow'.

Konbiniance
To cope with this hypermobile lifestyle Tokyo's *homo movens* relies on a set of basic architectural typologies, the most notorious example being the Japanese capsule hotels, a derivative of architectural inventions of Kurokawa himself. But of all the architectural devices in *homo movens*' survival kit, perhaps none is as omnipresent in the routines of old, young, rich, and poor as a quick visit to the convenience store, also known as *konbini*.

The virtual network of convenience stores that colonizes Japan certainly appears as a concrete embodiment of the decentralized, non-hierarchical vision of the urban that Kurokawa proposes, or as the 'Harvard Project on the city II: Guide to shopping' puts it: 'Their urban presence is pure process—a Metabolist's dream'.[13] On the other hand, convenience stores are easily viewed as a textbook example of the opposite of biological symbiosis: parasitism.

When I started working in Tokyo, as a healthy and ecologically inspired European I naturally kept a distance from these piece by piece identical shops containing the same processed foods stuffed with chemicals and wrapped in three layers of plastic, ready to instantly appease the slightest urge for consumption of the passer-by at all times. However, I finally gave in, thinking 'oh well what's the harm in buying a banana?' And soon enough Tokyo's flow had turned me into a loyal customer of konbiniance. My curiosity for the trash and treasures on the *konbini*'s trays evolved into a fascination for the role of convenience stores in the urban fabric and the array of spaces they occupy.

Tatami Urbanism

Although the convenience store was invented in America and I have found the same ones in Mexico, China, and Sweden, one could argue that the *konbini* is the heir of a typically Japanese urban tradition. Urbanity remains hard to define but anyone would agree that it is related to density. Density? In a European city this density might be reflected in the diversity of architectural forms and functions neatly stitched together in the city centre. American skyscraper cities display a density of critical mass, a vertical multiplication of functional space. There, the degree of urbanity of a city is measured by the number of floors in its buildings. The Japanese version of density that endows its cities with urbanity stands in direct contrast to the pluralism in European cities and the 'bigness' of American cities. It is a density based on the flexibility of smallness and generic space. I call it tatami urbanism.

The *tatami* serves as a basic unit of space in traditional Japanese construction. It is in fact a standardized floor mat of approximately 0.9 by 1.8 metres that serves as a neutral ground on which all domestic activities are accommodated and alternate, within a single room. The *tatami* provided compactness in cities that were long forced to stay low-rise due to the hazards of earthquakes and fires. Furthermore, standardized building components allowed households to detach and save the most valuable elements of their house whenever a raging fire threatened to reduce the neighbourhood to ashes. But even in contemporary concrete blocks, tatami are a popular tool to realize minimal housing.

魚民
わらわら
7
ELEVEN

The Westernization of construction in Japan challenges tatami urbanism. The West's sparkling white kitchens and bathrooms require a room of their own and thus claim back half of the space saved by *tatami*. Traditionally, bathing takes place in the public realm. Men and women go to the neighbourhood *sentō* to bathe and shave. In contemporary Tokyo, where time is scarce and convenience is crucial, *sentō* have a hard time competing with modern private bathrooms. Thus, in the minuscule apartments the pressure to save space is now on the kitchen. *Homo movens* has no time to cook anyway, nor for elaborate restaurant service. And so the kitchen, banished from the home, is put onto the street and turns into a convenience store.

The *konbini* is expected to be close-by, open, and packed with fresh food at all times. Essentially, they are used as public fridges, comparable in a way to the public baths of the old days. In Tokyo, the cumulative area of the tiny *konbini* add up to roughly the same floor area as the sum of all the city's huge department stores.[14] Omnipresent, identical, and utterly commercial, *konbini* are easily dismissed as another disastrous effect of a globalized neoliberal economy that will end up making every place the same and put all local shop owners out of business. To a large extent this has happened already, but the Japanese accept *konbini* as evident in their lives because they relate to it as a peripheral device of their homes, just like the *sentō* used to be. You may climb down the stairs in your nightgown at two a.m. and hop into your local *konbini* for a midnight snack. In any other public space, this would be considered quite rude. In Tokyo it is hard to spot someone who is not neatly dressed but since a *konbini* is considered a collective extension of the home, other rules apply. You will find a microwave to heat your *bentō* and water boilers to prepare your instant noodles. Even deep in the suburbs, the *konbini* will be waiting, 24/7.

By placing the bathroom in the public realm, bathing naturally acquires new qualities. The *sentō* is a social place where one can meet neighbours, and good friends can strengthen their bond by drying each other's backs. Likewise, our 'urban fridge' performs a public duty, providing local disaster relief in case of an earthquake, recycling bins in a city without trash cans, easy access to basic necessities for an ageing population and most of all: a minimal dose of human contact.

1 Quote taken from R. Kaku, 'The Path of Kyōsei', *Harvard Business Review,* July-August 1997, 11.

2 In the Japanese Lexicon of philosophy and thought (1998) *kyōsei* is described as follows: 'In ecology the word is used in opposition to parasitism, and in the world of ideas of Japan today it is employed in different contexts, as in "symbiosis of human being and nature," "symbiosis with disabled persons," "symbiosis of diverse ethnics and cultures," even "symbiosis of woman and man"'.

3 R. Ophüls-Kashima, 'The concept of kyōsei – Symbiosis or Conviviality in Japan: Social-ecological thinking after "Fukushima"', *Journal of Environmental Thought and Education* 8 (2015), 2.

4 Ibid., 14.

5 R. Kaku, 'The Path of Kyōsei', *Harvard Business Review,* July-August 1997.

6 Ibid., 12-13.

7 R. Ophüls-Kashima, op. cit., 4.

8 Ibid., 2.

9 R. Koolhaas and H.U. Obrist, *Project Japan: Metabolism talks* (Köln: TASCHEN, 2011), 451-461.

10 R. Ophüls-Kashima, op. cit., 7.

11 Rhizome is a philosophical concept developed by Gilles Deleuze and Félix Guattari in their 'Capitalism and Schizophrenia' (1972–1980) project. Deleuze and Guattari use the terms 'rhizome' and 'rhizomatic' to describe theory and research that allows for multiple, non-hierarchical entry and exit points in data representation and interpretation.

12 R. Ophüls-Kashima, op. cit. 8.

13 R. Koolhaas, et al., *Project on the City II: The Harvard Guide to Shopping* (Köln: TASCHEN, 2001), 756.

14 Ibid.

H

Resurrection of the Construction State (1945-1960)

Recovering Industry

On August 30 1945, General Douglas McArthur, the Supreme Commander of Allied Powers (SCAP), landed in Tokyo to impose lasting democracy on a defeated nation. Three weeks earlier, the Japanese empire had been forced into unconditional surrender after nuclear attacks on Hiroshima and Nagasaki. The subsequent American occupation, lasting from 1945 to 1952, marked the first and only time that Japan has ever been occupied by a foreign power. Although officially, this post-war occupation of Japan was to be shared with the other allied powers, including the Soviet Union, the USA claimed a monopoly on the Japanese reconstruction.[1] The occupiers felt that before the Japanese state could be remodelled, the old system had to be dismantled. While the bureaucracy was left largely in place as a necessary support for the occupation, the imperial army and navy, as well as the *zaibatsu*[2] conglomerates, were disbanded.[3] Initially, economic reconstruction was not included in the plan to democratize and demilitarize Japan. The occupiers were convinced that private big business was largely to blame for Japanese imperialism, and besides, plans were made to relocate Japan's remaining industrial infrastructure to its former enemies as war reparations.[4]

Tracing the Japanese construction industry back to its colonial roots, William Steele explains how giants of the cement industry, owning state-of-the art factories across the old empire, were now targeted by General MacArthur's ambitious zaibatsu dissolution programme.[5] The persecution ended by 1949, as the Allied Occupation came to rely on Japanese industry to undertake comprehensive economic reconstruction plans. Controls on the production of basic industries such as coal, iron, steel, and concrete were lifted, and private corporations were allowed to export goods again. Steele identifies the outbreak of the Korean War a year later as the defining event lifting cement production back to pre-war levels and beyond, as it gave the industry access to markets in Southeast Asia, India, and Australia.[6] The *zaibatsu* recovered their monopoly on the economy and production kept increasing until, in 1956, Japan possessed the largest cement export industry in the world.[7]

Housing Japan

Concocted from domestic soil, Japanese concrete was viewed as a practical but also a patriotic building material by the architects in charge of alleviating the post-war housing crisis.[8] Over four million homes, most of them in urban centres, had been destroyed in the napalm firebomb raids. In addition to the existing homes that had to be rebuilt, 2.1 million extra dwellings for the colonists returning from Japan's lost territories had to be provided.[9] Yet recovery was slow and millions of people were forced to live in slums and make-shift structures. Four years after the end of the war, a mere 6.8 percent of Tokyo's burnt down neighbourhoods had been rebuilt.[10] New housing projects only really started to pop up by the end of the 1940s, with the provision of multi-story apartment buildings known as *danchi* planned in new town developments.[11] After reconstruction, the Japan Housing Corporation was founded as a semi-public institution in 1955 to respond to another increase in housing demand due to an exploding population. It continued to build many *danchi* in suburban areas throughout the sixties and seventies.

Japan Inc.

Japan's political economy known as the 'Construction State', was only firmly established as a governing policy after a major political upheaval in 1960. Before officially ending the occupation in 1952, the Americans had concluded a security treaty with Japan that allowed US troops to be stationed on Japanese territory, securing Japan's role as an industrial and security ally during the Korean War. In exchange, Japan, which, according to article 9 of its American imposed 'Peace Constitution', was no longer allowed to have its own military force, received nuclear protection from the U.S. army. In 1960, a renewal of the treaty was drafted and passed through the Diet[12] by the Liberal Democratic Party (LDP)[13], ignoring large-scale demonstrations and nationwide protests. At the time, many Japanese did not want to see Japan involved in another war, least of all with the United States. Opponents would claim the new treaty to be in violation of Japan's constitutional status as a pacifist nation, a political issue that remains unresolved to this day[14].

In *Inventing Japan*, Ian Buruma describes how in a deliberate move to bury this political unrest, Prime Minister Hayato Ikeda promised to make all Japanese richer with an ambitious 'Plan to Double Individual Income' published in December 1960.[15] In 1959 a new industrial policy from the Ministry of Trade and Industry had already been devised to steer the Japanese economy towards the production of high-quality and high-technology products. But a strategic part of the Ikeda deal was a new economic programme of relentless construction. A nationwide building campaign was set in motion to profit Japanese industry and construction business while politicians of the ruling LDP could satisfy their constituents by bringing back business to rural areas. The Japanese population could see the plan working as the national GDP quadrupled over the course of a decade.[16] This semi-planned economy, bringing about a 'Japanese miracle' culminated in a confluence of state, business, and urban planning, dubbed 'Japan Incorporated' by the Americans, who were forced to sit by and watch as the Japanese economy shoots up the global rankings.[17]

Mountain City

Architect: Uzō Nishiyama
Publication: 1946

Uzō Nishiyama, known for translating his findings from history into modern housing proposals[18], believed that the greatest problem facing Japan at the end of the war, and in the future, was overpopulation.[19] It was clear that Japan's territorial resources were drastically reduced after losing the colonies. Japan was now facing the challenge of sustaining a high-density population on scarce land. When severe food shortages hit the country after the war, people called for undeveloped land to be cleared from deep within the forests and plains. Nishiyama believed there had to be a better solution, as he remembered watching some of the best fields being demolished to make space for industrial structures such as munition factories during the war. Since, officially, lasting world peace was established, Nishiyama admitted that food self-sufficiency might not necessarily be essential, but then again, neither were munition factories.[20]

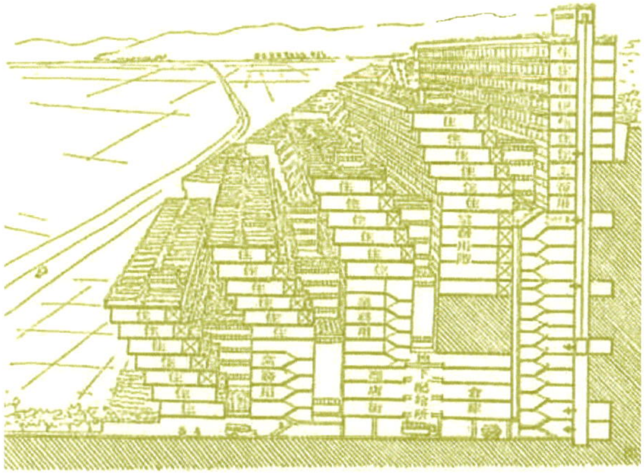

Nishiyama's mountain city designs aim to demonstrate that with the possibilities of modern construction and transport technology, the need to urbanize Japan's resourceful plains should not be taken for granted. Overlooking a horizon of rice paddies, this example of a 'highly concentrated' residential city using a south-facing slope features business and shopping areas, an underground supply centre, and an express train stop.

Concentrating urbanization in Japan's scarce arable plains is standard practice. The feudal cities of Japan typically relied on a hinterland for agriculture and on waterways for commercial transport. But now this productive hinterland was under pressure from urban sprawl. The architect observed that in Kobe[21] after the war, new territories were spontaneously explored: mountains behind the city were shaved and land was claimed from the sea to satisfy the needs of the population. In order to preserve the valuable acres, which make up a small fraction of the archipelago's largely mountainous surface, Nishiyama worked out a proposal to relocate urbanization to sloping terrain.[22] Although these mountain cities were never integrated in planning policy, the quasi-militaristic attempt to overcome Japan's inherent structural weakness with modern construction technology prefigured a Japanese obsession with agricultural megastructures and marine cities in the decades to come.

Yamato

Planner: Hisaakira Kano
Publication: 1958

From 1947 to 1948, the American occupation supported Japan's first socialist prime minister Tetsu Katagawa as he enforced a sweeping reform, redistributing land from big landowners to their tenants.[23] Although the measure had the desired effect of levelling social inequality while keeping a communist revolution[24] at bay, fragmented landownership also made any ambitious masterplan for metropolitan reconstruction almost impossible to realize. Meanwhile, the capital's population exploded from 3.5 million in 1945 to 9.5 million in 1960. Ten years after the reforms, the chairman of the Japan Housing Corporation acknowledged the fact that Tokyo had been left to expand beyond control and was now 'a huge mess'.[25] Following chairman Hisaakira Kano's idea of 'creating an estate where there are no landowners', the bureaucrat's team proposed an ambitious plan for the development of Tokyo Bay.

Since the plan was commissioned by the state-owned enterprise Electric Power Central Research Institute, Kano boldly proposed to use the atomic bomb as a tool to create a city rather than destroy one.[26] In 1954, 230 million yen were cleared for Japan's first nuclear energy programme with the Atomic Energy Basic Law limiting activities to peaceful purposes. Envisioning that even nuclear bombs may serve a peaceful purpose, Kano wanted to pulverize one of the neighbouring mountains to provide enough soil to fill up two thirds of Tokyo Bay, a no-man's land where architects and technocrats would have carte-blanche to implement the modern masterplan the city so desperately needed.[27]

The plan was later passed on to Kenzō Tange[28] who worked out a detailed architectural design for Tokyo Bay with his students at Tokyo University. On the first of January 1961, Tange presented the scheme on national television (NHK) against the backdrop of the 'Income Doubling Plan,' announced by the Ikeda administration in 1960. The Tange team had calculated that the plan would cost 18 trillion Yen over a period of twenty years, a reasonable sum compared to the 12 trillion that construction in Tokyo had cost during that time.[29]

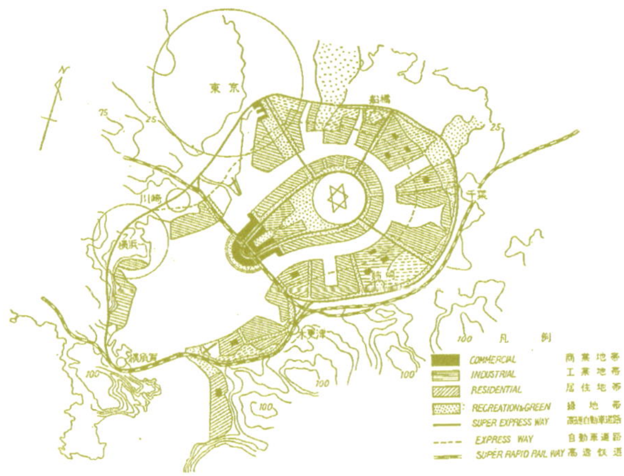

Kano called his new city 'Yamato', an old name for Japan and most recently a World War II battleship.[30] Following the approval of the Council for Industrial Planning, a committee of technocrats from the Ministry of construction, led by Kano, produced a new masterplan of the proposal under the name 'Neo Tokyo'.[31] Islands were divided into commercial, industrial, residential, and recreational zones, centred around a huge new airport.

New National Comprehensive Development Plan

Architect: Atsushi Shimokobe and Kishō Kurokawa
Publication: 1969

The booming economy under the Ikeda policy strengthened the faith in government planning but the fast growth inevitably brought about environmental problems of urban sprawl, congestion, and pollution. Atsushi Shimokobe, an old student of Tange who later pursued a career within the Japanese bureaucracy, believed that these urban problems needed to be addressed at the national scale. Taking on the task of masterplanning the future archipelago, he enlisted the help of his former classmate at the 'Tange Lab' Kishō Kurokawa, who had just founded a new think-tank: the Institute for Social Engineering.[32] In *Project Japan*, Rem Koolhaas and Hans Ulrich Obrist retrace Shimokobe and Kurokawa's assessment of the structural weaknesses of the archipelago: unstable ground, lack of space, lack of resources, pixelated land-ownership, and a population over-concentrated in Tokyo, culminating in a systematic redesign of the nation striving to spread its wealth more evenly.[33] Their New National Comprehensive Development Plan envisioned interregional redistribution of wealth by running a continuous urban belt along the length of the Japanese islands, linking isolated regions to a central spine via bridges, expressways and bullet trains. Koolhaas and Obrist point out that the Institute for Social Engineering took into account the coming of a leisure society, speculating that 'people's time will be equally divided between work and leisure from the latter half of the 1980s'.[34]

The comprehensive national plan was comparable to research by Tange on the Tōkaidō Megalopolis[35] and work of Uzō Nishiyama at his Kyoto University lab on 'Design for Life Space in the Nation'[36] of the same period. Popular support for plans reimagining the nation as a whole was proven when Minister of International Trade Kakuei Tanaka's book *Building a New Nation: Remodelling the Japanese Archipelago*, which promoted dispersed urbanism and connecting infrastructure, sold 910.000 copies.[37] The man himself was a licensed architect[38] and had a background in the construction business, which later funded his political career.[39] In 1972, the year he published his ambitious plan, Tanaka was elected Prime Minister, promising to turn the whole archipelago into a building site by spreading infrastructure and industrial activity over the entire territory: 'If we put together our sweat and power as well as the wisdom and technology that enabled us to construct the Japan of today from the debris of fire in World War II, I do not think it impossible to have a new era of "human restoration" in which society, man, sun, and green will take the initiative away from big cities and industries.'[40]

The cover of the Premier Tanaka's book shows an endless grid, expanding over the Japanese islands and seas. Envisioned construction plans included the making of new cities of 250,000 people, each including industrial, residential, service, and academic areas, and air, rail, and freeway improvements bringing every place in Japan within one day's travel time from any other.

1 I. Buruma, *Inventing Japan: 1853-1964* (London: Weidenfeld & Nicholson, 2003), 131.

2 The *zaibatsu* business conglomerates originated in the early Meiji period when the State had to sell of much of its infrastructure to private entrepreneurs. The *zaibatsu* went on to monopolize much of the Japanese economy. Classic examples are Mitsui and Mitsubishi.

3 I. Buruma, op. cit., 132.

4 W. Steele, 'Constructing the Construction State: Cement and Post-war Japan', *The Asia-Pacific Journal* 5 (2017), 2.

5 Ibid.

6 Ibid., 3.

7 Ibid., 1.

8 Ibid., 7.

9 R. Koolhaas and H.U. Obrist, *Project Japan: Metabolism talks* (Köln: TASCHEN, 2011), 642.

10 W. Steele, 'Constructing the Construction State: Cement and Post-war Japan', *The Asia-Pacific Journal* 5 (2017), 4.

11 W. Steele, op. cit., 7.

12 The National Diet (*Kokkai*) is Japan's bicameral legislature.

13 The Liberal Democratic Party (LDP) has been in power almost continuously since its foundation in 1955, with the exception of a period between 1993 and 1994, and again from 2009 to 2012.

14 Craig Martin, '"Reinterpreting' Article 9 endangers Japan's rule of law"', *The Japan Times*, June 27, 2014; Simon Cameron-Moore and Robert Birsel, 'Japan's Abe hopes for reform of pacifist charter by 2020', *Reuters*, May 3, 2017.

15 I. Buruma, op. cit., 166-167.

16 Ibid., 16

17 Koolhaas and H.U. Obrist, op. cit., 661.

18 Looking at the traditional separation of spaces in Japanese houses of hard surfaces (pounded earth) from those with soft ones (*tatami*), Nishiyama argued for further dividing tatami rooms for sleeping from living/dining/ kitchen areas (LDK) with wooden floors. The new organization of housing led to characteristic post-war housing projects: nLDK with 'n' indicating the number of bedrooms.

19 U. Nishiyama, 'Mountain Cities', in C. Hein, *Reflections on Urban, Regional and National Space: Three Essays* (New York: Routledge, 2018), 125.

20 Ibid., 121.

21 Kobe is a port city near Osaka characterized by the closeness of the mountains to the ocean. Consequently, the city extends along a thin strip of land along the coast.

22 U. Nishiyama, 'Mountain Cities', in C. Hein, *Reflections on Urban, Regional and National Space: Three Essays* (New York: Routledge, 2018), 122.

23 I. Buruma, op. cit., 148.

24 Such as the Maoist revolution taking place in China at that time.

25 R. Koolhaas and H.U. Obrist, *op. cit.*, 266.

26 H. Cho, 'Competing Futures: War Narratives in Post-war Japanese Architecture 1945-1970', PhD diss., University of Southern California (2011), 67.

27 R. Koolhaas and H.U. Obrist, op. cit., 275.

28 As vice-president of the Japanese Committee on International design Kano had the opportunity to meet Tange and discussed the plan with him. The architect immediately saw potential in the idea.

29 R. Koolhaas and H.U. Obrist, op. cit., 284.

30 Yamato and her sister ship, Musashi, were the heaviest and most powerfully armed battleships ever constructed.

31 R. Koolhaas and H.U. Obrist, op. cit., 276.

32 The Institute for Social Engineering, formed in 1969 researches the social use of engineering technology and produces regular reports for various ministries.

33 R. Koolhaas and H.U. Obrist, *op. cit.*, 683.

34 Ibid., 685.

35 At the request of the government, Tange worked at an official think-tank from 1967 to 1970, and published his vision of the Tōkaidō Metropolis as a guiding policy for the nation's future development.

36 U. Nishiyama, op. cit., 72-120.

37 R. Koolhaas and H.U. Obrist, op. cit., 650.

38 Tanaka was registered as a first-class architect after he passed the first-class architects law as a congressman in 1950.

39 I. Buruma, op. cit., 171.

40 Richard Halloran, 'New Japanese Premier Urges Fast Changes in Nation's Ways', *New York Times*, August 22, 1972.

D

'Construction is the hope of twentieth-century man'

Kenzo Tange, quoted in Cho, 'Competing Futures,' 183.

A city rebuilt in concrete.
Hiroshima, 17 March 2017

Call of the Catfish

In a 2012 lecture on 'Eco-topia and Eco-cities' architect Mitchell Joachim pointed out that during World War II, when the USA was attacked by the Japanese, America reacted by realigning its food, waste, and industrial systems within the timespan of a mere three days.[1] Details of the larger systems were worked out in the following months, but the principle was quickly in place. Joachim argues that a similar state of crisis is necessary in contemporary society in order to overcome political and social inertia when it comes to restructuring our modes of production and consumption. The astounding environmental recovery which came as a by-product of the global responses to the outbreak of the Covid-19 virus seem to support his theory. The hasty lockdowns instantaneously cleared the smog in cities where pollution seemed as insoluble as it was distressful. Cities such as Paris and Milan have seized the impetus to roll out ambitious urban plans to prioritize pedestrians and cyclists in the metropolitan area. And while we have not yet fully aligned our value system according to the environmental challenge we are facing, Joachim points to Hiroshima as the first crisis to inspire such action.

> I think the environmental debate began at that exact point, at least as we understand it in the contemporaneous fashion ... Hiroshima[2] was our first profound connection to what happens when we erase everything that we know.
>
> –Mitchell Joachim, architect

The direct impact of the radioactive contamination in Fukushima, coincidently a powerful reminder of the attacks on Hiroshima and Nagasaki, has indeed been the starting point for the Japanese government to get rid of its nuclear energy industry.[3] It also seems to be drawing Japan towards a new value system of which Itō and Kuma's anti-modernist architectural tenets[4]—drawing a clear line with the twentieth-century era of concrete architecture—represent the architectural parallel.

> In 2011, many parts of the Japanese coast were protected by huge retaining walls that were built to withstand a tsunami. The nuclear plant itself was supposedly designed to resist even a massive earthquake. Yet the walls were easily broken and the plant was irreparably damaged. The catastrophe showed that you cannot isolate a building or a city from the environment. That kind of modernist thinking has reached its limit.[5]
>
> –Toyo Itō, architect

When the government announced a plan to build a new 400-kilometre concrete seawall along the Northeast coast of Japan to protect the affected area from future tsunamis, it faced strong political opposition. The plan was devised under influence of Japan's construction lobby, asserting that the seawall would provide safety but also jobs to the economically devastated area.[6] But opponents of the concrete wall argued that technocratic solutions entailing further segregation from the natural environment have proved ineffective.

> After the earthquake in 2011, the tsunami destroyed hard concrete barriers. On the other hand, coastal Shintō shrines and temples survived, protected by forests of native trees.[7]
>
> –Akira Miyawaki, ecologist

Former prime minister Morihiro Hosokawa and the famous ecologist Akira Miyawaki are leading a movement that imagined, and is now building, a seawall of trees alongside the concrete wall. The protective forest will be able to limit the destructive power of even the largest tsunami, precisely by not aiming to block it completely.[8] This seawall of trees also promises to be more than a pragmatic return to nature by offering a way of recovering spiritually.[9] As Miyawaki already suggests, building the wall of trees may be viewed as an extension of Japanese religious typologies. The semi-regular plantings of trees for the wall have become ceremonies for life starting anew in the Tōhoku region.[10]

> The Great East Japan Earthquake taught us this lesson: Science and technology are not meant to control nature, but to be used as pieces of wisdom making it possible for us to coexist with nature… Now is a turning point of history. We have to shift from the age when materialism was central to an age where every life and soul will be loved tenderly. The Green Tide Embankment that protects life is a wisdom for living with nature.[11]
>
> –Doryu Hioki, Rinno Temple priest and chairman of the Green Tide Embankment association

Interestingly, in so far as the contemporary environmental crisis is the result of the materialism and uninhibited development of technology we are urged to overcome, it has origins as a solution to, or a distraction from Hiroshima, and the subsequent threat of global environmental disaster in the form of nuclear warfare. Japan's first seven post-war years were spent under American supervision, and the Japanese leadership thereafter chose economic growth under the protection of the U.S.' nuclear umbrella over political autonomy. Therefore, the post-war commemoration of the bomb emphasized urban transformation and the discourse of science, rather than dwelling on the traumatic experience itself.[12] As a matter of fact, there was even an American proposal to build Japan's first nuclear reactor in Hiroshima, an idea that was embraced by the city's mayor.

> The fact that Hiroshima will become the 'first nuclear power city' will comfort the souls of the dead. The citizens themselves, I think, would like to see death replaced by life.[13]
>
> –Shinzō Hamai, Hiroshima Mayor

The adoption of nuclear technology in Japan initially sparked controversy, which was fuelled by an incident in 1954 when a U.S. army hydrogen bomb test on the Bikini Atoll claimed the lives of several Japanese fishermen. While some believed economic development was paramount for the recovering nation, others warned that nuclear cooperation with the U.S. would imply entanglement in the Cold War. Drawing on his experience as a *hibakusha* (A-bomb victim), physicist Mimura Yoshitaka argues:

> Japan should not embark on nuclear research until the tension between the U.S. and the USSR is eased... If that meant there is a delay to Japanese civilization, so be it.[14]
>
> –Mimura Yoshitaka, nuclear physicist

Taketani Mitsuo, who had been involved in the government project for developing nuclear weapons during the war but later became an enthusiastic anti-nuclear bomb critic[15], did not agree with Yoshitaka. To him, the 'delay of civilization' was not an option. On the contrary, the bombing of Hiroshima, he felt, should be seized by Japan as an opportunity to demand international support in the development of nuclear power.

> The Japanese being the casualties of atomic warfare are entitled to have the strongest say in the development of atomic power...[and] possess the greatest moral right to carry out research. Other nations are obliged to help Japan's effort.[16]
>
> –Taketani Mitsuo, nuclear physicist

In the Hiroshima Peace City law of 1949, the endeavour to rebuild Hiroshima as a city of peace was equated with building a rational metropolis.[17] Nuclear energy, as a key component of future civilization, would be a logical extension of this rational metropolis.[18] In a dialogue with architect Takashi Asada, Kenzō Tange's assistant on the Hiroshima Peace Memorial project, nuclear physicist Taketani Mitsuo encouraged architects to build a new civilization of the 'Atomic Age' by overcoming the 'Atomic Bomb Age'.[19] Tange, who is considered the 'national architect' of post-war Japan, saw an era of great but potentially destructive power in the start of the 'Atomic Age', which he believed to be a justification for a technocratic planning approach to national reconstruction.

> As we leave the earlier half of the twentieth century and proceed into the second half, I have the feeling that we are experiencing vital changes in cultural forms in social structure, and in human environment. There is no way to predict the future, but I believe we can say this much: the current great change is resulting from the development of atomic energy and electronics, and the direction of the change is not toward unregulated expansion of energy but toward the controlling and planning of its development.[20]
>
> –Kenzō Tange, architect

In spite of the recent trauma of Hiroshima and Nagasaki, the pro-nuclear camp was able to present the choice as self-evident by, among other things, tapping into long-held fears about Japan being without significant natural resources, a so-called *motazaru kuni* (have-not-country)[21]. Unlimited energy in combination with limestone for cement, for which Japan remains a country-that-has[22], are the basic ingredients to build a new, future-oriented Japan. As a modern material extracted from domestic soil, concrete is perceived by post-war Japanese architects, including Tange Kenzō, Maekawa Kunio, and Ōtaka Masato as an ideal material out of which to construct a post-nuclear Japan, stripped of its past[23].

> Concrete is our material. Concrete is a material which comes out of Japan. We don't have to go to Manchuria or wherever, to get it, and we can't afford sophisticated American goods. We build with concrete.[24]
>
> –Masato Ōtaka, architect

Construction Culture

Hiroshima had come to represent a critical point from which science and technology could no longer be presented as inherently good. In this post-nuclear context, construction came to represent the positive, or literally the 'constructive', aspect of science and the opposite of war.

> We believe that the civilization and economy of the world are about to undergo a tremendous development. At the same time, we cannot help fearing that surpluses created in this expansion will be poured into the destructive consumption known as war. The wisdom of mankind must put the expansion in production to peaceful constructive uses. Construction is the hope of twentieth-century man and, at the same time, the responsibility to the men of the twenty-first century.[25]
>
> –Kenzō Tange, architect

Tange declared construction the 'hope of twentieth-century man', at the World Design Conference in 1960, the first significant international conference about architecture held in Japan. Here, architects from around the world arrived in a country rebuilt from material and spiritual ruin in a time span of just 15 years. This impressive feat has been an important lesson for the Japanese architects as it should be for their international visitors. While Japan was the first and until now the only atomic bomb victim, the architects of the 'Atomic Age' were reminded that the same could happen anywhere. In his opening speech to the conference, Kunio Maekawa, then president of the Japanese Architects Association, addressed the architectural elite[26] as if they would have a deciding role in putting science and technology to the right use:

> The good old memories of humanity as it existed at the end of the 19th century and the beginning of the 20th century were driven out by the First World War and the slightest remaining hope in this mechanical age was wiped out by the Second World War. Fourteen years since then, we are now facing the fatal moment when we have to choose between pleasant travel to space or space war.[27]
>
> –Kunio Maekawa, architect

His speech basically posited the commodification of advanced technology as the alternative, maybe even the antidote, to its potentially destructive nature. For Maekawa, the question was how we will conquer space, rather than whether we really needed to. The USA and the USSR were engaged in an unstoppable space race as well as an arms race. In this context, there was no point in asking whether these technologies should be developed in the first place. The contemporary race against the clock for the greening of technology in many ways mirrors the Cold War race for technology, alternating the promise of a futuristic dream with the threat of an apocalyptic nightmare. The ambivalent vision of the future, which prompted architects to envision building a brave new world in the 1960s, comes back today in depictions of a future where green skyscraper cities contrast with ruinous urban landscapes ravaged by a turbulent climate. In this sense, construction is still the hope of man in the twenty-first century. But this faith in new construction to save us from the past only keeps old mechanisms of consumption in place. If the crisis in Fukushima really is a wake-up call, it is a warning not to let history repeat itself. There, concrete construction and nuclear power, Japan's means to overcome the threat of nuclear warfare, have brought the nation back to square one. Japan's heavy retaining walls, it seems, were just a facade upholding the illusion of safety and of a government in control. Unfortunately, this illusion led many people to disregard the warnings on the day of the disaster and to perish in the storm.

1 European Graduate School, 'Mitchell Joachim. Ecotopia and Eco-Cities. 2012.', *YouTube*, https://www.youtube.com/watch?v=6sRe8msqa90

2 In his presentation Joachim refers to the vivid description of the aftermath of the bomb by John Hershey, who visited the site right after the bombing.

3 European Graduate School, ibid.

4 See K. Kuma, *The Principles of Place* (2011), and T. Itō, *The Great Transformation in Architecture* (2012).

5 J. Rose, 'The building after', *Artforum* 1 (2013).

6 Elaine Kurtenbach, 'Japan opts for massive, costly seawall to fend off tsunamis', *phys.org,* March 22, 2015, https://phys.org/news/2015-03-japan-opts-massive-costly-sea.html

7 Brian Lufkin, 'Akira Miyawaki has planted 40 million trees as a tidal-wave shield', *Wired*, January 6, 2014, https://www.wired.co.uk/article/the-tree-whisperer

8 As opposed to a massive breakwater that needs only prove to be inadequate in one location for the whole defensive line to collapse (as in March 2011)

9 Editorial, 'Tōhoku's Great Forest Wall Project', *Japan Times*, November 23, 2013, https://www.japantimes.co.jp/opinion/2013/11/23/editorials/tohokus-great-forest-wall-project/

10 Ibid.

11 Unsinkable Japan, 'Making Forests of Life for the Ones You Love "The Green Tide Embankment"', *YouTube*, https://www.youtube.com/watch?v=-nGr3LQxyyA

12 R. Zwigenberg, '"The Coming of a Second Sun": The 1956 Atoms for Peace Exhibit in Hiroshima and Japan's Embrace of Nuclear Power', *The Asia-Pacific Journal* 1 (2012), 5-6.

13 Ibid., 5.

14 Ibid., 3.

15 H. Cho, 'Competing Futures: War Narratives in Post-war Japanese Architecture 1945-1970', PhD diss., University of Southern California (2011), 183.

16 R. Zwigenberg, op. cit., 3.

17 Ibid., 5.

18 Ibid., 6.

19 The conversation is published in the *Shinkenchiku* architectural journal of August 1955.

20 H. Cho, op. cit., 79-80.

21 R. Zwigenberg, op. cit., 5.

22 W. Steele, 'Constructing the Construction State: Cement and Post-war Japan', *The Asia-Pacific Journal* 5 (2017), 6.

23 Ibid., 7.

24 Ibid., 6.

25 H. Cho, op. cit., 183.

26 The World Design Conference, intended as a platform to put Japanese architecture on the map, attracted Japan's most famous architects but also masters from abroad, such as Louis Kahn, Paul Rudolph, and Jean Prouvé.

27 H. Cho, op. cit. 183.

H

Cold War Architecture (1952-1973)

A Dynamic Geopolitical Context

The atomic bomb ended World War II but set the stage for the Cold War, during which the threat of nuclear warfare became a scenario to be reckoned with. In her doctoral study of postwar narratives in Japanese architecture, Hyunjung Cho traces the meaning and impact of the war trauma, continually evolving against the background of Japan's ties to the international Cold War context.[1] For instance, under the Allied occupation, the representation of the atomic bomb tragedy was strictly censored and the project for a 'Peace Memorial' in Hiroshima, the centrepiece of the city's reconstruction, was designed in the future-oriented style of international modernism. But the narrative of Hiroshima as a city of world peace was challenged at the end of the occupation, when nationalist sentiments resurface.[2] In 1954 in particular, when the U.S. army performed a hydrogen bomb test on the Bikini Atoll and a nearby crew of Japanese fishermen died from radiation sickness, anti-nuclear and anti-U.S. sentiment lighted up. Cho shows how architecture adapted to this dynamic geopolitical context as architect Kenzō Tange gradually integrated traditional elements into the design of the Hiroshima Peace Memorial as well as in the discourse surrounding the project.[3]

When the occupation ended, the renewal of the US-Japan security treaty, placing Japan under America's military protection, marked another paradigm shift. The ratification of the new treaty in 1960 coincided with the World Design Conference held in Tokyo, in an effort to put Japanese architecture on the map. At the event, the Metabolist group, including Kiyonori Kikutake, Kisho Kurokawa and Fumihiko Maki, and groomed by 'national architect' Kenzō Tange during the previous years, launched a manifesto advocating utopian plans to facilitate radical social change by architectural means.[4] While the architects of this progressive utopia opposed the political conservatism behind the 1960 Security Treaty, architectural historian Zhongjie Lin argues that ironically, the policies they opposed effectively led to the unilateral focus on economic growth which facilitated their visionary urban plans.[5] Thus, the decade of the 'Income Doubling Plan' gradually transformed Metabolism from a marxist-utopian movement into an architecture synthesising technocracy and the pop culture of mass-consumption.

Techno-Utopia

Here, Hyunjung Cho adds that the concept of metabolism itself is borrowed from Marx' and Engels' ideas about the material exchange between natural conditions and human society.[6] The writers of *Capital* and the *The Communist Manifesto* used the term 'metabolism' in their publications to criticize alienation from nature and the ecological crisis caused by capitalism. Cho points to the fact that, at the time, left-wing intellectuals in Japan took an interest in the problem of the domination of nature by technology since the atomic bomb in particular, symbolized both nuclear terror and the promise of scientific and technological innovation.[7] Thus, Marxism's ecological concept of metabolism appears as a legitimate alternative to the abuses of technology in modern society. The Metabolists'[8] emphasis on the 'city as process' can be understood as a socialist attempt to apply the law of nature to civilization. But the future city imagined as a second nature undergoing processes of evolution and modular reproduction was equally, if not more, inspired by contemporary scientific breakthroughs. Lin reminds us that the 1950s were regarded as 'the decade of genetic molecular biology' after Watson and Crick determined the molecular structure of DNA in 1953.[9] As Japan allied with the US, a Cold War notion equating American science with progress, freedom, and other positive values became the dominant frame. In the name of science and technology, rivalling superpowers explored hitherto uncharted territories such as Antarctica and outer space, combining the setup of their strategic defence with a narrative stressing the progress of mankind.

Mega Event

Japan eagerly participated in the celebration of industrial technology that propelled the nation's economy from an all-time low to a second place in world rankings, in just a quarter of a century. In 1964, Japan had officially 'rejoined the world' after hosting the Olympic Games in a sanitized and modernized capital city. Six years later, the nation, at the height of its economic power, stunned an unprecedented 64 million international visitors with a prototype of 'the city of the future' at Expo 70 in Osaka. The scheme, originally designed by local architect Uzō Nishiyama, was handed over to architects of the Metabolist group led by Kenzō Tange, who, according to Zhongjie Lin, probably enjoyed the preference of big industrialists and bankers for his abilities to create iconic structures as he had done for the '64 Olympics.[10] Inevitably, the grand show, featuring Japan's first bullet train, capsule towers and performing robots, exposed the crisis of Techno-Utopia. As commercialism took over the event, the technology conceived as a means to stimulate social change was reduced to an instrument of popular entertainment.[11] Soon after, the first oil crisis brought the Japanese economy to a grinding halt and forced the nation to reconsider this uninhibited materialism.

Tokyo Metropolitan Government office

Architect: Kenzō Tange
Completion: 1957

The new Tokyo Metropolitan Government Building is one in a series of office blocks the rising star Kenzō Tange designed throughout the 1950s. Its design featured Japan's first high-rise steel and glass facade, until now considered vulnerable to earthquakes.[12] But at the beginning of the Cold War, the debate over the safety of steel and glass architecture was not confined to earthquake-prone countries like Japan. The atomic age made it one of the most recurrent themes in contemporary U.S. architectural discourse.[13] In 'Competing Futures' Cho brings up the Japanese counterpart, a so-called 'anxiety debate', opposing construction engineer Takeyama Kenzaburo and architectural critic Hamaguchi Ryūichi.[14] The engineer warns that the pervasive use of glass in modern buildings would make Japanese cities even more vulnerable in case of earthquakes, typhoons, or nuclear blasts. As a critic, Hamaguchi defends the symbolic value of glass, praising the qualities of 'the sensibility of light openness and uneasy fragility of glass' as a metaphor for freedom and ephemerality in contemporary society.

At a time when private bunkers were being constructed across America, glass towers such as Skidmore Owings and Merrill's Lever House (1952) and Mies van der Rohe's Seagram Building (1958), confidently boasting their faith in a promising future, stood in sharp contrast with trends towards fortification in architecture. Tange contributed with a steel and glass high-rise of his own. The structure remained of concrete however, and the tower featured in the scheme was not built.

Antarctic Housing Project

Architect: Takashi Asada
Publication: 1957

In combination with fear of overpopulation, nuclear anxiety prompted an exploration of the uninhabited polar continents as a potential retreat from an impending environmental crisis. With an eye on the future survival of mankind, Antarctica was viewed as a promising frontier providing a strategic military location but also a 'rich repository of natural resources'.[15] Before the Antarctic Treaty was opened for signature in 1959, several countries[16] started making claims on the uncharted territory. The treaty, concluded in 1961, prevented further claiming and prohibited military use of the territory, explicitly forbidding 'nuclear explosions or disposal of radioactive waste' in a separate article.

After working on several proposals for circular-shaped pneumatic structures in 1956, Asada moved on to a modular panel system made of rectangular slabs. In his quest for 'perfect prefabrication', Asada stated that 'each part of the building was linked directly with the survival of the crews'. From 1957, Japan's Antarctic Showa Station was built up in different phases as an agglomeration of these prefabricated containers.

The Japanese Antarctic project was initiated as part of the International Geographical Year (IGY) from 1957 to 1958; a scientific research collaboration among the international community. During this Antarctic 'construction boom'[17], the Japan Institute of Architects was solicited in the construction of the living quarters for Japanese crews. The Antarctic stations were in fact designed as architectural symbols of national advancement rather than purely technical challenges.[18] In 1956, the Institute formed a temporary Antarctic architectural committee with a design team headed by Takashi Asada, who's primary goal for the project was to 'achieve a perfect prefabrication'.[19] As Asada mentors the Metabolist architects, the Antarctic housing project can be considered the forerunner of capsule architecture.

Nakagin Capsule Tower

Architect: Kishō Kurokawa
Completion: 1972

Kurokawa's experimentation with capsules in the sixties and early seventies marks a shift from 'hardware', a megastructural approach to overcoming the structural weakness of Japanese cities, to the age of 'software', as the national economy shifted its focus from reconstruction to mass-consumption and the organization of an 'information society'. While small in size, the capsules of the Nakagin tower are generously equipped with the latest electronic devices. 'From now on', the architect declares, 'architecture will increasingly take on the character of equipment'.[20] The 144 capsules of the tower are produced by a factory specialized in shipping containers.[21] The standardized capsules are intended to be mass-produced, disposed of, and replaced with newer models according to the fast-changing needs of society.

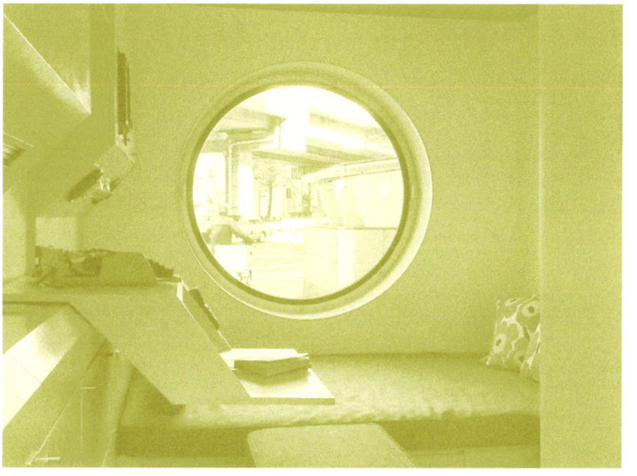

In his essay 'Capsule declaration,'[24] the architect explains that the spaceship is a capsule and the capsule is like a spaceship: a controlled environment within which the device and the life within depend on each other for survival.

The capsule corresponds to an idealized capitalist dream of affluence and comfort, albeit in the shadow of the communist threat[22]. But it also derives from a view of architecture as a survival machine. As the city is flooded by ever more movement and information, Kurokawa speculates that Tokyo could soon become as harsh an environment as Antarctica or the moon: 'Just as an astronaut is protected from solar winds and cosmic rays, individuals should be protected by capsules in which they can reject information they do not need...thereby allowing an individual to recover his subjectivity and independence.'[23]

1 H. Cho, 'Competing Futures: War Narratives in Post-war Japanese Architecture 1945-1970', PhD diss., University of Southern California (2011), 175.

2 Ibid., 50.

3 Ibid.

4 Literally, metabolism translates as *shinchin taisha*, meaning 'in with the new, out with the old'.

5 Z. Lin, *Kenzo Tange and the Metabolist Movement: Urban Utopias of Modern Japan*, (London: Routledge, 2010), 61.

6 H. Cho, op. cit., 195.

7 Ibid.

8 Especially critic Noboru Kawazoe was concerned with integrating Marxism in the Metabolist principles.

9 Z. Lin, op. cit., 23.

10 Ibid., 208.

11 Ibid., 200-201.

12 R. Koolhaas and H.U. Obrist, *Project Japan: Metabolism talks* (Köln: TASCHEN, 2011), 124.

13 H. Cho, op. cit., 174.

14 Ibid., 174.

15 Ibid., 185.

16 The first countries with significant stakes in Antarctica include Argentina, Australia, Belgium, Chile, France, Japan, New Zealand, Norway, South Africa, the Soviet Union, the United Kingdom and the United States.

17 These countries establish over 50 Antarctic stations for the International Geographic Year.

18 H. Cho, op. cit., 185-186.

19 Ibid., 187.

20 R. Koolhaas and H.U. Obrist, op. cit., 388.

21 Ibid.

22 H. Cho, op. cit., 215.

23 R. Koolhaas and H.U. Obrist, op. cit., 388.

24 Quotes are taken from Kurokawa's 1969 essay 'Capsule Declaration'.

D

'A gigantic monster on the brink of extinction'

Sin from City Demolition Inc. (Arata Isozaki), quoted in Koolhaas and Obrist, *Project Japan*, 52.

'3.6m above sea level' Ubiquitous municipal signs call attention to the looming threat of natural disaster. Minami Shinagawa, Tokyo, 17 February, 2017

Cleanliness and Order

On the seventh day of the 1964 Olympic Games, a group of artists took to the streets of Tokyo to perform a 'Campaign to promote Cleanliness and Order in the Metropolitan Area'. Disguised as a group of officials executing an urban beautification programme, the members of the Hi Red Centre proceeded to scrub the Ginza's pavement with toothbrushes, mocking the technocratic effort to turn the capital into a sanitized metropolis for the big event.[1] The technocratic clean-up of the city strived to erase the last traces of wartime destruction, and presented a gleaming metropolis as the embodiment of Japan's advance among its democratic peers. In response, the artists provocatively tried to expose how in the excitement for the games, Tokyo's citizens were letting their city become a product of decisions taken by national authorities and big corporations.[2] The fact that the group was barely noticed by passers-by, who mistook their performance for an official programme, indicates the normality and social acceptance of this situation in Japan. While at the time of the '64 Olympic Games, architects, Kenzō Tange for example, still firmly believed in construction and centralized planning as a means to achieve social progress, the failure of technocratic planning in March 2011 has reversed the situation. In a recent interview, Yoshiharu Tsukamoto of Atelier Bow-Wow talks about how central planning and big building contractors are driving a wedge between architects and society.

> In the reconstruction of the devastated area of Tōhoku, architects could not do so many things. Everything was mainly about infrastructure and a new residential area that was built by a series of engineering consultancies and big construction companies under decisions from the central government... so there is a barrier between architects and society, which is produced by the 20th century, the industrialization process and construction culture.[3]
>
> –Yoshiharu Tsukamoto, architect (Atelier Bow-Wow)

Tsukamoto calls on architects to raise their voices in protest.[4] It would be a pity for society, he argues, if people no longer had access to architects who, as opposed to politicians and corporations, are capable of formulating a long-term vision for the living environment.

> Politicians have a very short time perspective; maybe they are thinking about the next elections. Big companies think with short time perspectives also in order to gain profits. These trends bring people into unhappy conditions.[5]
>
> –Yoshiharu Tsukamoto, architect (Atelier Bow-Wow)

Rather than trying to fit in with the technocratic system like Tange did, Toyo Itō's and Kengo Kuma's post-3/11 architectural tenets can be qualified as a counter-architecture. As he lays the blame for the disastrous consequences of the Tōhoku earthquake at the feet of Japan's 'urban-centric' culture, Kengo Kuma believes that now is the time for architecture to evolve, from 'monumental objects' built for profits, towards human-scaled 'places' built for communities.[6] His 'anti-object' architecture, presented in a book with that very title: *Anti-Object: The Dissolution and Disintegration of Architecture*, aims to bring back the sense of place in each region which disappeared with twentieth-century urbanization by building with small elements, as opposed to monolithic concrete.

> The architecture of small elements is a democratic architecture. It is grass-roots architecture, not from the top down but from the bottom up.[7]
>
> –Kengo Kuma, architect

Anti-Object, Anti-Urban?

In a book outlining his 'post-earthquake and post-tsunami architectural tenets' entitled *The Principles of Place*, Kuma further opposes the modernist myth of progress that motivated the erection of concrete blocks. He suggests that improvements in the built environment arise in response to great crises rather than economic growth, or technological advancement.

> Architectural theses have all, up to now, represented theories based on the notion that society's evolution brings on architecture's evolution. ... But, in actuality, architecture has been diverted by tragedies. Great catastrophes and economic depressions ... have immensely transformed design.[8]
>
> –Kengo Kuma, architect

The architect refers to the great earthquake of 1755 in Lisbon. He recognizes the earthquake as an era-defining moment that changed the course of architecture, prompting the invention of 'the modern'. The new Lisbon was planned and built on a grid pattern, connecting big public squares with wide boulevards in, according to Kuma, a physical rejection of the dark, closed world of Portuguese Catholicism.[9] By causing more than 60,000 deaths, the devastating earthquake and tsunami in Lisbon planted a popular distrust of God, leading to the concepts of liberty and equality that inspired the French Revolution 34 years later. In his writings, Voltaire had put God and nature on trial and found both guilty.[10] In response, Rousseau wrote a letter to Voltaire reprimanding his insults—not to God but to nature. The horrific death toll, in Rousseau's view, was due to the fact that people had locked themselves into crowded cities rather than living a natural life, dispersed in nature. Although Kuma gives no mention of Rousseau, the latter's anti-urban philosophy directly applies to the architect's vision for the future of his country.

> I sensed that 3/11 had reversed the course of history, I felt, in a word, that the Tokyo-centric era was over, or, perhaps put more clearly, the era where cities themselves were at the center of everything was over.[11]
>
> –Kengo Kuma, architect

Kuma's view of architecture evolving as a consequence of major disasters rather than in proportion to the economic and technological progress of society is not new: it echoes the message of Arata Isozaki who in the 1960s distanced himself from his comrades in the Metabolist movement for this very reason.[12] Unlike his peers who were focused on a 'genetic' evolution in architecture, Isozaki sceptically reminded us that architecture and destruction would always be two sides of the same coin. He illustrated his schizophrenic take on urban growth in a story involving Arata, a visionary architect and urban planner, and his long-time friend Sin (also the Chinese reading of the character 'Arata'), a retired professional killer. It is interesting to note that Kengo Kuma, in his rebellious stance against the modern concrete machine, ideologically stands much closer to Sin than to Arata, the architect. Sin is a poet in spirit for whom killing is not a job, it is a *métier*, a craft to be treated with care and dedication. He is a man of tradition. But modern times have made his trade the laughingstock as the bustling metropolis daily kills hundreds of innocent bodies in a blind, reckless and ugly manner.

The city, therefore, was the killer of all killers and, worse still, being anonymous, it was a curious enterprise to which no responsibilities were attached. And he felt that in order to create an age in which the killing profession would again be an art, and in which this human act could be performed with pleasure, there was nothing more urgent than to destroy these inhuman cities.[13]

Sin retires from his job as a hitman to start a company named City Demolition Incorporated. Its goal? 'The complete destruction of large cities which have been repeatedly engaged in vicious mass murder, and at the construction of a civilization in which elegant, pleasant and humanistic murder can be carried out easily' and this by any means. Sin's caricature of Tokyo is in line with Kuma's disapproval of the reckless faith in concrete and steel:

> 'A gigantic monster on the brink of extinction; a pig roasted whole; the ultimate evil of unintentional, inevitable mass massacre. . .'[14]

Arata admits that he too now has his doubts about urban planning and smiles when Sin argues that it is inexcusable for the professional to only make utopian plans. But Arata knows that if Sin executes his city demolition plan too hastily, it will 'bring prosperity rather than destruction and, against his will, the circumstances that would satisfy his artistic aspirations will not be brought forth.' The cynical Arata would fear the same of Kuma's architectural rebellion. Simply stating that existing cities are no good and that they should be replaced with better, more decent structures most likely results in perpetuating real estate speculation, the destructive force at the origin of the problem Kuma is dealing with. In fact, the architects' iconic contributions to the 2020 Olympics are instrumental in leveraging investment for countless new concrete towers all over Tokyo[15], although the man himself is hardly to blame for this.

Home For All

In the same spirit as Kuma, Toyo Itō co-authored the book *Great Transformation of Architecture: back to fundamentals* with anthropologist Shinichi Nakazawa in 2012, to discuss potential directions architecture could take to help communities 'navigate through the postmodern, post-3/11 earthquake world to pursue happiness'.[16]

> I have always felt that the world has become dominated by market economy, and architecture has become a tool to further enhance such a system. I've been trying to be cognisant about that. I've sought ways to push architecture back to its original purpose — which is to serve community, or to provide venues for people to share.[17]
>
> –Toyo Itō, architect

Itō is aware of the vicious circle in which modern architecture is trapped and in which he himself has played a significant role. In the ecological age we tend to question modernity's foundations and yet the opportunity of the crisis only appears to be selling the next modernity, accepting economic growth and technology as the implicit solution, rather than offering a way out. Meanwhile, architecture is being held hostage as a 'tool to visualize capital'. The second part of Itō's response appears at first sight as a modest, almost naïve horizon for architecture's future. But making social resilience paramount may just be the way to go if architecture wants to take a stand in the contemporary urban field. Linking ecological sustainability to social resilience is a move to reclaim the future of the city out of the hands of technicians. The combination is a task that clearly calls for the architects' ability to give expression to built form and the urbanists' expertise in handling typical 'urban questions'. In a talk given at the High Level Group meeting on Smart Cities, Brussels, 24 September 2014, Rem Koolhaas warned us that via the 'smart city' movement engineers and technicians are gradually claiming authorship over the design of cities.[18] In the meantime, we are forgetting that architecture and cities possess their own form of intelligence. By arguing that 'the fight against nature cannot be won' Japanese architects are effectively predicting that this technocratic response to the sustainability crisis is bound to fail.

> People say the Tōhoku Tsunami was a natural disaster, but I disagree. People blindly believed that existing embankments – big, hard and sturdy things made of concrete – would protect us from natural threats. We thought drawing explicit boundaries between nature and humans would solve all the problems. But it didn't. I think that thinking was fundamentally wrong.[19]
>
> –Toyo Itō, architect

The statement that strong architecture has failed the people should not be framed as an attack on the previous generation of architects, it is an attack on technocracy. By extension, this frame also addresses the problem of destructive real estate speculation. In Japan, cyclical destruction of the built environment due to earthquakes and war naturally feeds a huge construction industry, which has established a co-dependent relationship with the technocratic state. The latter relies on the construction sector as an economic lever to pull the country out of economic depressions in these times of crisis.[20] Alternately, in times of welfare, the technocratic state has to feed the construction industry with more roads and bridges to build and buildings to replace. The constant enforcement of improved technical standards is an effective method to ensure this constant demand for construction.

Together with Kengo Kuma, Kazuyo Sejima, Hiroshi Naito, and Riken Yamamoto, Itō formed a collective called *Kishin no Kai* to support communities affected by the earthquake. They each produced *Minna no Ie* (Home for all) projects. Itō confused many people with a surprisingly basic design showing no trace of starchitecture. As opposed to his previous work, which continually explored the limits of contemporary technology and spatial experimentation, 'Home for all' is based on a traditional Japanese home design that can best be described as familiar. 'Is this what Toyo Itō has to design? Should you be building something this ordinary?' A lot of people asked, says Itō.[21] But his design makes a strong point by showing that sustainability and resilience in architecture could really mean something else than what we are being sold.

1 R. Tomii, 'After the "descent to the everyday": Japanese collectivism from Hi Red Center to The Play, 1964-1973' In B. Stimson and G. Sholette, *Collectivism after Modernism: The Art of Social imagination after 1945* (Minneapolis: University of Minnesota Press, 2007), 54-55.

2 The flyer to their event features a list of fake corporate and government sponsors including:
-The Tokyo Metropolitan Cleansing Projects Department
-National Federation of Shopping Streets
-Rear End Society
-...

3 J. P. Urrutia, Juan Pablo. 'Yoshiharu Tsukamoto: We have to avoid treating people just like numbers', *Materia Arquitectura* 12 (2015).

4 Ibid.

5 Ibid.

6 R. Pulvers, 'Architect Kuma Kengo: "a product of place",' *Asia-Pacific Journal* 2 (2013), 2.

7 Roger Pulvers, 'Born of disaster, modern architecture is itself now an ongoing disaster.', *Japan Times,* May 13, 2012, https://www.japantimes.co.jp/opinion/2012/05/13/commentary/born-of-disaster-modern-architecture-is-itself-now-an-ongoing-disaster/

8 Ibid.

9 Ibid.

10 Roy Starrs, 'Zen, Japan and the art of democracy', *New Statesman*, July 7, 2011, https://www.newstatesman.com/asia/2011/07/japan-essay-nature-earthquake

11 Roger Pulvers, ibid.

12 R. Koolhaas and H.U. Obrist, *Project Japan: Metabolism talks* (Köln: TASCHEN, 2011), 25.

13 A. Isozaki, 'City Demolition Inc.', in R. Koolhaas and H.U. Obrist, *Project Japan: Metabolism talks* (Köln: TASCHEN, 2011), 52-53.

14 Ibid.

15 In addition to the new national stadium, Kengo Kuma Architects designed a new train station at the core of a new urban development in Shinagawa in prospect of the 2020 Games.

16 M. Fuji, 'Toyo Ito: 3.11 and "Great Transformation of Architecture."', *Zero = Abundance*, 2015, http://www.interactiongreen.com/toyo-ito-sustainable-architecture/

17 Ibid.

18 R. Koolhaas, 'My thoughts on the smart city', *European Commission*, September 24, 2014, http://ec.europa.eu/archives/ commission_2010-2014/kroes/en/content/my-thoughts-smart-cityrem-koolhaas.html

19 M. Fuji, ibid.

20 Benjamin Powell, 'Explaining Japan's recession', *Mises Institute*, NOVEMBER 19, 2002, https://mises.org/library/explaining-japans-recession

21 M. Fuji, ibid.

TIMELINE
Post-Nuclear Ecology

1945: Atomic bombing of Hiroshima and Nagasaki
1945-1952: American occupation
1946: Mountain City by Uzō Nishiyama
1947: Peace Constitution enacted
1947: American attempt to dissolve zaibatsu conglomerates
1947-1949: Major land reforms enacted
1948: Japan Export Corporation founded
1949: Controls lifted on industrial production of coal, iron, steel, concrete
1949: Hiroshima Peace Memorial design competition
1950-1953: Korean War
1954: U.S. army's hydrogen bomb test on the Bikini Atoll
1954: First Japanese Nuclear energy programme
1955: First nuclear cooperation agreement with United States
1955: Japan Housing Corporation founded as semi-public institution
1955-1975: Vietnam War
1957: Tokyo Metropolitan Government office by Kenzō Tange
1957: Antarctic housing project by Takashi Asada
1957-1958: Construction boom in Antarctica during International Geographic Year
1958: Yamato Tokyo Bay plan by Hisaakira Kano
1959: Ministry of Trade and Industry reforms Japanese industry to concentrate on high-quality, high-tech products
1960: Renewal of US-Japan Security treaty
1960: Resignation of Prime Minister Kishi Nobusuke following widespread protests and demonstrations
1960: Income Doubling Plan by Prime Minister Ikeda
1960: Launch of Metabolist manifesto at World Design Conference
1961: Kenzō Tange presents Tokyo Bay urban plan on national television (NHK)
1961: Antarctic Treaty
1961: President John F. Kennedy announces mission to the moon
1963: 31 metre building height regulation in Tokyo lifted
1964: Tokyo Olympics
1966: First nuclear power plant in Japan
1968: Japanese GDP becomes second largest in the world
1969: New National Comprehensive Development Plan by Atsushi Shimokobe and Kishō Kurokawa
1970: Expo 70 Osaka
1972: Nakagin Capsule Tower by Kishō Kurokawa
1972: *Building a New Japan: A Plan for Remodelling the Japanese Archipelago* published by Prime Minister Kakuei Tanaka
1973-1974: OPEC oil embargo
1982: Start Heisei Period
1986-1991: Japanese asset price bubble
1991: Dissolution of USSR marks end of Cold War

Island Ecology

source: The Economist. 'Japan's economy v rest of the world.' Accessed April 22, 2018, www.economist.com/graphicdetail

Even though Japan's regions can boast the GDP's of entire countries and the Exclusive Economic Zone granted by the U.N. Convention on the Law of the Sea (1982) has made it the seventh largest country of all, narratives stressing its insular isolation on a territory relatively poor in natural resources still prevail. Ever since the isolationism of premodern Japan, central authorities have relied on the image of Japan as an 'island nation', to convey a sense of homogeneity and harmony by equating national and natural borders. At a time when globalization, accelerated by neoliberalism and new information technology, is causing fragmentation between globally embedded urban centres and increasingly neglected regions, imagery of Japan as a coherent island ecology offers hope to the ones left behind and a sense of identity to the ones living in generic metropolitan environments...

Exclusive Economic Zone	**Regional GDP (2011)** (+nearest country equivalent), bn$			
	>1.000	750-500	500-250	<250

E

勿体無い
Mottainai

If you focus on what to throw away, you will lose sight of the real purpose of tidying. The best criterion for choosing what to keep is this: does it spark joy when you touch it?[1]

-Marie 'KonMari' Kondo, organizing consultant, 2017

Mottainai

The Japanese *mottainai* ethic is said to stem from Japan's isolation as an island with limited resources. *Mottainai* literally means 'essence'. It is a popular expression used to convey a feeling of regret at wasting the intrinsic value of a resource or object, and can be translated as 'what a waste!' or 'don't be wasteful'. From a Western perspective, *mottainai* can be interpreted as a concept adding 'Respect' to the three R's of conservation practice: reduce, reuse, recycle.[2] The concept has roots in Buddhism but according to Yuko Kawanishi, a sociologist at Tokyo Gakugei University, *mottainai* also has ties with shintō animism, promoting the idea that all things have a *kami*, or spirit.[3]

Mottainai does not just apply to tangible objects, however. Because of inflationary land prices, an empty lot in Tokyo can evoke a reaction of 'what a waste!' as well.[4] In *Made in Tokyo*, a study of urban constructions that reflect the metropolitan values of Tokyo's dwellers, the architects of Atelier Bow-Wow diagnose a 'void phobia'.[5] It corresponds to an ethic that naturally resists the simple public/private dichotomy of open and built space. Based on void phobia, Tokyo's organization is more akin to a rainforest-like section in which every inch of space and every ray of sunlight must be exploited to the max, resulting in what the authors identify as an 'automatic scaling' reflex. Viewed as a metropolitan counterpart of the traditional *mottainai* ethic, which raises a cultural awareness of both the interdependence and the impermanence things[6], the concept perfectly explains why empty lots are considered a waste but scrapping and rebuilding at rates three or four times faster than in Europe is not: in Tokyo, empty space is the real limited resource.

Nevertheless, the Japanese scrap-and-build approach to urban renewal is environmentally and financially unsustainable. As the demand for flexibility and constant change is imposed not just by the rules governing Tokyo's urbanity but also by the nature of our times, the Japanese have to ask themselves to what extent they can hold on to the existing building stock. There is no more excuse for ceaseless construction now that the Japanese population is decreasing fast and Tokyo is expected to start shrinking in the near future, like many other cities around the world. The question then is whether we can reduce, reuse, and recycle the city in a way that respects and reanimates its spirit.

Invisible City

The biotope of twenty-first-century man will be the city, and the possibilities this urban environment provides inevitably depend on its built form. Although in developed countries this form is not changing as much as it used to, the past few years have proven that the city is still capable of transformation. Without touching a single brick, new apps from Silicon Valley, such as Google Maps, Airbnb, Uber, or even Pokémon Go are reinventing urbanism from afar. Throughout the twentieth century, the city was adjusted to the needs of the times using concrete and steel. Hilton Hotels, for example, had to erect its empire tower by tower since its establishment a century ago. Today, we have the house sharing platform Airbnb, which in 2016, without building anything whatsoever, acquired a higher market value than the Hilton and the Hyatt corporations combined.[7] From this perspective, modernization no longer means expanding the tangible infrastructure, the 'hardware' if you will, but updating the 'software', thereby enabling the use, and reuse, of the existing patrimony.

Historically, the articulation of architectural form and materiality has codified the hierarchy, continuity, and meaning of urban spaces. Mobile internet has introduced a new means of organizing urbanity that is at odds with this architectural tradition. Users now have the power to overwrite architectural code with binary code, effectively enveloping the city in a new layer of text. For instance, when Pokémon Go[8] projects a virtual layer over the city, magically transforming every open space into play-ground, whether this open space is an empty parking lot or the central square doesn't matter all that much. The physical attributes and corresponding hierarchy between these spaces make way for a new order, that emphasizes the distinction between players and non-players instead.

For the first time, we no longer read urban space with the naked eye as smartphones provide an increasingly indispensable lens to navigate the city. This is especially true in Tokyo, a formless, incoherent and ever-changing agglomeration of buildings where streets have no names, and only the postman knows the addresses. In the virtual streets of Google maps, 'virtual facades' have the power to give existing buildings a new appearance, using a scale of stars, a short description, and the comments of previous users. Architecture as 'interface' is silenced, letting new functions worm their way into old shells. Virtual space is able to unlock real space where the architecture of the city fails to guide us.

CAPCA / IE-project
The public space of the Facebook generation is an ephemeral phenomenon. It can appear—and disappear—in interior and exterior spaces, at the centre or in the periphery. It consists of spontaneous collaborations of like-minded folk and ignores the state monopoly on public space that was chiselled in the city over the centuries.

This new operating system enables the city to draw urbanity into the darkest corners of its 'rainforest section' by giving spaces that lacked visibility a chance to maximize their potential. Whenever I hit the city, I needed my smartphone, not just to find my way in Tokyo's labyrinthine streets, but also to find access to the myriad of urban functions hiding underground, enveloped in generic towers, or cast away in sleepy residential neighbourhoods, which is where I found Capca.[9]

Capca, aka the IE-project[10], was launched in Toshima, a 'local' residential neighbourhood, home to commuters and elders. I found Capca listed on Airbnb as a 'shared style host', and picked it simply because it was the cheapest option. Upon arrival, it became clear that guests were expected to share the space, not only with fellow travellers, but also with artists working there, and locals enjoying the small café downstairs.

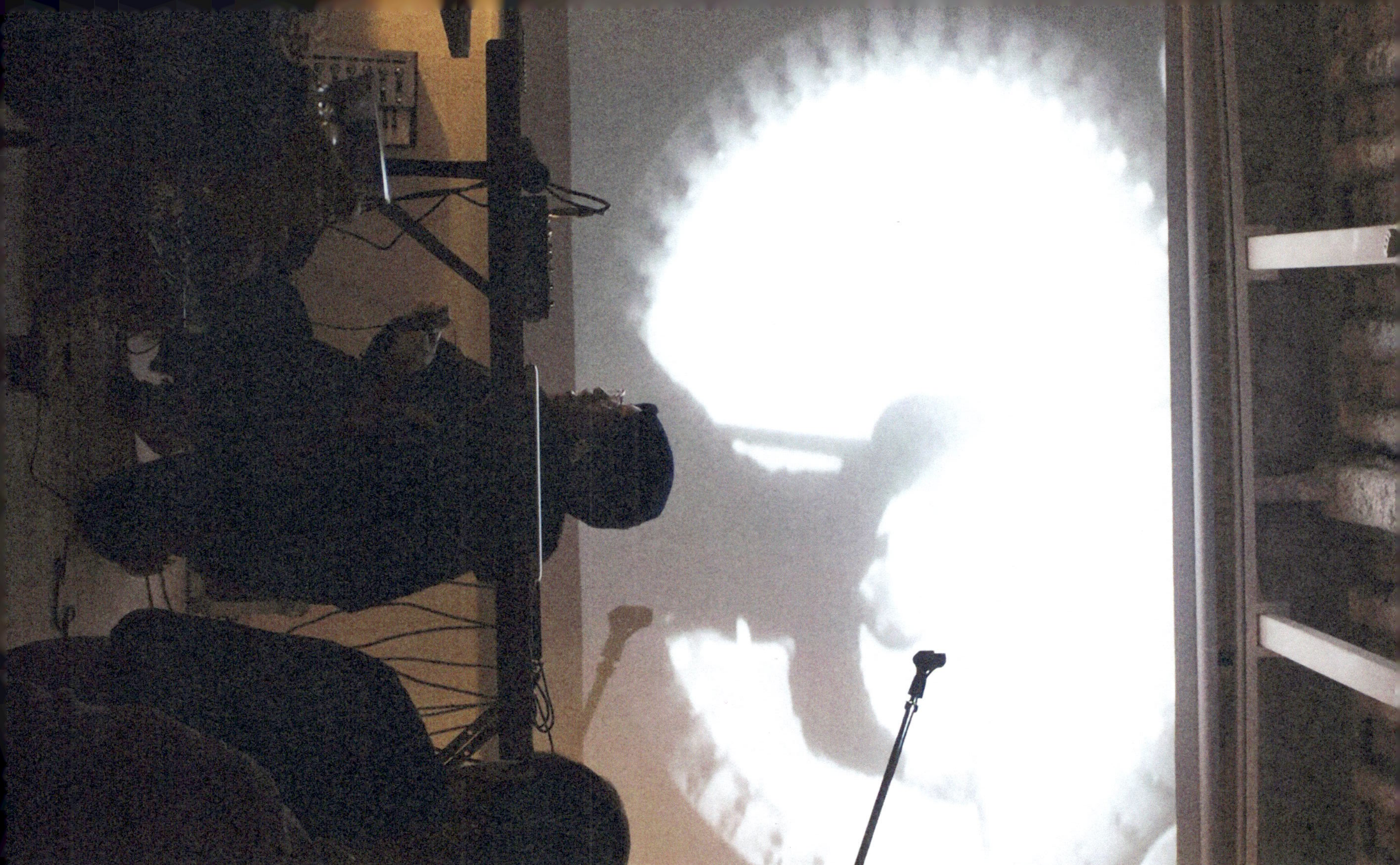

Daisuke Komatsu, the owner, conceived Capca as a place where he and other artists can produce and exhibit their work, and organize events that reach a wider public. Although money probably played its part in the decision, Daisuke told me he chose a location outside the popular centre of Tokyo in an attempt to reanimate a residential neighbourhood that is increasingly left empty during the daytime. The underlying idea is that the dormitory suburbs of Tokyo have preserved more of the Japanese culture than the busy centre and that this culture can stay alive and be stimulated by sharing it with artists and foreigners.

By organizing a serial use of the building, in which international guests get a place to sleep at night, Daisuke and other artists compose music or make paintings in the morning, and the café opens in the afternoon, giving the neighbourhood a social space, a broad range of users is attracted to the building. While the different users more or less succeed each other during the day, in the evening all users come together and share ideas, experiences, art, and their Facebook page.

The artists benefit from international exposure, locals get a rich programme of events to liven up their neighbourhood, and travellers from abroad can use the opportunity to have a real exchange with Japanese communities. This may all be a bit idealistic but sure enough, when I came back a year later, I found people from these three categories coming back there too.

A time-based scheme, in which various functions overlap and succeed each other during a 24hour cycle implies a flexible spatial layout. Yet Capca did not require a specific architectural typology. Daisuke just bought a little house in which the spatial management of activities is facilitated by the creative use of furniture within a recycled envelope. At night, hammocks are hung from the ceiling for the Airbnb'ers. For an exhibition, hangers and branches can be fixed to the ceiling beams. Since there is no space for a shower, the city's 'furniture' is used as well. Bathing takes place at the local *sentō*, or public bathhouse.

In urbanist discourse, the use of Airbnb is often framed as a parasitic way to thrive off of these existing urban resources. Virtual space in general is still often associated with a dystopian vision of the future in which the social fabric would deteriorate and a homogeneous globalization would lead to the loss of culture and tradition. Indeed, the coexistence of heterogeneous functions in this tiny space can be framed as a purely economic logic, enabling these activities to resist the real estate pressures of the metropolis. However, while using Airbnb's technology, Capca effortlessly achieves the opposite of what critics would expect: more freedom, diversity, creativity, and cooperation.

As a model, Capca challenges us to imagine the software of the city in a way that does not hijack our everyday environment, but brings it closer to the citizen. Before I left, Daisuke warned me that the house was planned for demolition soon, to make space for a road-widening project in view of the 2020 Olympics. The plans must have changed perhaps due to the postponement of the games. The little house is still there, run by Daisuke's friend who turned the house into an artisanal bakery that, like Capca, shows us how to reuse, reduce, recycle, and respect the city. Meanwhile, Daisuke moved further off-centre to the rural prefecture of Niigata, where he has renovated a traditional *minka* house and raises a young family.

1 M. Kondo, *The Life-changing Manga of Tidying Up: A Magical Story* (New York: Ten Speed Press, 2017), 54.

2 Mary Wallace, 'Mottainai, How the Japanese Say "Waste Not, Want Not"', *We hate to waste*, January, 2014, http://www.wehatetowaste.com/mottainai/

3 Kevin Taylor, 'Avoiding waste with the Japanese concept of "mottainai"', *ABC*, August 25, 2015, http://www.abc.net.au/radionational/programs/philosopherszone/mottainai/6722728

4 J. Kuroda, M. Kaijima, Y. Tsukamoto, *Made in Tokyo* (Tokyo: Kajima Institute, 2001), 24.

5 Ibid.

6 Kevin Taylor, ibid.

7 Deanna Ting, 'Airbnb's Latest Investment Values It as Much as Hilton and Hyatt Combined', *Skift,* September 23, 2016, https://skift.com/2016/09/23/airbnbs-latest-investment-values-it-as-much-as-hilton-and-hyatt-combined/

8 Pokémon Go is an augmented reality (AR) game that uses the mobile device's GPS to locate, capture, battle, and train virtual creatures, called Pokémon, which appear as if they are in the player's real-world location.

9 CAPCA is short for the Japanese onomatopoeia 'PukkaPukka' referring to droplets falling in a pool of water. It is used to describe a relaxed mood or atmosphere.

10 *Ie* (家) means house or household in Japanese.

H

Architecture of Dispersal (2011-2020)

Decentralization

Japan is well known as a country in which a strong, centralized power oversees a pyramidal hierarchy. This power structure has materialized over the past century in the form of a Tokyo-centric urban agglomeration[1] that quietly carries through concentration, in spite of official planning policies that consistently promote 'dispersal'.[2] In *Cities, Autonomy, and Decentralization in Japan*, Carola Hein has compiled detail studies of plans and discourses of decentralization in Japan. She goes through the prewar era and on to the radical postwar reconstruction plan of Hideaki Ishikawa. Inspired by the erasure of half of the capital's inhabited surface in World War II, Ishikawa envisioned a reduction of Tokyo's population from its prewar 6.5 million to a maximum of 3.5 million.[3] His plans to let nature permeate the formerly overcrowded city were soon abandoned as the capital's population quickly rose above prewar levels. Then, in spite of the dispersal promoted again in the National Capital Regional Development Plan of 1958, the subsequent era of rapid economic growth was characterized by an efficient industrial concentration within Tokyo's metropolitan area and along the Pacific belt region.[4]

Hein shows that the New City Planning Act of 1968, too, saw many of its ambitions unrealized and that the attempt to decentralize power in favour of citizens and local governments with the creation of the National Land Agency in 1974 remained theoretical.[5] Policies initiated in the 1980s to redistribute parts of the capital city functions and government agencies to satellite cities were abandoned due to economic stagnation in the following decade.[6] In 1995, decentralization was promoted once again in the new Law for the Promotion of Decentralization, but in effect, Hein notes, the transfer of national power to local institutions was counteracted by other policies reducing the overall number of institutions at the same time.[7] Even before 2011, the politics of 'decentralization' led to an unprecedented level of discussion at the beginning of the twenty-first century, with centralized authority and its expressions being questioned on various levels of Japanese government, among citizens, and in academia.[8]

Disaster Relief

The triple disaster of March 2011 inflicted a major blow to the Japanese economy, but most importantly, it killed over 15,000 people and left hundreds of thousands without a home in the peripheral region of Tōhoku. In their survey of 'disaster and political trust' in the aftermath of the events, Eric Uslaner and Eiji Yamamura found that while 2011 records a sharp decline in faith in the national government, the Prime Minister, and political parties, this does not appear to be the case for local governments.[9] When, in the eyes of the local population, the central government failed to deliver an efficient response, this became a catalyst for attempts at regaining autonomy and resilience on lower levels, including the neighbourhood, the city, the region, and the islands. Architects became involved in this trend with the *Minna No Ie* Home-for-All disaster relief project, conceived by the *kishin-no-kai* group.[10] The project offers 16 interventions intended as small-scale shelters fostering local organization and cooperation along the North-Eastern coast. This initiative, led by Tokyo-based architects with globalized practices, has received international acclaim[11] and is now widening its scope to remedy neglect and depopulation in other areas of rural Japan.[12] Nevertheless, from a pure business perspective, these humanitarian projects, located in areas left behind by the ongoing concentration and globalization of the national economy, find their reward in exhibitions and publications around the world.

By emphasizing the smaller scale, user participation, and 'soft' aspects of planning such as community building and scenery instead of 'hard' infrastructure, 'Home-for-All' inscribed itself in the Japanese *machizukuri* (literally, 'making a neighbourhood' or 'making a community') tradition. *Machizukuri* became a catchword in the 1980s as a reaction against centralized thinking and later found application in the reconstruction of Kobe after the Great Hanshin Awaji earthquake of 1995.[13] Carola Hein writes that besides disaster relief, the *machizukuri* tradition has brought back attention for urban form and architecture, and protection of monuments and townscapes at the beginning of the twenty-first century.[14] This longing for a renewed sense of community and a connection to the local environment has found its way back into the political discourse of central authorities. The recently (2020) resigned Prime Minister Shinzō Abe took office pledging to make 'a beautiful country, Japan', a statement clearly out of tune with Prime Minister Tanaka's popular promise in the early 1970s to 'turn the whole archipelago into a construction site'.[15]

Towards a Beautiful Country

The challenge of making 'A beautiful country, Japan,' Abe declared, was to rediscover what was 'wonderful' about the country, and reaffirm 'Japan's ideals, visions and uniqueness' to forge a new 'country identity' for the future.[16] In the same policy speech, however, Abe announced his endeavour to bring Asian and global economic growth to Japan by opening up the country to foreign visitors, working for an early realization of 24-hour operation of international airports in the major metropolitan areas, and double the amount of foreign investment in Japan. While the rhetoric of 'a beautiful country, Japan,' does convey a sense of harmony binding the Japanese archipelago, the actual policy is informed by ongoing economic trends of globalization and informatization, which are likely to cause further fragmentation between centre and periphery. Since the neoliberal reforms of the 1980s, the redistribution of political power has indeed gone hand in hand with globalization, causing the relocation of Japanese industries overseas as well as their concentration within the megalopolis.[17]

The unequal compromise between the local and the global, coating neoliberal structural reforms in vernacular imagery, is now taking concrete shape in preparation of the upcoming Olympic Games of 2021. Abe has repeated his vow to restore the beauty of Japan in the context of the upcoming event and Tokyo's mayor on her part has announced a plan to put Tokyo's electricity poles underground by this time.[18] There has even been talk of demolishing the highway that was built over the Nihonbashi river for the 1964 Olympics, at the time considered a symbol of modernization and progress.[19] The architecture of the venues is characterized by a taste for wood, white, and green, expressing a distinctly Japanese identity. While wasteful mega events like these are always justified as leverage for corporate investment, the question remains where this investment is going. Rather than supporting the structural recovery of the Japanese regions, the Games are most likely to promote concentration in the Tokyo area once again.[20] In response to prevalent anxieties concerning globalization and delocalization, a renewed taste for the vernacular is emerging, which paradoxically is not only facilitated by globalization, but in turn facilitates it by presenting a 'themed' Japan to the foreign consumer.

Toyo Itō Museum of Architecture

Architect: Toyo Itō
Completion: 2011

The year of the Tōhoku disaster, Toyo Itō completed a museum dedicated to his own work on 'Toyo Itō Island' Omishima. Other projects of his on this small island in the Inland Sea include the 'Ken Iwata mother and child museum', finished the same year, and a vacant house he has renovated into a Home-for-All community centre for the island's residents. After working on disaster relief plans Toyo Itō has been applying lessons learned in grassroots community engagement to these off-centre rural communities. Here, the aim is not to repair damage, but to revitalize the place culturally and economically.[21] Since little commercial and industrial development has taken place there, Omishima is now populated with just 6,400 residents, half of its peak population in the 1940s and 1950s.

The next phase of Itō's career, he says, will be dedicated to helping this island regain its vigour. In 2014, the museum held an exhibition entitled: 'Project Omishima: Transforming into the most beautiful island in Japan'.[24] To earn that title, Omishima will have some serious competition from other 'art and architecture islands'.

Since the 1990s, several art projects have emerged around the Inland Sea of Japan aiming to support this region, which is struggling with depopulation and economic decline.[22] Tadao Andō and SANAA have their own Inland Sea 'art island' on Naoshima and Inujima, respectively, where they aim to support local economies by attracting tourists from the cities and from abroad. In his study of the art economy around the Inland Sea, Kentaro Yagi stresses that this 'soft' approach to revitalization is all the more relevant here since the 'hard' infrastructural approach has failed.[23] Before traffic via mainland routes became more convenient, the Inland Sea of Japan used to be a flourishing cultural and economic artery, with boat traffic linking the islands to the major mainland cities close-by. Industries of the area included shipbuilding, refining, salt and other chemical industries. In an effort to retain the remaining enterprises, three vehicular routes were built around the turn of the century, connecting some of the major islands within the Inland Sea. But while these connecting traffic routes were expected to revitalize the regional economy, they only accelerated the exodus of local industries and population.

Yoshino Cedar House

Architect: Go Hasegawa+Airbnb
Completion: 2016

The Cedar House project in Yoshino is inspired by an elderly woman in rural Japan who started an Airbnb dwelling and, exceeding all expectations, received so many visitors that she enlisted her neighbours as hiking guides, translators, and tour guides, sparking a miniature tourism economy.[25] Entertaining the idea that Airbnb could become a force not only in sharing homes, but in urban planning as well, the tech giant commissioned architect Go Hasegawa to design a communal housing project capable of revitalizing a small town full of empty homes.[26] The Cedar House he designed was conceived in response to three general trends: Ageing and intense urbanization is causing rural villages to shrink, community centres in rural villages are intensively used and are literally the centre of the community, and finally, for small communities, the presence of (foreign) tourists has the potential to create a ripple effect in the economy. Airbnb is looking into possibilities to replicate this model in other declining small towns in Japan, and across the world.

The result is a hybrid community centre/apartment, built on land donated by the town of Yoshino. The design seeks to blend into the surrounding landscape by using 28 types of local wood and a plan and section based on the traditional concept of *engawa*[29]. The image above shows a prototype exhibited at House Vision 2 in Tokyo.

The Yoshino House was featured as part of the 2016 'House Vision' exhibition in Tokyo addressing the future of housing. Under the theme of 'CO-DIVIDUAL Split and Connect/ Separate and Come Together', architects and design firms were tasked with addressing the idea of connectivity between individuals in a country struggling with economic stagnation, a decreasing population, an ageing society, disasters striking one after another, and increasing friction in interpersonal communication.[27] In the view of the curators, the key to the future of the house lies in a synergy between architecture, community, and a Japanese technological proficiency provided by industrial leaders like Panasonic, Toyota, Muji[28], and others who were invited to participate in the creation of these techno-vernacular prototypes.

New National Olympic Stadium

Architect: Kengo Kuma
Completion: 2020

After its implication in a string of controversies, the competition-winning design for the New National Olympic Stadium by Zaha Hadid Architects was finally scrapped by the government in 2015, amid complaints of citizens, officials, and a gathering of world-famous architects[30] about exceeded budgets, oversizing, and a neo-futuristic appearance deemed unrespectful of the historical surroundings. This concern was reflected in the new competition brief listing 'Consideration of Japaneseness' as an explicit part of the criteria for selecting the replacement.[31] In the final round, a well-received design by Kengo Kuma that was reminiscent of the wooden architecture of Shintō shrines and Buddhist temples was chosen over a comparable scheme from his rival Toyo Itō.

Kengo Kuma showcases different types of larch and cedar in the stadium, including wood from regions hit by the 2011 earthquake and tsunami, to symbolize the diversity of the Japanese regions and support their local economies.

Kuma plans to realize his ambition to 'go beyond the era of concrete'[32] with the simple method he usually applies: minimizing height and trying to use local natural materials.[33] Otherwise known as resource poor, two-thirds of Japan is indeed covered in trees. But the stadium has been targeted by action groups claiming that the wood used on the site is leading to deforestation in Borneo and Malaysia, threatening the rainforest and the livelihood of indigenous people.[34] Because imports from China or Indonesia remain cheaper than local resources[35], tropical plywood is being used in the moulds for the concrete structure that Kuma's cladding in local timbers is covering up.

1 Japan is now over 90 per cent urbanized, with a quarter of the population living in the greater Tokyo area, against 23 per cent urbanized in 1945.

2 H. Cho, 'Competing Futures: War Narratives in Post-war Japanese Architecture 1945-1970', PhD diss., University of Southern California (2011), 75.

3 C. Hein, *Rebuilding Japanese Cities After 1945* (London: Palgrave Macmillan, 2003), 9.

4 H. Cho, op. cit., 75.

5 C. Hein, 'Introduction: decentralization and the tension between global and local urban Japan', in *Cities, Autonomy, and Decentralization in Japan*, edited by Carola Hein and Philippe Pelletier (New York: Routledge, 2006), 1.

6 H. Ohno, 'Fibercity/Tokyo 2050,' *The Japan Architect* 63 (2006), 6.

7 C. Hein (2006), op. cit., 1.

8 Ibid.

9 E. Uslaner and E. Yamamura, Eiji, 'Disaster and political trust: The Japan Tsunami and Earthquake of 2011,' *MPRA Paper 70527,* University Library of Munich (2016), 13-14.

10 *Kishin-no-kai* or 'Group of contributors' includes five volunteer architects—Toyo Itō, Kazuyo Sejima, Riken Yamamoto, Junichi Kano and Yasuhiro Yamashita—leading a call for action to young architects to lend a helping hand.

11 The Toyo Itō curated exhibition 'Architecture. Possible here? Home for all' won the Golden Lion at the Venice Biennale in 2012.

12 See case 1 in Omishima.

13 C. Hein, 'Toshikeikaku and Machizukuri in Japanese Urban Planning-The Reconstruction of Inner City Neighborhoods in Kobe,' *Japanstudien* (2001), 222.

14 Ibid., 222-224.

15 Like Tanaka's Plan for Remodelling the Archipelago, Abe's book 'Toward A Beautiful Country' became a bestseller and helped him win the election for office.

16 S. Abe, Policy Speech to the 166th Session of the Diet (2007), https://japan.kantei.go.jp/abespeech/2007/01/26speech_e.html

17 C. Hein (2006) op. cit., 1.

18 Tsuyoshi Inajima and Emi Urabe, 'Koike's plan for Tepco to remove utility poles in Tokyo an Olympian task', *Japan Times*, April 3, 2017, https://www.japantimes.co.jp/news/2017/04/03/business/koikes-plan-tepco-remove-utility-poles-tokyo-olympian-task/

19 Masaaki Kameda, 'Nihonbashi highway is urged to go under', *Japan Times*, February 26, 2014, https://www.japantimes.co.jp/news/2014/02/26/national/nihonbashi-highway-is-urged-to-go-under/

20 Japanese authorities placed a bid to host the 2016 Olympics while still facing a huge debt and many unresolved problems in the aftermath of the economic and environmental disaster of two years before. Due to a lack of public support, Tokyo did not get the nomination, but eventually secured the Games for 2020, which have been postponed because of the Covid-19 pandemic.

21 Zach Mortice, 'Toyo Itō's Next Architectural Feat', *Redshift*, October 25, 2016, https://www.autodesk.com/redshift/toyo-ito/

22 T. Ito, *Toyo Ito: Collected Works 2002-2014* (Tokyo: TOTO, 2014), 210.

23 K. Yagi, 'Art on Water: Art that Revitalizes Insular Communities Facing Depopulation and Economic Decline', *Nakhara* 6, 2010, 119.

24 Ibid., 120.

25 Cliff Kuang, 'An Exclusive Look At Airbnb's First Foray Into Urban Planning', *Co.Design*, February 8, 2016, https://www.fastcodesign.com/3062246/an-exclusive-look-at-airbnbs-first-foray-into-urban-planning

26 Ibid.

27 Jason Sayer, '"House Vision 2" in Tokyo tackles a simple question: How can architecture connect people?', *Archpaper*, August 18, 2016.

28 Muji is the Japanese equivalent to Ikea. The House Vision exhibition was curated by Muji's creative director Kenya Hara.

29 Engawa is a ledge that extends beyond the border of the house.

30 Japanese architect Fumihiko Maki had gathered other world-renowned architects to protest ZHA's design in a 2013 symposium entitled 'Rethinking the National stadium in the historical context of Gaien'.

31 Jonathan Soble, 'Japan Selects New Plan for 2020 Olympic Stadium in Tokyo', *New York Times*, December 22, 2015, https://www.nytimes.com/2015/12/23/world/asia/tokyo-2020-olympics-stadium.html

32 Aya Takada and Katsuyo Kuwako, 'Olympics Architect Wants to Bring Wood Back to Tokyo's Concrete Jungle', *Bloomberg*, May 24, 2017, https://www.bloomberg.com/news/articles/2017-05-23/olympic-architect-sees-wood-as-answer-to-tokyo-s-concrete-legacy

33 Ibid.

34 Aidan Imanova, 'Petition urges end to using deforestation-led wood for Kengo Kuma's Olympic stadium', *Middle East Architect*, May 14, 2017, https://www.middleeastarchitect.com/thoughts/petition-urges-end-to-using-deforestation-led-wood-for-kengo-kumas-olympic-stadium

35 The government is trying to address this issue by offering subsidies to builders of wooden public constructions and lumber producers.

D

‘I refuse to play the role of the Japanese architect’

[illegible] Isozaki [illegible] Lee and Baumeister, *The Domestic and the Foreign in Architecture*, 281.

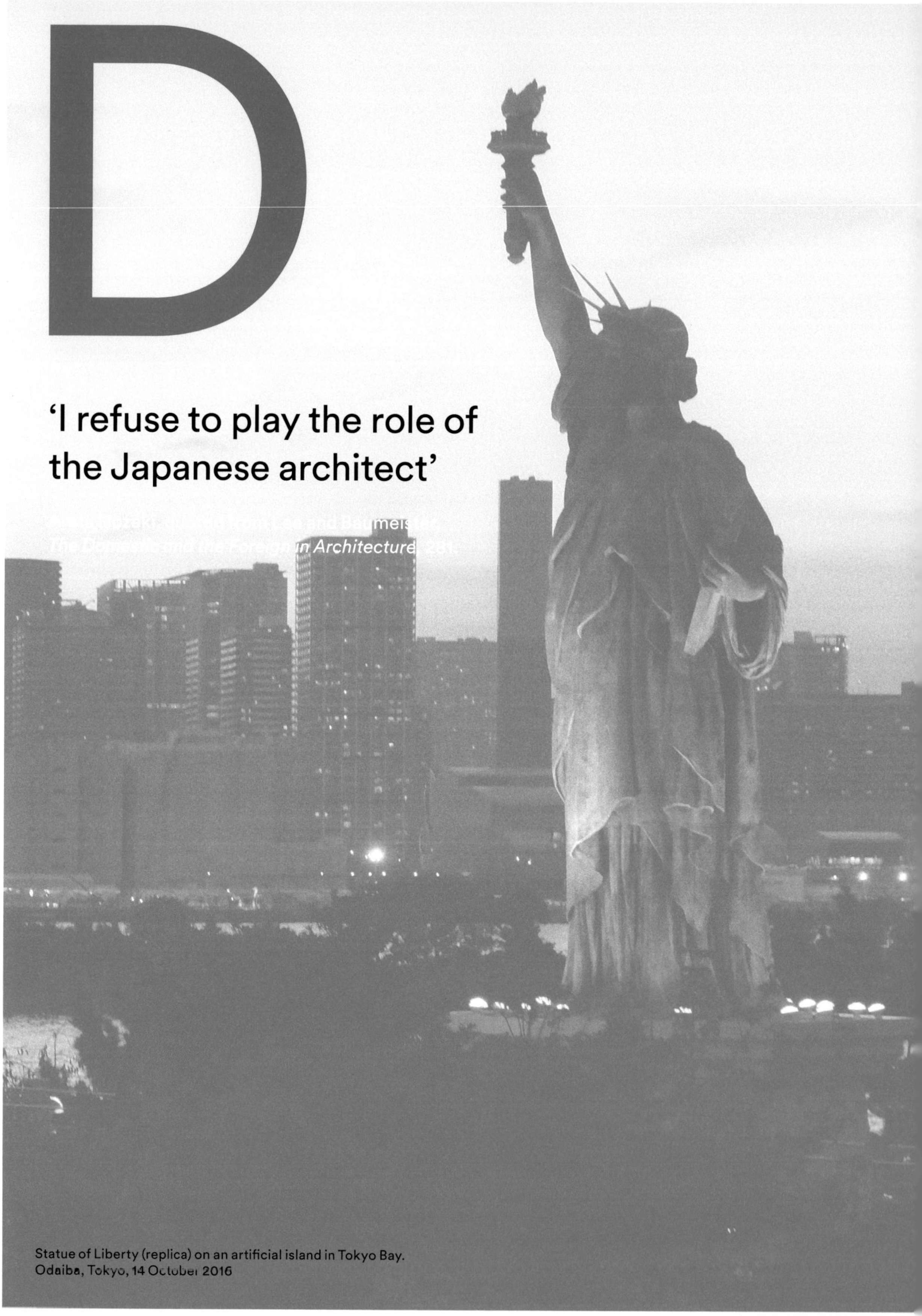

Statue of Liberty (replica) on an artificial island in Tokyo Bay.
Odaiba, Tokyo, 14 October 2016

Opening Japan

Japan is a country of so-called global architects. Over the past three decades it has produced seven Pritzker Prize[1] laureates[2], more even than the USA, which come in second with four laureates. Japan's 'global architects' receive prestigious commissions around the world, building landmark cultural institutions in foreign countries known to be protective of their heritage. In France, for instance, Shigeru Ban and SANAA architects have recently completed sister galleries of the Centre Pompidou in Metz (2010) and the Louvre museum in Lens (2006). Reflecting on similar projects including a Serpentine gallery pavilion in London (2009) and The New Museum of Contemporary Art in New York (2007) in an interview with *The Guardian*, Kazuyo Sejima distanced her practice from direct associations with Japan.[3]

> We may be influenced by Japanese architecture subconsciously, but we don't think of ourselves as particularly Japanese architects.[4]
>
> –Kazuyo Sejima (SANAA), architect

This comment may come as a surprise for those who know SANAA from architectural reviews in which their work is widely recognized as having acquired distinctly Japanese overtones by consciously exploring lightness, transparency, and ephemerality. In fact, Sejima is not denying this here, as she acknowledges potential influences of (traditional) Japanese architecture. It seems instead that she would like us to reflect on the nuance between SANAA as 'architects from Japan', and a portrayal as 'Japanese architects', which lumps together all architects from Japan into a homogeneous bunch, and by extension, implies their alignment with the Japanese nation. This in turn, would further imply the absence of critical distancing and self-reflection. Besides the fact that it entails a caricature of their work, the label of 'Japanese architect' threatens the modus operandi of a generation of Japanese architects receiving a substantial part of their commissions abroad. In conversation with Jörg Gleiter, Arata Isozaki, wishing to be called 'a cosmopolitan architect', addressed the problem explicitly.

> Of course, I have a Japanese passport, so I am a Japanese national. But psychologically I do not want to belong to Japan, especially Japan as a modern nation-state... Almost everywhere in today's so-called globalized world people want to pin me down to a representative of Japanese architects. It is always the same stereotypical questions I am asked: why as a Japanese I want to come to a foreign country and do a project there.[5]
>
> –Arata Isozaki, architect

Stereotypes are not without consequences, says Isozaki. After winning an international competition for a new entrance to the Uffizi museum in Florence for example, construction was cancelled at the last moment due to this discriminatory attitude.

> I already secured the contract and we were ready to start construction, but at the last minute they decided that this was too important a museum to be built by a 'Japanese' architect. One of the arguments was that as a Japanese I would just be the kind to destroy or violate the Italian treasures... In China recently I won three first prizes for projects but eventually lost them because of this kind of attitude. That is why I refuse to play the role of the Japanese architect.[6]
>
> –Arata Isozaki, architect

The 'Japanese architect' accused of 'violating' treasures abroad, in Isozaki's experience, is cast in the opposite role of the overly chauvinistic conservative when the situation is reversed. As a 'global architect' winning the competition for the New National stadium in Tokyo, Zaha Hadid encountered the same situation as Isozaki did in Florence. Only this time, it is the non-Japanese architect coming to build a cultural icon in Japan who gets shut down, just before construction is about to start. Although officially Hadid is decommissioned on the grounds of exceeding budgets, she explains that the inflated price tag of her landmark stadium is caused by rising costs for construction and materials in Japan's tight labour market, concluding that the 'Japanese' are in fact simply being chauvinistic.[7] She adds that her critics, including a group of world-renowned Japanese architects who voiced concern over the design's lack of sensitivity to local context[8], are only embarrassing themselves by showing the world that 'they don't want a foreigner to build in Tokyo for a national stadium'.[9]

> Sadly, the Japanese authorities, with the support of some of those from our own profession in Japan, have colluded to close the doors on the project to the world.[10]
>
> –Zaha Hadid, architect

Arata Isozaki, empathizing with Hadid's situation, came to her defence in the face of criticism, blaming the lack of vision in the design on the organizers. In an open letter to the Japanese Sports Council he blamed their plethora of restrictions and stipulations for the fact that the revised version of the design looks 'like a turtle waiting for Japan to sink so that it can swim away'.[11] Knowing the restraints of the Japanese construction culture, Isozaki radically argued for Hadid to make a new proposal without any help of Japanese firms.

> I can't find Zaha's hand anymore, I can only see the pressures of the council.[12]
>
> –Arata Isozaki, architect

Island Nation

Although in objective terms, the globalization of Japan's architecture and its construction industry have been very successful, the 'Japanese architect' is still haunted by the stereotype of a Japan that is unable to 'think globally'. This view is in part a stereotype cast on Japan by foreigners as shown in the cases above, but it is also a self-image carried by the Japanese. Rooted in eugenics theories imported from Germany, the self-portrayal as an 'insular' and 'homogeneous' nation was actually much more contested in the prewar era, when a 'mixed blood theory' fit the general mood of Asian expansion, then it is now.[13] In fact, as historical sociologist Eiji Oguma argues in *A Genealogy of 'Japanese' Self-images*, the cultural myth viewing Japan as a historically isolated society only really started spreading after defeat in World War II, when confidence in the ability to engage in international relations hit a low point.[14] Today, the myth persists, casting doubts over Japan's ability to integrate a migrant workforce and attract sufficient foreign investment now that its population is ageing rapidly and the recession of 'the lost decades' is lagging. Accordingly, the current Prime Minister defines the coming generation's ability to 'open' Japan to the world as the measure of its future success.

> When I assumed the office of the Prime Minister in September last year, I laid out to the people of Japan the vision that the Abe Administration will pursue: 'A beautiful country, Japan.' A country which is full of vitality, opportunity and compassion; a country which cherishes the spirit of self-discipline; a country which is open to the world; so that it is admired and respected by people all over the world, and our children's generation can possess self-confidence and pride.[15]
>
> –Shinzō Abe, current Prime Minister

As the coming Olympics obviously play an instrumental role in overcoming Japan's perceived isolation, the selection of the national stadium design should express the commitment to opening the country to knowledge exchange, trade, and immigration henceforth. To make this political statement, Tadao Andō launched the idea to organize an international competition for the main stadium while he is masterplanning Tokyo's 2016 Olympic bid.[16] His scheme envisions a series of locations on wooded islands in Tokyo Bay, at once displaying Japan's insular character and transcending it, by embracing visitors from around the world.

> Here's what I want to do: Right now Japan is kind of closed towards the world. I want to open Japan, and create a symbol of the openness. To create a country full of more possibilities for younger Japanese people, and to show young architects and young people worldwide that they can work and live and invest in Japan. So having a competition for the new stadium would be symbolic.[17]
>
> –Tadao Andō, architect

When he was later appointed chairman of the judging panel in charge of selecting Tokyo's new stadium design, Andō presented the first prize to Zaha Hadid Architects stating that:

> The entry's dynamic and futuristic design embodies the messages Japan would like to convey to the world.[18]
>
> –Tadao Andō, architect

Intended as a monument for Japan's 'open' future, Zaha Hadid's stadium design ends up symbolizing something entirely different in the eyes of the Japanese people. According to Kengo Kuma at least, in the eyes of the people the scheme comes to stand for waste and destruction.[19] It is unpopular because despite its neo-futuristic allure, the message associated with Hadid's landmark is one that belongs to the twenty-first century.

> I believe that society's perception of 'architecture' is going through a big change. It's being transformed. In the twentieth century, when we had a very industrial society, architecture was at the leading edge of technology, of the economy, and so on. Then we entered the twenty-first century, which is an 'environmentally conscious' era. Architecture often wastes taxpayer money, or it destroys the surrounding environment. Architecture began to have a very negative image, I think. I think one symbol of the change is these events that happened with the design for the new Olympic stadium. At least, that's how I see it.[20]
>
> –Kengo Kuma, architect

National Architect

After Hadid was officially decommissioned in 2015, Kuma's entry for the new National Stadium was selected in a subsequent competition. Compact and cheap, Kuma's design represents the antithesis of Hadid's soaring and technically daring design. Most strikingly however, in contrast to Hadid, the visual language of Kuma's design refers to the architecture of preindustrial Japan's pristine wooden shrines and temples. With the choice for a Japanese architect, presenting a Japanese design, it appears as though Andō's ambition to open Japan to the world swam away along with Hadid's 'turtle'. After all, 'Consideration of Japaneseness' is stipulated as a requirement in the new competition brief.[21] But to Kuma, there is no contradiction between the globalization of Japan, and a return to the values of its traditional society.

> Don't do the same thing as last time. Don't do the same thing as Beijing. Do something completely different. If we can do that in 2020, people will say, 'Wow, Japan has really entered a new era. A more modest and subdued era. They're leading the way towards something different.' I think we can get that message across. My ambition is to make a stadium that serves as a symbol of this new era. That's what I'm hoping to do.[22]
>
> –Kengo Kuma, architect

As we enter the age of environmentalism, Kuma basically argues that what he perceives to be the quintessence of Japan-ness: simplicity, modesty, and closeness to nature, will become universal values.

> I want my work to embody Japan, and show Japan to the world. I don't want to just do 'Japanese architecture' though. That's not what I mean. It's about this natural cycle that's at the heart of Japan. It will be great if I can create architecture that makes people feel that natural cycle. I think that will give meaning to having the Olympics a second time in Tokyo.[23]
>
> –Kengo Kuma, architect

Kuma presents his ideas as innovative by linking them to twenty-first-century environmentalism. He stresses this point by framing his twenty-first-century stadium in contrast with Tange's concrete stadium for the Tokyo Olympics of 1964. As that technologically innovative masterpiece gave meaning to the era of industrialism, his stadium will give meaning to the 'environmentally conscious' era. Looking back at Tange's discourse of the time however, we can see that Kuma's reasoning actually holds much in common with that of his predecessor. The national stadium in Yoyogi was the summum of Tange's post-war endeavour to fuse Japanese tradition and modern architecture. In 1959 the architect joined 43 architects from around the world in Otterlo, the Netherlands, for what is to be the last CIAM[24] meeting, where his proposal to revive modern architecture with tradition met with reluctance.

> It just so happens, by accident of history, that the aesthetic of the old Japanese architecture, which has a certain openness in its construction, corresponds to a feeling we have for an open aesthetic with its possibilities of cycles of fixed things, of changed things, and so on... We simply do not have Tange's possibilities. As a rule, I can see no point in suggesting that we should look into our stylistic past in each country.[25]
>
> –Peter Smithson, architect

But in the same vein as Kuma, Tange did not want to just do 'Japanese architecture'. He sought in tradition a vital energy he felt was lacking in a European modernism that had reached its limitations.

> One strong current in the Western hemisphere is something which I call 'aestheticism'. I see that aestheticism arises from the acceptance of existing order and is an effort to set abstract beauty in their wishful situation. It is strikingly stylistic and has failed to convey any fresh breath of naked human being. Typical examples can be found in the 'decorativism' now popular in the United States. On the other hand, against aestheticism, there is an emerging force, which I call 'vitalism'. No matter how chaotic the reality is, I believe there is always the vitality of the masses underneath. Though their voice is suppressed

> and their energy is hidden, this is something which we should dig out and make resound through our work.[26]
>
> –Kenzō Tange, architect

In Tange's view, the architecture of 'the Western hemisphere', 'accepting the existing order', is an architecture stuck in the past, much like the architecture of Hadid is to Kuma. And likewise, Tange prophesied the beginning of a new era in architecture, presenting himself as the interpreter of a popular movement. The lack of vitality he detected in the 'Western hemisphere' is not a mere reflection of Tange's wishful thinking however. The modern paradigm according to which the West would lead the world towards cultural progress and enlightenment was indeed entering a state crisis at the time, manifest in the new independence of African and Asian countries. In this context of global decentralization, questions of identity and traditional heritage regained interest.

> Vitalism itself is not regionalism... the popular tendency to use regional characteristics for decorating facades of buildings must be rejected. The same should be said of tradition. In my thinking, tradition can be developed through challenging its own shortcoming and pursuing the meaning of continuum within it.[27]
>
> –Kenzō Tange, architect

Both Tange and Kuma aim to uncover deeper principles in their appraisal of tradition. They reject superficial mimicking. At first sight, this appears to fit them into the category of critical regionalism, an architectural movement defined by architectural critic Kenneth Frampton as an 'arrière-garde'.[28] That is, a movement that keeps a critical distance from 'the Enlightenment myth of progress' as well as from the 'reactionary, unrealistic impulse' to return to the architectonic forms of the preindustrial past. But, at second thought, Kuma does portray Japan as a country which remains exceptionally close to its traditions and to the 'natural cycle that's at the heart of Japan', while Tange argues that the 'Western hemisphere' has kept only a superficial relationship with its traditional culture. In this respect, they go along with the narrative of nineteenth-century orientalism, which, based on 'the Enlightenment myth of progress', portrayed Japan as a mystical, isolated country that kept in much closer contact to nature and tradition—implying a relative freeze in time of Japanese society. Only now, the conclusion is reversed. Rather than standing in the way of progress, tradition is conceived as the catalyst that keeps humanity moving forward. This plot twist in the European myth of progress suddenly opposes a flexible and dynamic Japan against a static and ideologically exhausted West. From this perspective, rather than an effort to keep the 'myth of progress' and 'reactionary impulses' at a critical distance, one could more radically state that Japan's 'national architects' are trying to achieve both at the same time. Although Kuma presents his path-breaking architecture as rebellious and anti-system, his line of thought actually follows the self-images of the Japanese nation-state, as did the discourse of Japan's twentieth-century 'national architect' Kenzō Tange. Unrivalled until now, Tange was charged to give monumental expression to Japan each time the nation would 'open up to the world': starting with the 1942 monument for the Greater East-Asia Co-prosperity Sphere, then doing the Hiroshima Peace Memorial, the 1964 Olympic Stadium, and finally the 'Big Roof', centrepiece of Expo 70. Each of these buildings mirrored the different 'egos' adopted by the nation-state ranging from Japan as 'the roof of Asia' to a 'peaceful and isolated island' to Japan as the 'high-tech future'. Eager to overcome the past after the triple disaster of 2011, and anxious about a future facing the challenges of globalization, the Japanese nation sees in the National Stadium the next self-defining monument. Has it found a new national architect?

> Instead of the old-fashioned idea of putting up a huge monument, my idea is to create a stadium that people will remember as part of the Meiji Shrine outer gardens, the wooded area in which it's located.[29]
>
> –Kengo Kuma, architect

Kuma discards 'old-fashioned' monumentality and claims to replace it with closeness to nature, which ironically brings him close to Tange's old conception of a Japanese monumentality for the Greater East Asia Co-prosperity Sphere of 1942. The latter had defended a ground-hugging architecture inspired by shintō shrines by contrasting it with the monumentality of the 'West', which was characterized by 'ascending forms' that have 'lost contact with nature and territorial realities'.[30] This alleged inherent closeness to nature, unique to the Japanese, resurfaces in Kuma's formal gestures.

> I wanted to keep it low. Make it as low as possible. And, in addition to that… I wanted to add trees to the outer walls. Normally, with a big stadium, when you look at it from the outside you just see a hunk of concrete. But if you look at this from the outside, it's low, it's got these trees, and it has eaves.[31]
>
> –Kengo Kuma, architect

Kuma is not wrong when he denounces consumerism and argues that we can and should aim to heal our bond with the natural environment. But when he promises to 'show the model of a mature society in the stadium', by saying 'that's the way to live a happy life relying on limited natural resources from a small land'[32] the primary focus seems to lie in the representation of the Japanese nation. Relying on the myth that the Japanese have inhabited an isolated island ecology with scarce resources since times immemorial[33], Kuma implies that self-sufficiency and sustainability are deeply engrained in Japanese society. The fact that Japan is in reality anything but self-sufficient[34], having one of the lowest food self-sufficiencies among developed countries, for example[35], is conveniently concealed by mapping the modern nation-state onto a priori conceptions of its natural environment. While in Kuma's discourse the insular quality distinguishes Japan from other nations, it simultaneously posits Japan-ness as an ideal for the rest of the world, as planet earth becomes one big island, steadily running out of resources. Tange too stressed internalized 'ecological ethics' in his 1943 competition entry for a Japanese Cultural Centre in Bangkok, claiming that the 'Japanese' conception of environmental order featured in his design expresses 'deep ethical principles'.[36]

> These ethical principles and the Japanese tradition of state planning represent the form of our 'character', they reveal our 'reverence' to these values … It has nothing to do with the individualistic structure of Western architecture, there is only the Japanese way of planning an environmental order that can help us.[37]
>
> –Kenzō Tange, architect

Giving concrete examples of what this environmental order might be, seemed less important than underlining what it is not: 'the individualistic West'. Of course, this should not come as a surprise as the head of the jury asked the competitors 'to express with simplicity and refinement the identity of Japan'.[38] Encouraged to do this 'based on a traditional architectural style' but at the same time not to 'carry on solely imitation of the past', the two finalists, Kunio Maekawa and Kenzō Tange handed in very similar designs. Likewise, the competition brief for the 2020 Olympic stadium asking for 'consideration of Japan-ness' produced strikingly similar proposals by finalists Toyo Itō and Kengo Kuma—which in fact also resemble Maekawa and Tange's schemes for Bangkok in many ways.

In contrast to what the contestants claim, it is hard to conclude that the 'Japan-ness' in their designs is not a form of the empty formal mimicking they despise. When architecture aligns itself too closely with the nation, it has no choice but to turn to the myth, an a priori idea that prevents critical thinking and dealing with the realities of the present. Posed in this context, the question of 'Japan-ness' receives a rhetorical answer that, by affirming the nation's self-image, ultimately only serves to stress its boundaries. Ideologically, the ecological revolution in Japan is not necessarily joining the world in a fourth industrial revolution, or a new modernity. When the discourse on nature is associated with nation-building efforts, ecology can be like a window looking forward to the past. Not a historical past, but a mythical natural state of Japanese society. For the architects who wish to keep a critical distance as to what Japan is, the phrase 'I am not a Japanese architect' makes a lot of sense.

1 The Pritzker Prize is widely recognized as the most prestigious award in architecture, often dubbed the 'Nobel Prize of architecture'.

2 Kenzō Tange, Fumihiko Maki, Tadao Ando, Kazuyo Sejima and Ryue Nishizawa (SANAA), Toyo Itō, Shigeru Ban, and Arata Isozaki.

3 Jonathan Glancey, 'Sanaa's summer pavilion brings sunshine to the Serpentine', *The Guardian*, July 8, 2009, https://www.theguardian.com/artanddesign/2009/jul/08/sanaa-summer-pavilion-serpentine

4 Ibid.

5 Jörg Gleiter and Arata Isozaki, 'Comments on the Production of International Architecture'. In R. Baumeister and S. Lee, *The Domestic and the Foreign in Architecture* (Rotterdam: 010 publishers, 2007), 280.

6 Ibid., 281.

7 Jonathan Soble, 'Japan Selects New Plan for 2020 Olympic Stadium in Tokyo', *The New York Times*, December 22, 2015, https://www.nytimes.com/2015/12/23/world/asia/tokyo-2020-olympics-stadium.html

8 Fumihiko gathered a group of Japanese architects, including Toyo Ito, Sou Fujimoto, Riken Yamamoto, and Kengo Kuma for a symposium entitled 'Rethinking the New National Olympic stadium in the historical context of Gaien' in 2013 to protest the size of Hadid's icon.

9 Amy Qin and Robin Pogrebin, 'National Pride at a Steep Price', *The New York Times*, January 5, 2015, https://www.nytimes.com/2015/01/05/arts/design/olympic-stadium-in-tokyo-is-dogged-by-controversy.html

10 Jonathan Soble, ibid.

11 Amy Frearson, 'Zaha Hadid's Tokyo stadium will be "a disgrace to future generations" says Arata Isozaki', *Dezeen*, 10 November, 2014, https://www.dezeen.com/2014/11/10/zaha-hadid-tokyo-stadium-olympic-disgrace-arata-isozaki/

12 Amy Qin and Robin Pogrebin, ibid.

13 E. Oguma, *A Genealogy of 'Japanese' Self-Images*, trans. David Askew (Melbourne: Trans Pacific Press, 2002), 210-214.

14 Ibid., 319.

15 S. Abe, Policy Speech to the 166th Session of the Diet (2007), https://japan.kantei.go.jp/abespeech/2007/ 01/26speech_e.html

16 Edward Lifson, 'Tadao Ando', *Archpaper*, September 3, 2009, https://archpaper.com/2009/09/tadao-ando/

17 Ibid.

18 Edward Lifson, 'Tadao Ando: New Stadium Tokyo 2020', *A as architecture*, July 23, 2012. http://aasarchitecture.com/2012/07/tadao-ando-new-stadium-tokio-2020.html

19 Kengo Kuma interview, 'Tokyo 2020: Designing the Olympic Stadium', *NHK World*, May 12, 2018, https://www3.nhk.or.jp/nhkworld/en/tv/directtalk/articles/20160405/index.html

20 Ibid.

21 Jonathan Soble, ibid.

22 Kengo Kuma interview, ibid.

23 Ibid.

24 The 'Congrès International d'Architecture Moderne' was an organization operating from 1928 until 1959, gathering the world's (but mainly Europe's) leading architects of the modern movement. CIAM produced a series of events and congresses to debate and spread the principles of modernism in architecture and urbanism.

25 R. Koolhaas and H.U. Obrist, *Project Japan: Metabolism talks* (Köln: TASCHEN, 2011), 126.

26 Ibid.

27 Ibid.

28 K. Frampton, 'Towards a Critical Regionalism: Six Points for an Architecture of Resistance', In H. Foster, *The Anti-Aesthetic. Essays on Postmodern Culture* (Seattle: Bay Press, 1983), 20.

29 Y. Kiyono, 'Architect Kuma Kengo Shares His Thinking Behind Japan's New National Stadium Design', *Nippon*, June 30, 2016, https://www.nippon.com/en/people/e00101/

30 B. Jacquet, 'Compromising Modernity: Japanese Monumentality during World War II', New York University, Institute of Fine Arts (2009), 6.

31 Kengo Kuma interview, ibid.

32 Aya Takada and Katsuyo Kuwako, 'Olympics Architect Wants to Bring Wood Back to Tokyo's Concrete Jungle', *Bloomberg*, May 24, 2017, https://www.bloomberg.com/news/articles/2017-05-23/olympic-architect-sees-wood-as-answer-to-tokyo-s-concrete-legacy

33 E. Oguma, op. cit., 316-319.

34 Even in the sectors were Japan is self-sufficient, like timber for construction, the industry favours cheaper imports from countries suffering deforestation. See case 2020 Olympic Stadium in History section.

35 B. Jacquet, op. cit., 8.

36 Ibid.

37 Ibid., 7.

38 Ibid.

H

After Growth (1992-2050)

Lost Decades

Ian Buruma concludes his historical account of 'invented Japan' by presenting a nation that, after nearly half a century of high-speed growth, looks like it is 'about to swallow the world'.[1] The Japanese economy, Buruma tells us, is inflated to the point that by the late 1980s Japanese authors were writing about the coming 'Japanese century'. This bubble economy crashed in 1992, and the country seems unable to snap out of the recession ever since. The 1990s and 2000s are now commonly referred to as 'the lost decades'. But although real estate prices haven't returned to the vertiginous heights of the 1980s, according to more recent analyses, the idea that the Japanese economy has been lagging behind is largely a myth.[2] The misconception is partly due to the fact that demographics are not taken into account when comparing GDP's with the U.S. or Europe.[3] The United States' working-age population has grown by 0.8 per cent, whereas that of Japan has shrunk at about the same rate. Reporting for the *New York Times*, Eamonn Fingleton suggests that the 'doom and gloom story' of the Lost Decades is purposely repeated by the Japanese political and economic class, who noticed a 'sweetening of the mood' in trade with the West after the 1990 stock market crash.[4] He argues that as Japan's financial outgrowing of Europe and America in the 1970s and 1980s began steering the latter towards protectionist measures, Japanese negotiators realized they could harvest more foreign sympathy from a self-portrayal as Asia's 'fallen giant'.

Deconstruction

Lost decades or not, construction did not stand still: in the two decades following the crash, 81 high-rise buildings taller than 150 metres were constructed in Tokyo against 64 in New York, 48 in Chicago, and 7 in Los Angeles.[5] The Japanese construction lobby, headed by powerful players within the so-called 'Iron Triangle'[6], appeared able to push for further deficit spending in economic stimulus programmes[7] so that, despite a shrinking population, the construction industry was still projected to grow at a rate of 1.2 per cent annually through 2019.[8] The short life-span of buildings, 26 years on average, guarantees this constant demand for construction.[9] But the fast metabolism of ongoing construction is leading to environmental problems. Construction waste for example, uses about 40 per cent of disposal volume in landfills in Japan and makes up 90 per cent of all illegal dumping.[10] Furthermore, Japan will have to find a way to manage abandoned houses and infrastructure in the near future, and later maybe entire cities.

The country's population peaked at 128 million inhabitants in 2011 and is expected to decline to about 100 million in 2050, a drop of 22 per cent.[11] As the number of vacant houses increases, these are expected to become breeding grounds for local crime[12], and infrastructure that expanded in response to the enlargement of cities will probably no longer be maintained. Deconstruction technology is emerging in this context as the systematic disassembly of buildings in order to reuse or recycle recovered materials. Enacted in 2000, the Construction Material Recycling Act already made Japanese contractors responsible for sorting and recycling construction and demolition waste. As a result, recyclability became a significant aspect of construction methods. In 2012, about 96 per cent of materials were recycled.[13] Nevertheless, this emerging industry still wastes a lot of time and energy due to the fact that existing architectural components have not been designed with dismantling in mind, while the necessary tools for dismantling often do not exist yet.

Lean Island

To pave the way for standardization, automation, and robotics in deconstruction, the Japanese construction industry can rely on a long history of using modular design and prefabrication. In their study of automated deconstruction, Maged Helal and Thomas Bock notice that, looking to further minimize time waste and labour costs, the construction industry in Japan benefits from a valuable transfer of experiences, technologies, and concepts with leading manufacturers in domestic sectors such as the automotive industry.[14] Said to have evolved as a problem solving system in a social environment characterized by the scarcity of habitable space and natural resources, Toyota's lean production and management philosophy has found a wide range of applications as a systematic method for waste minimization.[15] Toyota was the first corporation to apply the lean production systems of its car manufacturing to prefabricated housing[16], and later inspired its competitors in the prefab industry.[17] Today 'lean' is also found in the urbanist policies of the Tokyo Metropolitan Government in their efforts to transform the capital into a 'zero waste' sustainable city.[18] In his promise to cut bureaucratic inefficiency, Shinzō Abe even spoke of political reforms aimed at 'zero waste', and a 'lean government'.[19]

In a market analysis for European firms wishing to enter the Japanese sustainable building market, the EU-Japan Centre for Industrial Cooperation warns that Japan, as a relatively isolated archipelago, has 'created and enforced its own contracting culture'.[20] Although they assure that the notorious bid-rigging system known as *dango* inside cartels of contractors has recently disappeared, there still exists a hierarchy of large and small contractors which has, in most cases, business operation histories going back more than a century. To remedy the virtual absence of foreign construction companies, the government introduced a 'Major Project Arrangement' (MPA) in the beginning of the 1990s.[21] In that scheme, for a selected number of reference projects, all Japanese competitors were obliged to include a foreign partner in their consortium to be allowed to participate in competitive bidding. But after the establishment of GATT[22] and then WTO[23] rules, preventing 'structured' bids pre-designating authorized competitors, the foreign contractors withdrew from the market. To fill the gap left by a diminishing workforce as the domestic population ages, construction companies are increasingly looking towards automation and robotics. While restrictions on immigration are already being loosened to supplement the lack of manpower[24], the foray into robotics is spurred by anxiety about the possibility of collisions between immigrants and locals due to a lack of experience in Japanese society in living with foreigners.[25]

Aichi Expo 2005

Architect: Kiyonori Kikutake
Completion: 2005

After the expos in Osaka (1970) and Tsukuba (1995), Aichi 2005 was planned once again by a (former) member of the Metabolist movement, architect Kiyonori Kikutake. The architect's masterplan for the world fair took modularity and reuse as a central starting point. While in the decade of rapid growth Kikutake's Metabolism was based on the premise of consumerism and mass production, Metabolism was reinvented here as a recycling concept. In conventional world expositions, participating countries freely construct original pavilions based on their own ideas. However, to ensure the reuse of construction materials, the masterplan of EXPO 2005 Aichi requested that all participating countries set up their exhibition facilities within standardized modules, each of which is 18 meters long, 18 meters wide and 9 meters high, constructed and provided by the association.[26] Since this modular building system was cost-effective, it enabled many more countries to participate. When the exhibition closed, the modules were deconstructed for future reuse, thus avoiding the production of a huge amount of building scrap.

While the modular building system was presented in the context of the Expo as a visionary approach to the coming age[27], it simultaneously referenced the Japanese architectural heritage. The past was present as a blown-up Japanese garden (the Expo grounds). In it, the white containers of the national pavilions represented a scaled-up version of the Japanese vernacular, which with its modular and standardized elements took on a symbolic role as the precursor of the architecture of the future.

Akasaka Prince Hotel (deconstruction)

Contractor: Taisei Corporation
Deconstruction: 2013

Taisei Corporation, one of Japan's major contractors, developed a deconstruction technique to dismantle high-rise buildings, which can reduce carbon emissions by 85 per cent, according to the company. In 2013 they successfully dismantled Kenzō Tange's Akasaka Grand Prince Hotel in Tokyo (1982), the tallest building torn down in Japan to date. The deconstruction process cuts the elements from the top down, four floors at a time. Green energy is harvested by the system when lowering heavy construction materials from the top of the tower to ground level. Kajima corporation, a similar enterprise, has successfully applied a variant that tackles deconstruction from the bottom up. Four other major Japanese contractors have followed and today six of Japan's largest general contractors are actively exploring these new deconstruction techniques.[28] While deconstruction generally struggles with cost-effectiveness due to the high cost of labour and low waste disposal costs, the size of Japanese construction companies enables these large contractors to offer packages that include the construction and disassembly of a building in a single price.[29] This policy makes demolition cheaper, since there is a discount from the companies.

Based on the assumption that skyscrapers in Japan over 100 meters can be expected to be torn down after 30 to 40 years, about a hundred high-rise buildings will follow the dismantling of the Grand Prince Hotel (2013) within a decade.[31]

High-rise buildings have suddenly appeared as part of Japan's cityscape starting in 1963 as a result of the withdrawal of the 31-metre building height limit following a construction boom leveraged by the 1964 Olympics. This first generation of Japanese high-rises is now reaching a critical age limit, creating a sudden demand for methods offering a safe way to demolish a building higher than 100 metres in densely built areas.[30]

Fibercity 2050

Architect: Hideyoshi Ohno
Publication: 2006

Economic recession brought the visionary planning of the fast-growth era to a standstill and for a long time, Japanese architects confined their experiments to single structures, mainly detached houses. Still, the visionary urbanism that disappeared with stagnation could make a comeback once Japanese cities start shrinking at the pace they were once growing. At least, this is the premise of Tokyo Fibercity 2050 published as the 63rd edition of *The Japan Architect*. Envisioning the long-term population decrease as a large-scale urban renewal project, this plan proposes a set of tools and guidelines for the systematic deconstruction of the world's largest metropolis.

The Fibercity is a new paradigm for shrinking cities, a strategy for urban renewal that envisions fibres (linear components) and cloth as organizational models.[32] The underlying assumption is that while the changes that tend to be realized in contemporary Japanese cities are either point interventions in the form of objects, or minor surface interventions such as theme parks and gated communities, the longer perimeter of linear surfaces could achieve a big effect with a relatively small effort.[33]

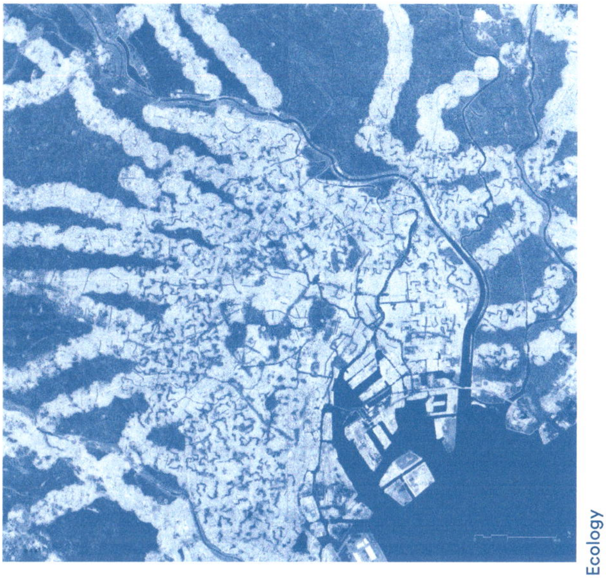

Fibercity proposes four design elements to restructure the radically reduced metropolitan space[34]:

1. 'Green Finger' is a proposal to reorganize the suburban areas severely affected by population decline around zones within walking distance of stations along railway lines and the greening of outlying areas beyond, creating a web of linear compact cities linked by Tokyo's railway lines.
2. 'Green Partition' encloses the city centre and high-risk urban disaster areas with a high density of wooden structures with green strips.
3. 'Green Web' is a traffic conversion strategy transforming the central ring road of the Tokyo Metropolitan Expressway into roads for emergency disaster relief and green roads.
4. 'Urban Wrinkle' highlights linear spots of interest, or *meisho*[35], optimizing local scenery and history within a homogenized and monotonous urban space.

1 I. Buruma, *Inventing Japan: 1853-1964* (London: Weidenfeld & Nicholson, 2003), 172.

2 Various articles have been published on the subject in 2011 and 2012 by *Forbes*, *The New York Times*, *The Atlantic*, *The Guardian*, and others.

3 Daniel Gros, 'The myth of Japan's lost decade', *The Guardian*, January 17, 2011, https://www.theguardian.com/commentisfree/2011/jan/17/japan-myth-lostdecade

4 Eamonn Fingleton, 'The Myth of Japan's Failure', *The New York Times*, January 6, 2012, https://www.nytimes.com/2012/01/08/opinion/sunday/the-true-story-of-japans-economic-success.html

5 Ibid.

6 The 'Iron Triangle' refers to the interplay of ministerial bureaucracy, politics, and business in Japan.

7 W. Flüchter, 'Shrinking Cities in Japan: Between Megalopolises and Rural Peripheries', in P. Oswalt and T. Reniets, *Shrinking Cities Complete Works 3, Case Study: Japan,* (Project Office Philipp Oswalt: Berlin, 2008), 3.

8 J. Littlefair, 'Building Products and Sustainable Construction: A Market Assessment Tool for U.S. Exporters', *2016 ITA Building Products and Sustainable Construction Top Markets Report*, May (2016), 50.

9 Danielle Demetriou, 'Why design buffs must visit Tokyo, an architectural riddle of a city', *The Telegraph*, April 10, 2017, https://www.telegraph.co.uk/travel/destinations/asia/japan/articles/why-design-buffs-must-visit-tokyo/

10 A. Chini et al, 'Deconstruction as an essential component of sustainable construction', *CIB World Building Congress,* April (2001), 1.

11 W. Flüchter, op cit., 3.

12 H. Ohno, 'Fibercity/Tokyo 2050', *The Japan Architect* 63 (2006), 3.

13 INGÉROSEC Corporation, 'Sustainable Building and Construction Sector in Japan and Analysis of Opportunities for European firms', *EU-Japan Centre for Industrial Cooperation*, March (2015), 65.

14 M. Helal, T. Bock, 'Towards a Sustainable Construction Industry: Automated Deconstruction and Recycling', *Sustainable Building Conference Cairo*, November (2013), 613.

15 K. Fujita and R. Hill, 'The Zero Waste City: Tokyo's Quest for a Sustainable Environment', *Journal of Comparative Policy Analysis* 4 (2007), 9.

16 Toyota started prefabricating housing in the 1970s. In 2004 the industrial giant established a whole new branch to begin full-scale production of factory-built homes. That year Toyota Home built 4,700 homes.

17 R. Smith, 'History of Prefabrication: A Cultural Survey', *Proceedings of the Third International Congress on Construction History* (2009), 7.

18 K. Fujita and R. Hill, 'The Zero Waste City: Tokyo's Quest for a Sustainable Environment', *Journal of Comparative Policy Analysis* 4 (2007), 11.

19 S. Abe, Policy Speech to the 166th Session of the Diet (2007), https://japan.kantei.go.jp/abespeech/2007/01/26speech_e.html

20 INGÉROSEC Corporation, 'Sustainable Building and Construction Sector in Japan and Analysis of Opportunities for European firms', *EU-Japan Centre for Industrial Cooperation*, March (2015), 65.

21 M. Helal, T. Bock, op. cit., 613.

22 The General Agreement on Tariffs and Trade

23 The World Trade Organization

24 David Green, 'As Its Population Ages, Japan Quietly Turns to Immigration', *Migration Policy Institute*, March 28, 2017, https://www.migrationpolicy.org/article/its-population-ages-japan-quietly-turns-immigration

25 H. Ohno, op. cit., 4.

26 M-C. Tsunoda et al, 'Design for Reuse- Case study of World Exposition 2005 Aichi Japan', *Building Stock Activation Conference* (2007), 188.

27 Ibid., 190.

28 T. Bock et al., 'Vertical Shipyard: Technology Transfer for Automated Con- and Deconstruction Methods', *International Association for Automation and Robotics in Construction* (2011), 652-658.

29 M. Helal, T. Bock, op. cit., 614.

30 Ibid., 615.

31 Elisabeth Graw, 'Japan's disposable home culture is an environmental and financial headache', *The Guardian*, May 2, 2014, https://www.theguardian.com/sustainable-business/disposable-homes-japan-environment-lifespan-sustainability

32 H. Ohno, op. cit, 8.

33 Ibid.

34 Ibid., 10-13.

35 In the Edo period, *meisho* were informal places where local history and personal memories had accumulated, places where fragments of the nature latent in the substratum of the city would appear, openings for escape from the artificiality of the city.

D

‘We are not in the century of construction anymore’

Yoshiharu Tsukamoto quoted from J. P. Urrutia, ‘Yoshiharu Tsukamoto’, 24.

Florian Bush Architects’ Floating Stadium passing under the Tokyo Gate bridge in Tokyo Bay.
courtesy of FBA

Floating the Stadium

> We are still not quite sure what happened a couple of weeks ago. A package was delivered and placed, perhaps because of its appearance (it was a small, almost squared black box, an exercise in reduction except for a rather gaudily large quick response code on its top), in the Applications section of the mail shelf. Later that day, someone in the office noticed that the postmark read '2020.12.22'.[1]
>
> **-Florian Busch Architects, Tokyo 2017**

In this 'box from the future', Florian Busch Architects allegedly found models, photographs, and magazines recounting the story of 'Tokyo's Olympic Odyssey'.[2] According to these documents, in another unexpected turn of events, Tokyo once again abandonded its plans to build a new National Stadium in Sendagaya, this time, however, in favour of an outlandish project: Tokyo's new National Stadium was to be a floating structure, docked onto the city in Tokyo Bay. Making the stadium Japan's 6,853rd island, it seemed, would make a perfect compromise and more. Locals living around the old site would now find a park at their doorstep rather than the dreaded white elephant. The city of Tokyo would not need to worry about the maintenance of an oversized stadium or a programme of events for it to be rentable, nor would any of the upcoming host cities. From now on, the stadium would float from harbour to harbour on demand, and every four years to a new Olympic destination. The innovative concept would generate tremendous publicity, and make sure the Tokyo Olympics would be remembered long after 2020. The Japanese government would truly keep its promise of organizing 'compact games'[3] so that, finally, even environmentalists, worried about the waste events like these can generate, could applaud the sustainable character of this recyclable stadium.[4]

In a brilliant public relations stunt for his office, covered by, among others, *The Japan Times*, Florian Busch, a Tokyo-based German architect who started his career under Toyo Itō, sets forth this alternative future.[5] His floating stadium design, conceived as a critique of the string of questionable decisions made in the conception of the New National Stadium, conveys in images what words cannot. Instead of simply pointing at where it all went wrong, Busch renders a version of what could have been. Utopian and pragmatic at the same time, the floating stadium effortlessly resolves the conflicts and compromises that have shaped the previous designs, thus exposing the narrow-mindedness of the agencies in charge of producing our contemporary urban environments. As the core decisions in urban projects are increasingly taken by technocrats and large general contractors, architects are left with the job of 'decoration'. Compared to the floating stadium, Zaha Hadid and Kengo Kuma's designs—which tried so hard to look different from each other—suddenly appeared quasi-identical, now revealing their true nature. In the tumultuous course of events, the stadium only changed its dress, exchanging a sparkling futuristic one for a 'Japanese' fabric of timbers and greenery. But the naked body of the building, the locus of the actual issues that need to be discussed, has remained under this surface.

> Out of all the gross mistakes that were made with regard to the stadium, one stood out from the beginning: the choice of the site. The only sensible response (and a very beautiful one at that) would have been to use the existing stadium. But if a new stadium was inevitable (which of course it wasn't), then surely not there.[6]
>
> –Florian Busch, architect

The floating stadium, as a theoretical project, has the luxury of going to the bottom of things. Stripped of its 'architecture', the underlying political, economic, and urbanist vision for the Olympic venue appears fundamentally flawed. Unfortunately, it is on this deeper level—from which architecture has been banished—that the profession could have made a difference. Instead of reusing the stadium built in 1958, authorities made the decision to demolish it and replace it with a newer and larger iconic structure in order to send a message to the world. Hadid's stadium says 'opening Japan', and Kuma's says 'considering Japanese-ness'. But just like their architectures, confined to cladding a predetermined form, their messages—equally predetermined—remain superficial. Unlike the floating stadium, which, as an expression of the Japanese *mottainai* ethic, and an insular extension of the archipelago connecting to other continents, can do both 'opening Japan', and do 'Japanese-ness'. Free to be the change that is needed, rather than just expressing it, it automatically transcends superficial contradictions. It shows the potential of architectural vision, and, most importantly, the lack of it in today's world.

Myth to Marketing

In response to the March 2011 triple disaster, Kengo Kuma and Toyo Itō emphasized the need to break away from the perverse building culture of the twentieth century. But when this anti-establishment architecture becomes entangled in nation-building efforts, as we have seen in Kuma's description of his own stadium[7], critical stances taken in response to the disaster degenerate into a facile promotion of national myths and self-portrayals. Sceptics may rightfully ask whether embodying idealized images is not an intrinsic aspect of architecture. Has an architecture free of myths ever even existed? Even historical sociologist Eiji Oguma concludes his study of 'Japanese' self-images admitting that stereotypes are to some degree necessary for society to function.[8] He warns us however, of the tendency to replace one distorted version of the truth with another.

> It is not sufficient to fight against myths by destroying one myth and replacing it with another... What is required is to liberate ourselves from all myths, something which will require some work.[9]
>
> –Eiji Oguma, *A Genealogy of 'Japanese' Self-images*

The reason why we need to stay aware of cultural myths is that they serve to cover up a state of denial in society.[10] We have compared Kuma's conception of the New National Stadium to Kenzō Tange's discourse on a Japanese counter-monumentality that 'overcomes modernity'. This project of 'overcoming modernity' focused on attacking the shortcomings of an essentialized 'Western oppressor', in order to avoid talking about a lingering domestic cultural malaise.[11] Although the comparison may be a bit of a stretch, we are therefore inclined to ask whether, just like Tange's prewar counter-monuments, Itō and Kuma's anti-modernist architectural tenets are not concealing a deeper problem. In his study of Japanese 'ultranationalism', Alain-Marc Rieu warns us that 'overcoming modernity' still operates today, as 'modern society's mythology'.[12]

> It is short-sighted to reject the project of overcoming modernity in the past: indeed, it remains as a project today in different parts of the world. It seems to emerge when the cycle of modernization in a society is reaching its end. When its projection in the future and its promises are contradicted by daily life.[13]
>
> –Alain-Marc Rieu, *'Syndrome of "overcoming modernity"'*

Following Rieu's reasoning, we see that the events in Tōhoku severely contradicted the promises of twentieth-century modernization and consumerism, and have consequently disrupted the faith in centralized technocratic planning. But the renewed taste for 'Japan-ness' in contemporary architecture also coincides with a period of underlying cultural anxieties in the face of globalization. Japan will have to integrate a large number of migrants to make up for future labour shortages as its population ages. Furthermore, neoliberal reforms of the national economy are widening the rift between Japanese urban centres and the regional periphery, which now suffers from economic decline and an acute shrinkage of the population. The architectural representation of Japan as a coherent and harmonious entity becomes appealing in this context of fragmentation and identity loss. However, as this 'Japanese' architecture becomes an object of desire, it comes to serve the mechanisms it set out to counter. In the House Vision exhibitions of 2013 and 2016, as well as in the preparations for the Olympic Games we see this 'soft, natural, and humane' Japanese architecture being used to advertise consumption of the latest industrial products, and to leverage speculative investment in real estate.[14]

Absorbed by these marketing mechanisms, the architectural movement that emerged after the Tōhoku disaster could suffer the same fate as the Metabolist movement of the 1960s. The postwar avant-garde movement, launched in the heat of the 1960 political debates surrounding the ratification of the US-Japan Security Treaty, reached its apotheosis as a physical manifestation ten years later, during the mega event of Expo 70 in Osaka.[15] But in hindsight, Expo 70 has been described by historians as the moment when Metabolism reached an ideological crisis, as its revolutionary intentions were visibly consumed by corporate interests.

> The event was dominated by the Metabolists' iconic forms of megastructure and capsule, and brought great international visibility to their work. However, the crisis of techno-utopia also became evident in this grand show. The social ideals that had been associated with the Metabolists' urban schemes fell through, giving way to a commercialism that took complete control of the event.[16]
>
> –Zhongjie Lin, *Urban Utopias of Modern Japan*

Arata Isozaki, who had designed the central Festival Plaza, was so disillusioned by the event that he distanced himself from the work as soon as the Expo was over.[17]

> I was utterly exhausted with that dubious aftertaste of disgusting bitterness as if I had been engaging in war. I was unable to find an excuse to escape from the Expo and continued my official obligation to the end, although I was emotionally withdrawn from it. The first moment of emotional withdrawal came when I realized that the Expo was under the control of technocrats. We were indeed naïve. We had an illusion that Expo 70 would be a great opportunity for us to openly confront modern technology.[18]
>
> –Arata Isozaki, architect

Of course, as long as architects comply with the outline of official assignments, there is no way around technocrats safeguarding the status quo. Before entering the competition, Kengo Kuma was well aware that the task to 'redo' the stadium would be treacherous.

> I couldn't speak lightly about it. I was thinking that if another architect took on this job, it would be like catching a hot potato—and it never occurred to me that I'd be the one to catch it![19]
>
> –Kengo Kuma, architect

When asked why he entered the competition anyway, Kuma suggests that architects in Japan find themselves increasingly shut out of building processes. These are now dominated by big construction companies and a technocratic planning apparatus which view their designs as obsolete.

> Japan has become conservative, and these days it's virtually unheard of for a solo architect to get involved in a project of this scale. I made up my mind to give this job everything I've got partly because I want to keep the flame burning in the architectural profession.[20]
>
> -Kengo Kuma, architect

In Kuma's view, rather than an act of collaboration with architecture's enemy, realizing a design on this scale as an independent architect was an opportunity to react to the deplorable state of affairs. Although they each responded to the problem in their own way, here, Busch and Kuma's diagnoses overlap.

> If you look at architectural competitions in Japan today, they have become extremely boring and conservative, and a lot of them are so rigidly constrained that young architects —and there are so many really talented young minds in Japan—are not given the chance to compete. The requirements are absurd, with limiting regulations that mean you can only enter a competition if you're an established general contractor—a large corporate force already.[21]
>
> –Florian Busch, architect

State of Deconstruction

Defining architecture's continuing social mission holds special relevance, now that the need for architecture is being put into question. As ecological and economical constraints tighten, the design of the urban environment is increasingly monopolized by technicians.[22] Furthermore, Kengo Kuma has remarked that in the eyes of the citizen, too, architecture today is often seen as a waste of taxpayers' money and a threat to the natural environment.[23] In this context, despite their compromises with the mainstream, Kuma and Itō's post-tsunami legacy should not be underestimated. We have seen that by questioning the 'modern' paradigm, Kuma and Itō have provided a refreshing point of view on ecology in architecture, as it tends to be understood as a technical challenge, rather than an architectural one.[24] Their proposals emphasize the bond between social and environmental relations, and hint at the emancipatory potential of architecture in view of a paradigm shift in society. In a building culture increasingly focused on numbers, they conceive of sustainability in architecture as a design assignment that, besides technical requirements, equally revolves around local culture, community, and identity.

Admitting that the upcoming Olympics could entail an ideological crisis for this social movement in architecture, similar to the one Metabolism experienced after Expo 70, we must ask where to go from here. If the contemporary crisis of the 'modern' in architecture is diagnosed solely on the basis of a disaster that washed away its concrete structures, it is tempting to see this 'twentieth-century architecture' as the obsolete remnants of the past, to be replaced with newer, better, and more 'natural' architecture. Yet this cycle of perpetual rebuilding is what has been feeding the construction state all along. Discussing proposals to relocate the Tokyo Metropolitan Expressway, which conceals the sky above the otherwise scenic Nihonbashi river, Hidetoshi Ohno speaks of a 'patricidal' tendency in Japanese urban design.

> The radicalism of the conservative mindset manifests in the form of reproaching one's father's generation, and being nostalgically attached to one's grandfather's era, but in Japan this has actually become the destruction of relics from our father's era. In the Meiji Era, they tried to erase the Edo era; in the postwar era, the prewar days were rejected; now people speak ill of the period of high economic growth. Perhaps growth is always like this.[25]
>
> –Hidetoshi Ohno, Architect

Zooming out of the 2011-2021 timeframe, Japan finds itself in a broader, post-growth era. In this larger context it is clear that even if Japanese architecture does go 'beyond the era of concrete', Japan itself cannot, since the twentieth century has left an oversized world of concrete behind. Therefore, basing the architecture of the 'environmental age' on a rejection of the previous generation's achievements would be short-sighted, however tempting it may be. Citing his own ethnographic approach to architecture as a possible future direction, Yoshiharu Tsukamoto finds that first and foremost, architectural education needs a new orientation.[26]

> Considering that there was an explosion of the building industry in the twentieth century, architectural education is very much making- or construction-oriented. But this was a very special moment of the human being. Now, I really think about another way to confront our reality, our work as an architect, because, especially in Japan, we are not in the century of construction anymore.[27]
>
> -Yoshiharu Tsukamoto (Atelier Bow-Wow), architect

As we move into the twenty-first century the task should not be to build a new world, but to recycle the twentieth century. Japan's ubiquitous concrete landscapes could benefit from a view that accepts them as a resource, enabling their reuse to serve contemporary needs. This transition from a 'construction state' to a state of deconstruction, feeding on the old rather than the new, requires vision, and as Florian Busch demonstrates with his floating stadium, this can become a new, meaningful task for architecture, as the profession is increasingly shut out of building processes.

Incidentally, the current Covid-19 crisis may be a significant teaching moment in this respect. Over the past decades, the premise of perpetual growth has continually prioritized short-term efficiency over long-term resilience. And while the shock of the pandemic seems to be fuelling this trend in some ways, nudging us further towards automation, surveillance, and centralized control, without monitoring the social consequences, new forms of resilience are emerging. It has been interesting to see how in Tokyo, many hotels that were built in anticipation of the Summer Olympics were converted into quarantine towers. After the government secured hundreds of thousands of rooms to house infected patients, some hotel chains even followed up by offering special rates for 'Self-Quarantine Accommodation'. Efforts are made to offset the loss of mass tourism from abroad by subsidizing domestic travel, stimulating off-centre economies.[28] Meanwhile, sports stadiums are being reopened as test sites for social distancing measures, where high-precision cameras and beacons help define the safety limits of large gatherings.[29] In the hope of hosting the Olympics in 2021, the Japanese government has finally found an incentive to conceive truly 'compact', and thus greener Games. Tokyo has a mandate to radically rethink the existing model, and to set a precedent with consequences that may reach beyond the scope of the pandemic.

As Japan closed its borders, Florian Busch jokingly suggested[30] that the floating stadium would have been the perfect vessel for an 'Olympics in quarantine'. One can easily imagine gathering tested athletes from around the world on the floating structure, symbolically drifting around Tokyo Bay while keeping a healthy distance from the inhabitants of the host city. This idea of a closed archipelago Japan, reserving a single (and man-made) island for contact with the outside world may sound familiar: it brings us back to the artificial island of Dejima[31], a fan-shaped landfill of about 120 by 75 metres in Nagasaki Bay. Built in 1636 to segregate Portuguese inhabitants and control their catholic missionary activities, it was turned into a trading post for the more secular Dutch seafarers a few years later, after the Portuguese were expelled from the country. Yet even the Dutch were kept from entering the rest of Japan, apart from their yearly trip to Edo to pay homage to the shōgun. From 1641 onwards the Dutch enclave of Dejima became the focal point of knowledge transfer between Japan and the West. It lasted for over two centuries, up until the onset of Japan's modern era in 1853, the starting point of our story.

1 Florian Busch Architects, 'The Floating Stadium', http://www.florianbusch.com/projects/fsp/

2 Ibid.

3 One of the reasons Tokyo won the bid is that the city emphasized that the games would be compact and ecological. Japan Trends. 'Will the Tokyo 2020 Olympics be the "eco Olympics"?'

4 Apart from being reused for each Olympic Games, the stadium is 'built from over 80% recycled material'.

5 Kris Kosaka, 'Florian Busch, the architect who floated the Tokyo 2020 Olympic stadium', *The Japan Times*, March 28, 2018, https://www.japantimes.co.jp/community/2018/ 02/28/our-lives/florian-busch-architect-floated-tokyo-2020-olympic-stadium/

6 Lily Crossley-Baxter, 'Florian Busch and the floating stadium: A futuristic Olympic insight', *Rethink Tokyo*, April 18, 2018, https://www.rethinktokyo.com/2018/04/18/florian-busch-tokyo-olympic-odyssey-floating-stadium/152364 5336

7 See chapter 4, 'I refuse to play the role of the Japanese architect'.

8 E. Oguma, *A Genealogy of 'Japanese' Self-Images,* trans. David Askew (Melbourne: Trans Pacific Press, 2002), 348.

9 Ibid., 349.

10 Ibid., 348.

11 A. Rieu, 'The syndrome of "overcoming modernity": Learning from Japan about ultra-nationalism', *Journal of Global Cultural Studies* 9 (2014), 2.

12 Ibid.

13 Ibid.

14 See chapter 2, 'The Japanese must still remove his shoes at the doorway' and chapter 3, 'A gigantic monster on the brink of extinction'.

15 Z. Lin, *Kenzo Tange and the Metabolist Movement: Urban Utopias of Modern Japan*, (London: Routledge, 2010), 200.

16 Ibid.

17 H. Cho, 'Competing Futures: War Narratives in Post-war Japanese Architecture 1945-1970', PhD diss., University of Southern California (2011), 284.

18 Ibid..

19 Y. Kiyono, 'Architect Kuma Kengo Shares His Thinking Behind Japan's New National Stadium Design', *Nippon,* June 30, 2016, https://www.nippon.com/en/people/e00101/

20 Ibid.

21 Kris Kosaka, ibid.

22 R. Koolhaas, 'My thoughts on the smart city', *European Commission*, September 24, 2014, http://ec.europa.eu/archives/ commission_2010-2014/kroes/en/content/my-thoughts-smart-cityrem-koolhaas.html

23 See chapter 4, 'I refuse to play the role of the Japanese architect'.

24 See chapter 3, 'A gigantic monster on the brink of extinction'.

25 H. Ohno, 'Fibercity/Tokyo 2050,' *The Japan Architect* 63 (2006), 6.

26 J. P. Urrutia, 'Yoshiharu Tsukamoto: We have to avoid treating people just like numbers', *Materia Arquitectura* 12 (2015), 24.

27 Ibid.

28 The tourism ministry's Go To campaign (comprising Go To Travel, Go To Eat, Go To Event, and Go To Shotengai) is a ¥1.7 trillion initiative encompassing travel, food, and entertainment industries, offering to refund up to fifty percent of travel expenses.

29 Jack Tarrant, 'Olympics: Japan to test anti-virus measures at near-full baseball stadium', *Reuters*, 16 October, 2020, https://de.reuters.com/article/uk-olympics-2020-baseball-fans/japan-to-test-anti-virus-measures-at-near-full-baseball-stadium-idUSKBN2710HQ

30 By this time, I had started working as an architectural designer for Florian Busch Architects. The comments were made in private.

31 *Dejima* (出島) literally means 'exit island'.

TIMELINE
Island Ecology

1603: Start Tokugawa era/Edo period
1633-1853: *Sakōku* isolationism limits international relations and trade under the Tokugawa shōgunate
1634: Dejima (exit island), built as only official place of direct trade and exchange between Japan and the outside world
1690: First accurate domestically produced Japanese globe made with help of Dutch merchants in Nagasaki
1868: Start Meiji era
1912: Start Taishō era
1919: Japan acquires mandate over Germany's former territories in the South Pacific islands at Versailles Peace Conference
1919: Japanese bid for a racial equality clause at Peace Conference refused by the Western powers in Versailles
1924: *Shima no Jinsei* (Island Life) published by Kunio Yanagita
1926: Start Shōwa era
1930: Japanese Racial Hygiene Committee formed to advocate social reforms based on eugenics
1952: Treaty of San Francisco makes all former colonial subjects lose Japanese nationality
1972: *Limits to Growth* published by the Club of Rome
1973-1982: United Nations Conference on the Law of the Sea grants Japan a large Exclusive Economic Zone around its islands, making it the seventh largest nation in terms of EEZ
1982: Start Heisei era
1986-1991: Economic bubble inflates real estate and stock market prices in Japan
1992-2011: Collapse of the bubble followed by 'lost decades'
2000: Construction Material Recycling Act makes contractors liable for sorting and recycling construction and demolition waste
2004: Toyota Home established, builds 4,700 homes in the first year
2005: Expo Aichi
2006: Fibercity 2050 vision by Hidetoshi Ohno
2006-2007: Shinzō Abe Prime Minister
2007: *Towards a Beautiful Country: My Vision for Japan* published by Shinzō Abe
2011: Triple disaster in the Northern region of Tōhoku
2011: Toyo Itō Museum of Architecture by Toyo Itō
2012-2020: Shinzō Abe Prime Minister
2013: Tokyo selected to host 2020 Olympic Games
2013: Deconstruction Akasaka Prince Hotel by Taisei Corporation
2013-2017: Resident foreign workforce increases by 40 per cent
2015: Design for the New National Stadium by Zaha Hadid Architects scrapped
2016: Yoshino Cedar House by Go Hasegawa
2017: Shinzō Abe calls for 'rebirth of the Japanese nation in 2020' pushing for a review of Japan's Peace Constitution
2019: Start Reiwa era
2019: New National Olympic Stadium by Kengo Kuma
2020: (January) Central government of China imposes a lockdown in Wuhan and other cities in Hubei in effort to quarantine centre of coronavirus outbreak
2020: (March) Japan imposes travel restrictions following coronavirus outbreak
2020: (March) Tokyo Olympics postponed to 2021
2020: (April) Japan declares state of emergency following coronavirus outbreak

Live on Concrete, Love of Nature

Milan, 6 October 2018

I am about to cross a roundabout when I am startled by the sound of something hard dropping on the concrete next to my feet. I find a walnut, split in half. I look up at the sky and find the suspect. A crow, who now lands a few meters away. He acts nonchalant but I see him watching me out of the corner of his eye. Yes, I know you're a smart one. You cracked this nut to find a little snack inside. Let's cross the road to give him space.

The bird hesitates, then walks up to the half nut and takes a few bites. He picks up the shell with his beak, walks off of the sidewalk and drops it on the road. Cars are going around the roundabout and I start to think that maybe this fellow is not that smart after all. Watch out!!

"CRAAACKKK"

The crow escapes—but the nut is crushed right under the centre of the car tire. The bird happily hops back to pick up the last crumbs of his breakfast.

Amazed, I make a note in my sketchbook reminding myself to watch animals in the city more closely from now on. There is a story here. I think of how the crow reminds me of myself, when I was adapting to a new life in Japan. You can think of the bird in the city as the ultimate foreigner. Away from his natural habitat, the bird must be an artist. It borrows the anthropocentric urban environment as a 'ready-made' object, only to transform its purpose and meaning by using it in its own ways.

It was obvious that the bird had used the roundabout in this way before. It sees the roundabout as a giant nutcracker. I wonder if it enjoys this little routine. Routine has a negative connotation in our society. Especially when visiting a foreign country, consumerist logic commands us to see and do as many things as we can. When the saturation point is reached, where seeing too many 'unique' things ends up eroding this very quality, we think it may be time to go home.

Really, it is through rhythms, routines, and rituals that we establish a bond with a place. To inhabit is to in-habit. The routine is a double-edged sword. Following the example of others around us, the routine helps us live together. We adapt our manners to the conditions of the environment we share. In Japan, we are quiet on the train. We take off our shoes before entering the house and we eat with chopsticks. But other habits purposely break the norm and become an expression of who we are inside. They set us apart and help us sustain a sense of self in a city of millions.

Architecture, at its best, acts as a canvas for this 'in-habiting' performance. A building may only have a few functions, but it can have many more uses. When the bridge becomes a fishing range, when the river embankments become a golf course, when the abandoned poison gas factory becomes a rabbit paradise reviving the local economy—that is when our love of nature can live on concrete.

Although the research of this book focuses on theory more than on practice, it was written with the pragmatic outlook of an architect, welcoming the coexistence of critical and poetical points of view. The main concern has been to outline a layered view of the environment in which we build. One that, for instance, can see through the myth of Japan as an isolated, resource-scarce island, while acknowledging and praising the existing spirit of *mottainai*.

By bridging the Japanese nation-nature dialogue with 'building', we have grounded the discussion in the material situation of our living environment, thus enabling us to refrain from seeing the legacy of the past as an imposed identity to be accepted or rejected—and start seeing it as a resource.

In the essays at the beginning of each chapter, I have hinted at how the mechanisms at work in the production of the city already lend themselves to a reading in an ecological sense. This shows that rather than starting from scratch, progress can be achieved by seeing the existing building stock in a new light, and from different viewpoints. From there, tactical changes can be implemented. A realistic approach, inherently more ecological than the fantasy of a completely new world.

Tokyo Gate Bridge (aka the Dinosaur Bridge), Tokyo Bay, 23 June 2017

Always pragmatic, Tokyo is a city of landmarks, not of monuments. Fishing amateurs gather under the Tokyo Gate bridge.

Building demolition waste goes into landfills on Tokyo Bay. Originally planned as industrial sites, many of these artificial islands are turned into public parks.

Wakasu Seaside Park, Tokyo Bay, 23 June 2017

Garden gnomes, invading public space.

Kasai Rinkai Park, Tokyo Bay, 3 May 2017

Mount Nokogori,
Chiba, 29 April 2017

Pilgrimages to mountaintops are popular weekend getaways. Networked into the metropolitan train system, these holy sites and the urban fabric are one.

SUNBUILDER

Golf practice, on the river, under the cherry blossoms.

Shin-Kobe River, Kobe, 9 April 2017

Watersplash on pavement
Artist: unknown

Ueno Park,
Tokyo, 18 December 2016

The 'Rabbit Island' in Japan's inland sea does not need art to attract a tourist economy. Legend has it that its Wordl War II poison gas factory was abandoned to the test rabbits, who have multiplied into an impressive colony, attracting many visitors.

Ōkunoshima, 21 March 2017

‘There is something bordering on blithe dismissal in Banham’s use of the term: Ecologies, he seems to imply, are simply what we make of them.’
-Joe Day,
Foreword to Reyner Banham, Los Angeles: Architecture of Four Ecologies (2nd edition, 2009)

Murasaki River, Kitakyushu, 8 April 2017

Literature

Books

Baek, J., *Architecture as the Ethics of Climate* (New York: Routledge, 2016)

Banham, R., *Los Angeles: The Architecture of Four Ecologies* (London: The Penguin Press, 1971)

Buruma, I., *Inventing Japan: 1853-1964* (London: Weidenfeld & Nicolson, 2003)

Coaldrake, W., *Architecture and Authority in Japan* (Hove: Psychology Press, 1996)

Dale, P., *The Myth of Japanese Uniqueness* (New York: St. Martin's Press, 1986)

Imanishi, K., *A Japanese View of Nature: The World of Living Things*, translated by Pamela J. Asquith, Heita Kawakatsu, Shusuke Yagi, and Hiroyuki Takasaki (New York: Routledge, 2002)

Isozaki, A., *Japan-ness in Architecture* (Cambridge Massachusetts: MIT Press, 2006)

Ito, T., *Toyo Ito: Collected Works 2002-2014* (Tokyo: TOTO, 2014)

Kaijima, M. Kuroda, J., and Tsukamoto, Y., *Made in Tokyo* (Tokyo: Kajima Institute Publishing, 2015)

Kitayama, K. et al., *Tokyo Metabolizing* (Tokyo: TOTO, 2010)

Kondo, M., *The Life-changing Manga of Tidying Up: A Magical Story* (New York: Ten Speed Press, 2017)

Koolhaas, R., and Obrist, H. U., *Project Japan: Metabolism Talks* (Köln: TASCHEN, 2011)

Koolhaas, R., et al., *Project on the City II: The Harvard Guide to Shopping* (Köln: TASCHEN, 2001)

Kuroishi, I., and Traganou, J., *Design and Disaster: Kon Wajiro's Modernologio*, (New York: Parsons The New School for Design, 2014)

Lin, Z., *Kenzo Tange and the Metabolist Movement: Urban Utopias of Modern Japan* (London: Routledge, 2010)

Oguma, E., *A Genealogy of 'Japanese' Self-images*, translated by David Askew (Melbourne: Trans Pacific Press, 2002)

Sand, J., *House and Home in Modern Japan: Architecture, Domestic Space, and Bourgeois Culture, 1880-1930* (Cambridge Massachusetts: Harvard University Asia Centre, 2003)

Schencking, J. C., *The Great Kanto Earthquake and the Chimera of National Reconstruction in Japan* (New York: Columbia University Press, 2013)

Tanizaki, J., *In Praise of Shadows*, translated by Thomas J. Harper and Edward G. Seidensticker (Stony Creek, CT: Leete's Island Books, Inc., 1977)

Tsukamoto, Y., and Kaijima, M., *The Architectures of Atelier Bow-Wow: Behaviorology* (Milan: Rizzoli, 2010)

Watsuji, T., *A Climate: A Philosophical Study*, translated by Geoffrey Bownas (Tokyo: Ministry of Education Printing Bureau, 1961)

Weisenfeld, G., *Imaging Disaster: Tokyo and the Visual Culture of Japan's Great Earthquake of 1923*, (Berkeley: University of California Press, 2012)

Chapters in edited books

Asquith, P., 'Imanishi Kinji's Natural Ethic: The Contribution of a Twentieth-Century Japanese Scientist to Ideas of "Being in the World"'. In *Historical Consciousness, Historiography, and Modern Japanese Values*, edited by Baxter James, 201-206 (Kyoto: International Research Center for Japanese Studies, 2006)

Berkhoff, A., 'Feeling at home in Tokyo'. In *Tokyo Totem: A Guide to Tokyo*, edited by Christiaan Fruneaux and Edwin Gardner, 238-245 (Tokyo: Flick Studio, 2015)

Frampton, K., 'Towards a Critical Regionalism: Six Points for an Architecture of Resistance'. In *The Anti-Aesthetic. Essays on Postmodern Culture*, edited by Hal Foster, 16-30 (Seattle: Bay Press, 1983)

Gleiter J., 'Comments on the Production of International Architecture: Arata Isozaki In conversation with Jörg H. Gleiter'. In *The Domestic and the Foreign in Architecture*, edited by Sang Lee and Ruth Baumeister, 276-286 (Rotterdam: 010 Publishers, 2007)

Hein, C., and Pelletier, P., 'Introduction: decentralization and the tension between global and local urban Japan'. In *Cities, Autonomy, and Decentralization in Japan*, edited by Carola Hein and Philippe Pelletier, 1-24 (New York: Routledge, 2006)

Kuroishi, I., 'Domesticating Other's Space: Surveys and Reforms of Housing in Chosen and Japan by Wajiro Kon'. In *Constructing the Colonized Land: Entwined Perspectives of East Asia around WWII*, edited by Izumi Kuroishi, 215-252 (Surrey: Ashgate Publishing Ltd., 2014)

Nishiyama, U., 'An essay on the National Structure'. In *Reflections on Urban, Regional and National Space: Three Essays*, edited by Carola Hein (New York: Routledge, 2018)

Nishiyama, U., 'Mountain Cities'. In *Reflections on Urban, Regional and National Space: Three Essays*, edited by Carola Hein (New York: Routledge, 2018)

Tomii, R., 'After the "descent to the everyday": Japanese collectivism from Hi Red Center to The Play, 1964-1973'. In *Collectivism after Modernism: The Art of Social imagination after 1945*, edited by Blake Stimson and Gregory Sholette (Minneapolis: University of Minnesota Press, 2007)

Dissertations

Berkhof, A., 'Notion and appearance of home and nature in Tokyo street gardens' Masters diss., University of Groningen, 2014.

Cho, H., 'Competing Futures: War Narratives in Post-war Japanese Architecture 1945-1970' PhD diss., University of Southern California, 2011.

Clancey, G., 'Foreign Knowledge or Art Nation, Earthquake Nation: Architecture, Seismology, Carpentry, The West, and Japan, 1876-1923,' PhD diss., Massachusetts Institute of Technology, 1999.

Grunow, T., 'Empire by Design: Railways, Architecture, and Urban planning in Tokyo, Taipei, and Seoul,' PhD. diss. University of Oregon, 2014.

Journal Articles

Baek, J., 'Climate, Sustainability And The Space Of Ethics: Tetsuro Watsuji's Cultural Climatology and Residential Architecture', *Architectural Theory Review*, v.15, December (2010)

Baek, J., 'Fudo: An East Asian Notion of Climate and Sustainability', *Buildings*, v.3, September (2013)

Berque, A., 'La logique du lieu dépasse-t-elle la modernité?', *Approches critiques de la pensée japonaise du XXe siècle* (2001)

Beynon, D., 'So flat, so cute! Robots, superflatness and Asian architectural futures', *History in practice: 25th International Conference of the Society of Architectural Historians Australia and New Zealand*, Society of Architectural Historians, Australia and New Zealand, July, (2008)

Blaxell, V., 'Designs of Power: The "Japanization" of Urban an Rural Space in Colonial Hokkaidō', *The Asia-Pacific Journal*, v.7, no.2, August (2009)

Bock, T., et al. 'Vertical Shipyard: Technology Transfer for Automated Con- and Deconstruction Methods', *International Association for Automation and Robotics in Construction*, June (2011): 652-658.

Bognor, B., 'What Goes Up, Must Come Down', *Harvard Design Magazine*, no.3, Fall (1997)

Cabeza Lainez, J. M., and Jimenez Verdejo J. R., 'The Japanese Experience of Environmental Architecture through the Works of Bruno Taut and Antonin Raymond', *Journal of Asian Architecture and Building Engineering*, v.6, n.1, May (2007)

□apková, H., 'Influence of Spirit and Not of Form: Antonín Raymond, Le Corbusier, and Architectural Piracy in the Transwar Era'. In S. Inaga, *A Pirate's View of World History: A Reversed Perception of the Order of Things from a Global Perspective,* International Research Center for Japanese Studies (2017).

Chini, Abdol, et al. "Deconstruction as an essential component of sustainable construction," CIB World Building Congress, April (2001)

Da Silva, C. N., '"Principles of Human Geography" Revisited, By Paul Vidal de la Blache', *Belem: Revista GeoAmazônia*, v.3, June (2015)

De Waal, F., 'Without Walls', *New Scientist*, v.172, December (2001)

INGÉROSEC Corporation, 'Sustainable Building and Construction Sector in Japan and Analysis of Opportunities for European firms', *EU-Japan Centre for Industrial Cooperation*, March (2015)

Fujita, K., and Hill, R., 'The Zero Waste City: Tokyo's Quest for a Sustainable Environment', *The Journal of Comparative Policy Analysis*, Vol. 9, No. 4, December (2007)

Hein, C., 'Toshikeikaku and Machizukuri in Japanese Urban Planning-The Reconstruction of Inner City Neighborhoods in Kobe', *Japanstudien*, v.13, (2001): 221-252.

Helal, M., and Bock T., 'Towards a Sustainable Construction Industry: Automated Deconstruction and Recycling', *Sustainable Building Conference Cairo*, November (2013): 611-623.

Isozaki, A., and Asada, A., 'The After-image of Erewhon: On Mirage City, Another Utopia', *Intercommunication*, Summer (1997)

Jaquet, B., 'Compromising Modernity: Japanese Monumentality during World War II', New York University, Institute of Fine Arts, March (2009)

Littlefair, J., 'Building Products and Sustainable Construction: A Market Assessment Tool for U.S. Exporters', *2016 ITA Building Products and Sustainable Construction Top Markets Report*, May (2016)

MacNeill, A., 'From Nature to Nation: shizen and the Japanese national imaginary', *Contingent Horizons*, v.3, February (2017)

Morton, P., 'The uses and abuses of human geography', *Journal of Architecture*, v.16, no.6, December (2011): 805-820.

Oguma, E., 'Post-war Japanese Intellectuals' Changing Perspectives on "Asia" and Modernity', *The Asia-Pacific Journal*, v.5, no.2, February (2017)

Ohno, H., 'Fibercity/Tokyo 2050', *The Japan Architect*, no.63, Autumn (2006)

Omori, F., 'Preliminary Note on the Formosa Earthquake of March 17, 1906', *Bulletin of the Imperial EIC*, v.1, no.2, March (1907).

Ophüls-Kashima, R., 'The concept of kyōsei – Symbiosis or Convivality in Japan: Social-ecological thinking after "Fukushima"', *Journal of Environment Thought and Education* (no. 8, 2015): 89-98.

Pope, L.C., and Metzler, T., 'Has a Robotic Dog the Buddha-nature? Mu!', *Technical report WS-08-05 23-26,* Menlo Park, California: AAAI Press (2008)

Pulvers, R., 'Architect Kuma Kengo: "a product of place"', *The Asia-Pacific Journal*, v.11, no.2, June (2013)

Reitan, R., 'Ecology and Japanese History: Reactionary Environmentalism's Troubled Relationship with the Past', *The Asia-Pacific Journal*, v.15, no.2, February (2017)

Reitherman, R., 'Frank Lloyd Wright's Imperial Hotel: A Seismic Re-evaluation', NISEE – National Information Service for Earthquake Engineering. <http://nisee.berkeley.edu/kanto/kanto.html>

Rieu, A-M., 'The syndrome of "overcoming modernity": Learning from Japan about ultra-nationalism', *Journal of Global Cultural Studies*, v.9, (2014)

Schalk, M., 'The Architecture of Metabolism. Inventing a Culture of Resilience', *Arts 3* (2014): 279-297.

Shibata, K., 'The Origins of Japanese Planning Culture: Building a Nation-State, 1868-1945', *Research Papers in Environmental and Spatial Analysis*, no.128, May (2008)

Smith, H., 'Tokyo as an idea: An exploration of Japanese Urban Thought until 1945', *Journal of Japanese Studies*, v.4, no.1, Winter (1978): 45-80.

Smith, R., 'History of Prefabrication: A Cultural Survey', *Proceedings of the Third International Congress on Construction History*, Cottbus, May (2009)

Steele, W., 'Constructing the Construction State: Cement and Post-war Japan', *The Asia-Pacific Journal*, v.15, no.5, June (2017)

Tsunoda, M-C., et al., ''Design for Reuse-Case study of World Exposition 2005 Aichi Japan', *Building Stock Activation Conference*, Rotterdam, (2007)

Urrutia, J. P., 'Yoshiharu Tsukamoto: We have to avoid treating people just like numbers', *Materia Arquitectura*, no.12, November (2015): 20-27.

Uslaner, E., and Yamamura, E., 'Disaster and political trust: The Japan Tsunami and Earthquake of 2011', MPRA Paper 70527, University Library of Munich, Germany (2016)

W. Flüchter, 'Shrinking Cities in Japan: Between Megalopolises and Rural Peripheries', in P. Oswalt and T. Reniets, *Shrinking Cities Complete Works 3, Case Study: Japan,* Project Office Philipp Oswalt: Berlin (2008)

Yagi, K., 'Art on Water: Art that Revitalizes Insular Communities Facing Depopulation and Economic Decline', *Nakhara*, v.6, November (2010): 119-130.

Zwigenberg, R., '"The Coming of a Second Sun": The 1956 Atoms for Peace Exhibit in Hiroshima and Japan's Embrace of Nuclear Power', *The Asia-Pacific Journal*, v.10, no.1, February (2012)

Web articles

Abe, S., 'Policy Speech by Prime Minister Shinzo Abe to the 166th Session of the Diet', *Prime Minister of Japan and his cabinet*. Online. Available HTTP: http://japan.kantei.go.jp/abespeech/2007/01/26speech_e.html (accessed 10 May 2018)

Busch, F., 'The Floating Stadium', *Florian Busch Architects*. Online. Available HTTP: http://www.florianbusch.com/projects/fsp/ (accessed 31 May 2018)

Crossley-Baxter, L., 'Florian Busch and the floating stadium: A futuristic Olympic insight', *Rethink Tokyo*. Online. Available HTTP: https://www.rethinktokyo.com/2018/04/18/florian-busch-tokyo-olympic-odyssey-floating-stadium/1523645336 Accessed May 31, 2018.

Demetriou, D., 'Why design buffs must visit Tokyo, an architectural riddle of a city', *The Telegraph*. Online. Available HTTP: https://www.telegraph.co.uk/travel/destinations/asia/japan/articles/why-design-buffs-must-visit-tokyo/ (accessed 30 March 2018)

Didero, M., C., 'Toyo Ito: Re-building from disaster', *Domus*. Online. Available HTTP: http://www.domusweb.it/en/interviews/2012/01/26/toyo-ito-rebuilding-from-disaster.html (accessed 6 January 2018)

Editorial, 'Tohoku's Great Forest Wall Project', *The Japan Times*. Online. Available HTTP: https://www.japantimes.co.jp/opinion/2013/11/23/editorials/tohokusgreat-forest-wall-project/#.WwCVMDsoV-U (accessed 6 March 2018)

Fingleton, E., The New York Times. 'The Myth of Japan's Failure', *The New York Times*. Online. Available HTTP: https://www.nytimes.com/2012/01/08/opinion/sunday/the-true-story-of-japans-economic-success.html (accessed 16 April 2018)

Glancey, J., 'Sanaa's summer pavilion brings sunshine to the Serpentine', *The Guardian*. Online. Available HTTP: https://www.theguardian.com/artanddesign/2009/jul/08/sanaa-summer-pavilion-serpentine (accessed 12 May 2018)

Graw, E., 'Japan's disposable home culture', *The Guardian*. Online. Available HTTP: https://www.theguardian.com/sustainable-business/disposable-homes-japan-environmentlifespansustainability (accessed 28 September 2017)

Green, D., 'As Its Population Ages, Japan Quietly Turns to Immigration', *Migration Policy Institute*. Online. Available HTTP: https://www.migrationpolicy.org/article/its-population-ages-japan-quietly-turns-immigration (accessed 24 May 2018)

Gros, D., 'The myth of Japan's lost decade', *The Guardian*. Online. Available HTTP: https://www.theguardian.com/commentisfree/2011/jan/17/japan-myth-lostdecade (accessed 16 April 2018)

Halloran, R., 'New Japanese Premiere Urges fast changes in Nation's Ways', *New York Times*, August 22, 1972. Available HTTP: https://www.nytimes.com/1972/08/23/archives/new-japanese-premier-urges-vast-changes-in-nations-ways.html (accessed 1 November 2020)

Imanova, A., 'Petition urges end to using deforestation-led wood for Kengo Kuma's Olympic stadium', *designMENA*. Online. Available HTTP: http://www.designmena.com/thoughts/petition-urges-end-to-using-deforestation-led-wood-for-kengo-kumas-olympic-stadium (accessed 3 February 2018)

Ingle, S., 'Tokyo Olympics in 2021 at risk of cancellation admits Japan's PM', *The Guardian*. Online. Available HTTP: https://www.theguardian.com/sport/2020/apr/29/tokyo-olympics-not-reliant-on-covid-19-vaccine-senior-ioc-member (accessed 20 July 2020)

Kaku, R., 'The path of Kyosei', *Harvard Business Review*. Online. Available HTTP: https://hbr.org/1997/07/the-path-of-kyosei (accessed 25 March 2018)

Kameda, M., 'Nihonbashi highway is urged to go under', *The Japan Times*. Online. Available HTTP: https://www.japantimes.co.jp/news/2014/02/26/national/nihonbashi-highway-is-urged-to-go-under/#.WwCfzTsoWu4 (accessed 16 April 2018)

Katō, J., 'Itō Toyo and the "Minna No Ie" Project', *Nippon*. Online. Available HTTP: https://www.nippon.com/en/views/b03101/ (accessed 15 November 2017)

Kiyono, Y., 'Architect Kuma Kengo Shares His Thinking Behind Japan's New National Stadium Design', *Nippon*. Online. Available HTTP: https://www.nippon.com/en/people/e00101/ (accessed May 20, 2018)

Koolhaas, R., 'My thoughts on the smart city', *European Commission*. Online. Available HTTP: http://ec.europa.eu/archives/commission_2010-2014/kroes/en/content/my-thoughts-smart-city-rem-koolhaas.html (accessed 12 November 2017)

Kosaka, K., 'Florian Busch, the architect who floated the Tokyo 2020 Olympic stadium', *The Japan Times*. Online. Available HTTP: https://www.japantimes.co.jp/community/2018/02/28/our-lives/florian-busch-architect-floated-tokyo-2020-olympic-stadium/#.WxAwojulduY (accessed 31 May 2018)

Kuang, C., 'An Exclusive Look At Airbnb's First Foray Into Urban Planning', *Co.Design*. Online. Available HTTP: https://www.fastcodesign.com/3062246/an-exclusive-look-at-airbnbs-first-foray-into-urban-planning (accessed 2 May 2018)

Kuma, K., 'Tokyo 2020: Designing the Olympic Stadium', *NHK World*. Online. Available HTTP: https://www3.nhk.or.jp/nhkworld/en/tv/directtalk/articles/20160405/index.html (accessed 12 May 2018)

Kurtenbach, E., 'Japan opts for massive costly sea wall to fend off tsunamis' *Phys*. Online. Available HTTP: https://phys.org/news/2015-03-japan-opts-massive-costlysea.html (accessed 13 March 2018)

Lefebvre, B., 'Food, diapers, and free wifi: Japan relies on 7-11 to lead earthquake relief efforts', Quartz. Online. Available HTTP: https://qz.com/667567/food-diapersand-free-wi-fi-japan-relies-on-7-11-to-lead-earthquake-relief-efforts/ (accessed 25 April 2018)

Lifson, E., 'Tadao Ando', *Archpaper*. Online. Available HTTP: https://archpaper.com/2009/09/tadao-ando/ (accessed 20 April 2018)

Lifson, E., 'Tadao Ando: New Stadium Tokyo 2020'. *A as Architecture*. Online. Available HTTP: http://aasarchitecture.com/2012/07/tadao-ando-new-stadium-tokio-2020.html (accessed 20 April 2018)

Lufkin, B., 'Akira Miyawaki has planted 40 million trees as a tidal wave shield', *WiredUK*. Online. Available HTTP: http://www.wired.co.uk/article/the-tree-whisperer (accessed 11 March 2018)

Masaru, I. and Kazuyo, S., Shibaura House. 'Conversation: Between Kazuyo Sejima and Masaru Ito'. *Shibaura House*. Online. Available HTTP: http://www.shibaurahouse.jp/en/about/architecture (accessed 28 November 2017)

Mortice, Z., 'Toyo Itō's Next Architectural Feat', Redshift. Online. Available HTTP: https://www.autodesk.com/redshift/toyo-ito/ (accessed April 30, 2018)

Nagata, K., 'Japan needs imports to keep itself fed', *The Japan Times*. Online. Available HTTP: https://www.japantimes.co.jp/news/2008/02/26/reference/japanneeds-imports-to-keep-itself-fed/#.WwE5kTsoV-U (accessed 20 May 2018)

Plagens, P., 'Los Angeles: The Ecology of Evil', *Artforum* 11 (1972). Online. Available HTTP: http://www.art-agenda.com/reviews/los-angeles-the-architecture-of-four-ecologies/ (accessed 13 January 2018)

Pogrebin, R., 'National Pride at a Steep Price: Olympic Stadium in Tokyo Is Dogged by Controversy', *The New York Times*. Online. Available HTTP: https://www.nytimes.com/2015/01/05/arts/design/olympic-stadium-in-tokyo-is-dogged-by-controversy.html

Powell, B., 'Explaining Japan's recession', *Mises Institute*. Online. Available HTTP: https://mises.org/library/explaining-japans-recession (accessed 30 May 2018)

Pulvers, R., 'Born of disaster, modern architecture is itself now an ongoing disaster', *The Japan Times*. Online. Available HTTP: https://www.japantimes.co.jp/opinion/2012/05/13/commentary/born-of...dern-architecture-is-itself-now-an-ongoing-disaster/#.Wbr1yTsoVmA (accessed 5 April 2018)

Rose, J., 'The Building After: Toyo Ito interviewed by Julian Rose', *Artforum*. Online. Available HTTP: https://www.artforum.com/print/201307/toyo-ito-interviewed-by-julian-rose-42634 (accessed April 14, 2018)

Sayer, J., '"House Vision 2" in Tokyo tackles a simple question: How can architecture connect people?' *Archpaper*. Online. Available HTTP: https://www.archpaper.com/2016/08/house-vision-tokyo/ (accessed 25 April 2018)

Soble, J., 'Japan Selects New Plan for 2020 Olympic Stadium in Tokyo', *The New York Times*. Online. Available HTTP: https://www.nytimes.com/2015/12/23/world/asia/tokyo-2020-olympics-stadium.html (accessed 12 November 2017)

Starrs, R., 'Zen, Japan and the art of democracy', *New Statesman*. Online. Available HTTP: http://www.newstatesman.com/asia/2011/07/japan-essay-nature-earthquake (accessed 24 May 2018)

Takada, A., and Kuwako, K., 'Olympics Architect Wants to Bring Wood Back to Tokyo's Concrete Jungle', *Bloomberg*. Online. Available HTTP: https://www.bloomberg.com/news/articles/2017-05-23/olympic-architect-sees-wood-as-answer-to-tokyos-concrete-legacy, (accessed 12 March 2018)

Tarrant, J., 'Olympics: Japan to test anti-virus measures at near-full baseball stadium', *Reuters*, 16 October, 2020. Online. Available HTTP: https://de.reuters.com/article/uk-olympics-2020-baseball-fans/japan-to-test-anti-virus-measures-at-near-full-baseball-stadium-idUSKBN2710HQ (accessed 30 October 2020)

Taylor, K., 'Avoiding waste with the Japanese concept of "mottainai"', *ABC*. Online. Available HTTP: http://www.abc.net.au/radionational/programs/philosopherszone/mottainai/6722728 (accessed 30 April 2018)

Ting, D., 'Airbnb's Latest Investment Values It as Much as Hilton and Hyatt Combined', *Skift*. Online. Available HTTP: https://skift.com/2016/09/23/airbnbs-latestinvestment-values-it-as-much-as-hilton-and-hyatt-combined/ (accessed 12 May 2018)

Tsuyoshi, I., Urabe, E., 'Koike's plan for Tepco to remove utility poles in Tokyo an Olympian task', *The Japan Times*. Online. Available HTTP: https://www.japantimes.co.jp/news/2017/04/03/business/koikes-plan-tepco-remove-utility-poles-tokyo-olympian-task/#.WwCfQTsoWu4 (accessed 16 April 2018)

Unknown, 'Shigeru Ban: Connecting nature and human through natural disaster', *Zero = Abundance*. Online. Available HTTP: http://www.interactiongreen.com/shigeru-ban-disaster-architecture/ (accessed 19 December 2017)

Unknown, 'Toyo Ito: 3.11 and "Great Transformation of Architecture', *Zero = Abundance*. Online. Available HTTP: http://www.interactiongreen.com/toyo-ito-sustainable-architecture/ (accessed 6 January 2018)

Unknown, Zero = Abundance. 'Zero perspectives in "Small Architecture" by Kengo Kuma', Online. Available HTTP: http://www.interactiongreen.com/inspiring-zero-perspectives-small-architecture-kengo-kuma/ (accessed 6 January 2018)

Wade, S., 'Tokyo Olympic CEO: Games next year may not be "conventional"', *abcNews*. Online. Available HTTP: https://abcnews.go.com/Sports/wireStory/tokyo-olympic-ceo-games-year-conventional-70697759 (accessed 20 July 2020)

Wallace, M., 'Mottainai, How the Japanese Say "Waste Not, Want Not"', *We hate to waste*. Online. Available HTTP: http://www.wehatetowaste.com/mottainai/ (accessed 30 April 2018)

William, 'Will the Tokyo 2020 Olympics be the "eco Olympics"?', *Japan Trends*. Online. Available HTTP: http://www.japantrends.com/will-the-tokyo-2020-olympics-be-the-eco-olympics/ (accessed 30 May 2018)

Videos

European Graduate School, 'Mitchell Joachim. Ecotopia and Eco-Cities. 2012', *YouTube*. Online. Available HTTP: https://www.youtube.com/watch?v=6sRe8msqa90 (accessed 28 April 2018)

Unsinkable Japan, 'Making Forests of Life for the Ones You Love', *YouTube*. Online. Available HTTP: https://www.youtube.com/watch?v=-nGr3LQxyyA (accessed 7 March 2018)

Illustration credits

Tsukiji Hotel; Hiroshige Utagawa
courtesy of Waseda University Library 53

Ginza Bricktown; Kuniteru Utagawa
courtesy of Tokyo Metropolitan Library 54

Akasaka Palace; Kakidai
from Creative Commons (CC BY-SA 4.0) 55

Deer Cry Pavilion; Toyohara Chikanobu
from Wikimedia Commons 56

Shinko Sub-Prefectural Office; Fusakichi Omori
from Wikimedia Commons, source: *Preliminary Note of the Formosa Earthquake of March 17, 1906* 67

Daibutsuden; 663highland
from Creative Commons (CC BY 2.5) 68

Memorial for the Great Kantō Earthquake; author unknown
from Wikimedia Commons, source: *Dai Tōkyō shashin jō* 69

Electric Home; author unknown
courtesy of Uchida Seizo 101

Experimental house no. 5; Fujii Kōji
source: *The Japanese Dwelling-house* 102

Sketch of mountain hut in Nishitama-gun, Musashi from Nihon no Minka
courtesy of Kogakuin University Library, source: *Nihon no Minka*, 4th edition, 1954 103

Karuizawa summer house and studio; author unknown
courtesy of RIBA 104

Sketched map of research travels through Korea; Wajiro Kon
courtesy of Kogakuin University Library, source: *Chosen Buraku Chousa Tokubetu, Houkoku Daiisatu* 117

Japanese Cultural Centre in Bangkok; Kenzō Tange
courtesy of Tange Associates, source: *Kenchiku Zasshi* 118

Golconde Ashram Dormitory; Aleksandr Zykov
from Creative Commons (CC BY-SA 2.0) 119

Mountain City; Nishiyama Uzō
courtesy of NPO Nishiyama Uzō Memorial Library, source: *Chiiki Kūkan Ron* 149

Neo Tokyo Plan; Indutrial Planning Council
source: *7th Recommendation of Industrial Planning Council Recommendation on landfill of 200 million tsubo in Tokyo Bay* 150

Building a New Nation: Remodelling the Japanese Archipelago; Kakuei Tanaka
source: *Nikon Kogyo Shimbun* 151

Tokyo Metropolitan Government Office; author unknown
from Wikimedia Commons, source: *Shuto Tōkyō no tenbō* 165

Showa Station Antarctica; author unknown
courtesy of NIPR (National Institute of Polar Research) 166

Nakagin Capsule Tower; Dick Thomas Johnson
from Creative Commons (CC BY 2.0) 167

Toyo Itō Museum of Architecture; Daici Ano
courtesy of Daici Ano 197

Yoshino Cedar House; Edward Caruso
courtesy of Edward Caruso 198

New National Olympic Stadium; Dick Thomas Johnson
from Creative Commons (CC BY 2.0) 199

Aichi Expo 2005; Gnsin
from Creative Commons (CC BY-SA 3.0) 213

Akasaka Prince Hotel Deconstruction; feffreyl
from Creative Commons (CC BY-NC 2.0) 214

Fibercity 2050; Hidetoshi Ohno
courtesy of Hidetoshi Ohno, source: *Japan Architect* 63 215

Floating Stadium Project; Florian Busch
courtesy of Florian Busch Architects 218

Nagasaki Bay; Nabeshima Hofukai
from Wikimedia Commons cover

Floating Stadium Project; Florian Busch
courtesy of Florian Busch Architects cover

Nation Building Nature

Acknowledgements

The author wishes to acknowledge the following individuals and institutions

The author thanks the University of Ghent and the EU-Japan Centre for Industrial Cooperation for providing the time, support and resources necessary to conduct this study.

Parts of the essays published in this book have previously been published in Smple Magazine. Nijs is very grateful to the editors of Smple for their help and their ongoing interest in the future of architecture in Japan and elsewhere.

This publication was partly made possible through the generous support of many backers via the Nation Building Nature crowdfunding campaign on Kickstarter.

Special Thanks
for their feedback on the content and the overall concept of the book:
Prof. Johan Lagae, Prof. Andreas Niehaus, Prof. William Steele, Prof. Hera Van Sande, Prof. Tijl Vanmeirhaeghe, Dr. Yu Kishi

for their help with the photographic essays:
Carlos Conejo, Kaho Inoue, Daisuke Komatsu

for their generous support via Kickstarter:
familie Abdellatif, Niels Abdellatif, Sonia Ansiaux, Juan Azcarreta, Renaud Baeckelandt, Emmanuelle Bally, Shaikh Bechan, Gaëlle Beckers, Fredric Bender, Stephen Bill, Lumi Binakaj, Sami Biwer, Vic Bogaert, Pol Bosman, Michiel Burgelman, Senne Caroes, Clare Chapman, Chananchida Charoensri, famille Claren-Zeippen, Isabelle Dastroy, famille De Schepper-Oates, Felix Dijkstal, famille Eloy-Crochet, Joshua Menard Fiebak, Sophie Fochesato, Augustin Foly, Florence Fontanive, famille Frieden, Dino Ibrahimagic, Seleyman Ghafuri, familie Havenith, Cedric Havenith, Tim Holdsworth, Christopher Holgate, Adriano Infante, Masahiko Inoue, Kaho Inoue, Yumiko Inoue, Hodaka Kokeguchi, Ward Kromhout, Omer Kurtulus, Bernadette Lamesch, Teddy Lin, Pascale Mack-Merens, Claude Martine, Hikaru Matsubara, Ai Matsui, Euan McCartney, Victor Meng, Stany Miéwis, Arno Nijs, Alessandro Niro, Clara Nobels, Fanny Nobels, Ayako Noguchi, Peili Pey, Arne Platteau, Sven Post, M.J. Robles, Richard Rossi, Karl Sammut, Matt Shannon, Shreya Santra, Margarita Savova, Sven Schroeder, Yolande Servais, Clifford B. Spencer, Davide Spina, Caroline Stever, Charlotte Teulings, Shiina Tsunakawa, Manabu Ue, Jullya Ueno, Arne Vande Capelle, Melanie Vandevoir, Matea Točkica Večerić, Bram Verbauwhede, Robrecht Verstraete, Melvin Victorio, Lucas Volman, Joakim Wahlman, Pierre Westelynck, Martine Wintzerith, Astri Wright, Sigrid Wucherpfennig, Yuko Yokoyama, Didier Zeippen, Francine Zeippen, Ingrid Zeippen, William Zeippen, Yannik Zeippen

About the Author

Joachim Nijs (1994, Belgium) is a young designer trained in architecture and urban design at the University of Ghent, Belgium, where he graduated summa cum laude in 2018. He has worked in several architecture offices, both in Europe and in Japan, where he is currently based. Nijs' previous publications have appeared in Smple Magazine (Vancouver) and Trans Magazin (ETH Zürich).

Credits

Texts: Joachim Nijs
Copy editing: Leo Reijnen
Design: Studio Sander Boon
Photography: Joachim Nijs
Lithography and Printing: NPN Drukkers
Paper: Arctic Volume White, Lessebo Design White
Production coordination: Laurence Ostyn, nai010 publishers, Rotterdam
Publisher: nai010 publishers, Rotterdam

This publication was made possible through the generous financial support of many backers via the Nation Building Nature crowdfunding campaign on kickstarter.com.

nai010 publishers is an internationally orientated publisher specialized in developing, producing and distributing books in the fields of architecture, urbanism, art and design. www.nai010.com
nai010 books are available internationally at selected bookstores and from the following distribution partners:
North, Central and South America - Artbook | D.A.P., New York, USA, dap@dapinc.com
Rest of the world - Idea Books, Amsterdam, the Netherlands, idea@ideabooks.nl

For general questions, please contact nai010 publishers directly at sales@nai010.com or visit our website www.nai010.com for further information.

Printed and bound the Netherlands

ISBN 9789462086135
NUR 648
BISAC ARC000000

Title is also available as e-book:
ISBN 9789462086449 (e-book)

RAILROAD SEMANTICS

SPRING 2012 #6

tried to play it off by asking me if I knew where he could scrap the metal. I told him very seriously to leave, and he did, but I'm still wary of him. There can be some really shady characters out here sometimes.

2100- On a southbound DPU in the Eugene yard, and the Engineer must be a master. The train, with pusher and all, just sort of starts with no clanking at all, going from a dead stop to a light little roll, creaking to life ever so slightly . . . *slowly pulling out of the Eug yard . . . 7 miles per hour, easy to catch on the fly . . . rolling under Chambers Bridge at 8.8 miles per hour . . . coming out the other end at 9.1, and now back down to 9 miles per hour . . . a line of industry trains off on the wye to the west waiting to be backed into the yard . . . rolling a cool 8 mph through town . . . passing Van Buren crossing, car lots, barbwire fences, and abandoned buildings with loading-dock tracks no longer in use . . .* in the Whiteaker . . . *a decrepit graffiti wall . . . 8.6 mph—still catchable on the fly . . . down to the Grain Millers where cars are stopped on both sides of the crossing . . . passing the Wandering Goat . . . a dog wearing a headlamp turned on and a bike-light blinking red on its back, and two people with lights stopped on bikes waiting . . . passing the Grain Millers and two people sitting on the curb, along with another guy on a bike with a trailer . . . four cars sitting on one side of the tracks and three on the other . . . under the overpass in Washington-Jefferson Park at 9.3 mph—still slow enough to catch on the fly . . . REI (my savior) . . . crossing gates* dinging and cars stopped on Lawrence St. . . . rolling past the jail *at 9 mph on the low-speed secondary mainline . . .* conceivably, you could catch this train right at the Amtrak Station, which is true in other cities (like Sacramento, Spokane, and Pasco), but the funny thing about it here is that you'd essentially be catching the train right next door to the County Jail *. . . watching people in front of the Jackalope Bar . . . passing the Eugene depot at a consistent 9 mph . . . two crusty punks standing at a crossing beside a guy with a huge shopping cart full of shit—cans to sell and things to scrap . . . 11 mph under the bridge by the new Federal Courthouse—still slow enough to catch on the fly, though not more than two or three people . . . the train buckling for the first time, hitting 10 mph and then seeming to slow a little once clear of the streets . . . stopping, briefly . . . now moving again . . . this, the first southbound of the day since at least 10 a.m.. finally picking up speed . . . approaching Judkins—the Rivertrack—on the way to Springfield, the DPU now hitting 11... 12... gaining speed to go the distance . . . through Judkins at 23 mph—now much too fast to catch on the fly . . . under the I-5 into Glenwood, a small community that exists on the Willamette between Eugene and Springfield and that is basi-*